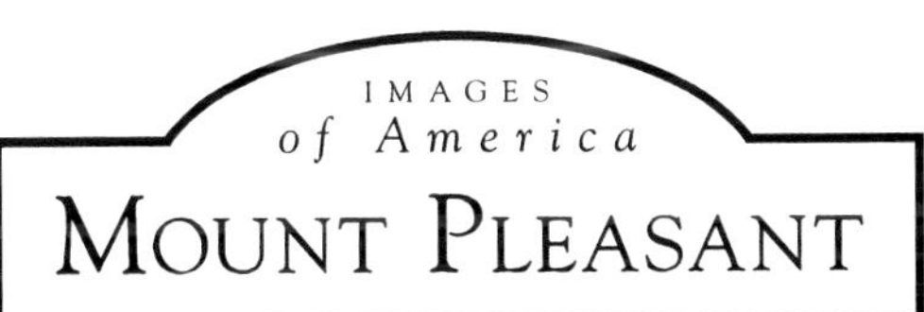
IMAGES
of America
MOUNT PLEASANT

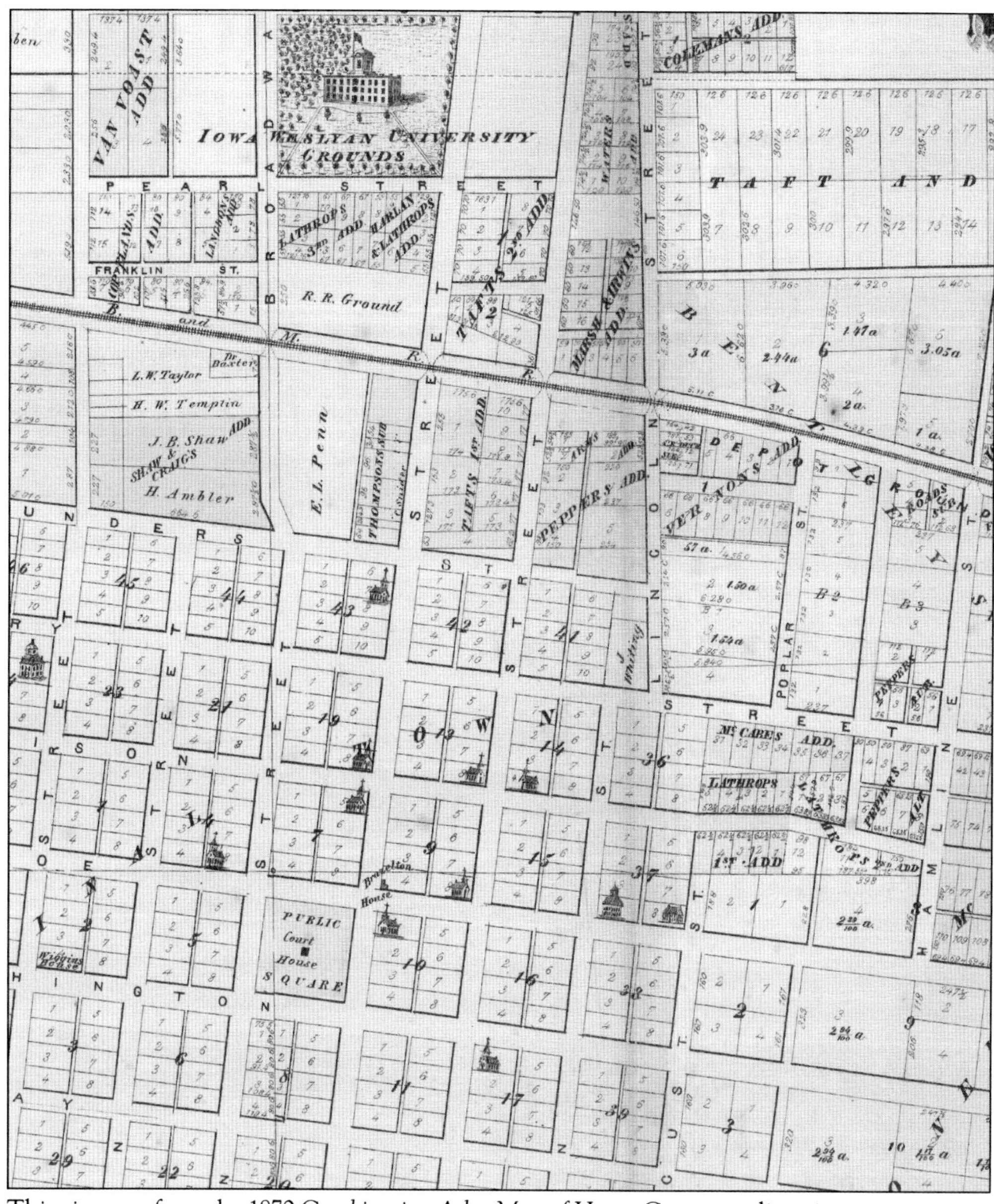

This city map from the 1870 *Combination Atlas Map of Henry County* outlines important streets and landmarks in Mount Pleasant. The square is visible in the southwest section of the image, where the courthouse was located in 1870. Just east of the square, in Block 37, two buildings mark the location of the Old Central School and Howe's Academy. Iowa Wesleyan University sits at the top of the map. Various churches are also marked. (Mount Pleasant Public Library.)

On the Cover: Gustaf Grau, the son of German immigrants, operated this cigar manufactory for about 35 years on North Main Street. Grau worked in the W.H. Schliep cigar factory while he was a young man; that building is now occupied by Breadeaux Pizza. Grau then opened his own cigar store in the 1890s. (Mount Pleasant Public Library.)

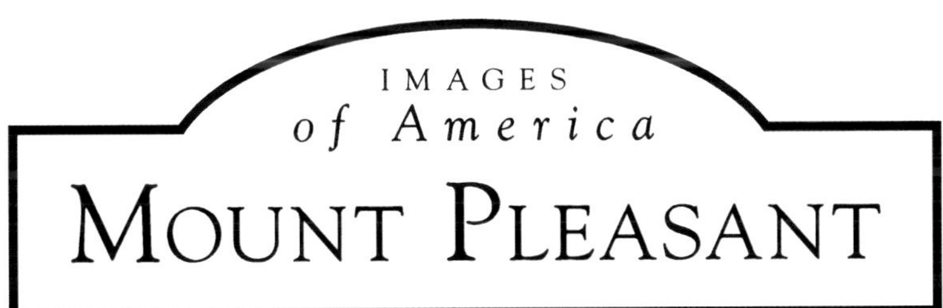

Jeffrey Meyer and John Hendrickson

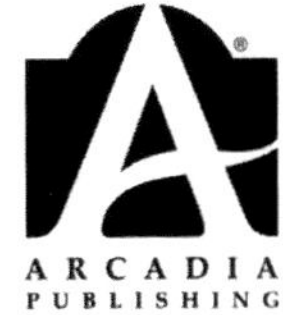

ISBN 978-1-4671-1678-7

Published by Arcadia Publishing
Charleston, South Carolina

Printed in the United States of America

Library of Congress Control Number: 2015959087

For all general information, please contact Arcadia Publishing:
Telephone 843-853-2070
Fax 843-853-0044
E-mail sales@arcadiapublishing.com
For customer service and orders:
Toll-Free 1-888-313-2665

Visit us on the Internet at www.arcadiapublishing.com

This book is dedicated to Don Young and Martha Hayes.

Contents

ACKNOWLEDGMENTS

This book would not have been possible without the work and dedication of Don Young and Martha Hayes. Young and Hayes were devoted to the Mount Pleasant community. Young's local history writings, available at the Mount Pleasant Public Library (MPPL), were instrumental resources. Young donated many resources to the community, including his collection of local history photographs, many of which appear in this book.

Pat White and Waunita Gibbons provided expert guidance. White and Gibbons both have an encyclopedic knowledge of local history. The Henry County Heritage Trust (HCHT) provided numerous images used in this work. At the time of this publication, the Henry County Heritage Trust board members are president Ken Vandevoort, vice president Terry McNair, secretary Waunita Gibbons, treasurer Pat Ryan White, Sheila Allender, Lea Bradley, Lynn Conrad, John Harnagle, David McCoid, and David Van Allen. Everybody in Henry County should visit the Trust's excellent museum at the old Saunders School.

Ruth Mallams's work on Mount Pleasant Methodist history provided significant information. Mary Ann Messer also provided church history resources. Coauthor Jeff Meyer would also like to thank his wife for her patience and understanding.

INTRODUCTION

Mount Pleasant is a small town with a big story. What began as a few log cabins in the 1830s developed into a significant educational, political, and ecclesiastical center in Iowa. Mount Pleasant quickly earned a reputation as the "Athens of Iowa." Presley Saunders, an early settler and community pillar, was very significant in this development. The 1888 *Portrait and Biographical Album of Henry County* recorded how this pioneer from Illinois founded a town here, stating:

> Struck with the beauty of the place, and finding water convenient, Mr. Saunders drove his stakes right there. The selection was a fortunate one for him. In February, 1835, he brought his family from Illinois, and knowing this must be near the center of the new county whenever formed, he laid out a plat for a village, which he called Mt. Pleasant, a most appropriate name.

Saunders planned a town square, which still serves as the community's center. Mount Pleasant received the distinguished honor as county seat, with the courthouse established during the town's infancy. Streets spread forth from the square. Churches were built, and banks appeared on the street corners. Businesses took root as industry developed. The railroad came, and with it, all the commodities and luxuries of the faraway cities.

The 1879 *History of Henry County* noted the remarkable transformation of the town after only one or two generations, recording that Mount Pleasant had some 6,000 residents in 1879. The *History of Henry County* remarked, "There are seventeen churches, two colleges, two seminaries, five public-school buildings, one railroad, with a prospect of another, one woolen-mill, one glove factory, hospital for the insane, one public library, gas works, two foundry and machine shops, one scale works, one pork-packing house, three newspapers," and many other businesses and services. In a sense, Mount Pleasant had, within the span of one or two generations, transformed from an assemblage of cabins to a center of culture and civilization.

Mount Pleasant emerged as an educational center. The earliest settlers held education as a critical necessity. School was first taught in a cabin during the pioneer days. A college was planned and begun in Mount Pleasant years before the arrival of the railroad. Private academies also formed during the community's infancy, and the public schools were functioning before the Civil War.

Mount Pleasant was also a center of progressive attitudes. The city's most honored resident, Sen. James Harlan, became a leading abolitionist in Washington, DC, during the traumatic years before and during the Civil War. His friendship and alliance with Pres. Abraham Lincoln fostered a courtship between Senator Harlan's daughter Mary and President Lincoln's son Robert Todd. Thus, Mount Pleasant was wedded into the story of the Lincoln family and the greater American narrative. Robert and Mary brought three children into the world; the family line of the fallen president yet alive in these grandchildren.

Mount Pleasant also produced a local political opponent to the Harlan family. Henry Clay Dean, a Peace Democrat who simultaneously opposed both slavery and the war, embodied many of the traits of the Mount Pleasant intellectual. "Dirty Shirt Dean," as the Methodist Episcopal preacher and lawyer was called, possessed a large personal library of thousands of books, participated in the life of the college, detested all manner of coercion and injustice, and attracted much attention for his political and religious oratory.

Prof. Samuel Luke Howe, the founder of an early school in Mount Pleasant, was also given to progressive ideals. In addition to his passion for education, Professor Howe was an ardent abolitionist. The 1879 *History of Henry County* recorded that his students "drew in Abolitionism with their Latin and their mathematics." Professor Howe also published Mount Pleasant's antislavery paper, the *Iowa True Democrat*.

Opportunities abounded for Mount Pleasant women in the 19th century. It is astonishing to realize that young women in this small town during the 19th century had at least five schools to attend. Young women and girls could attend public school, Howe's Academy, the Mount Pleasant Academy, the Female Seminary, or Iowa Wesleyan University. Nearly half a century before women received the right to vote, Mount Pleasant's *Free Press* in 1879 included an extended argument for women's suffrage on its front page, declaring: "The nation which has attained to the highest state of civilization, is the nation which fosters and encourages every means and instrumentality to confer the greatest amount of good upon the greatest number, making justice and equality the standard virtues to guide it forward in the ways of a more perfect existence."

Mount Pleasant public schools were racially integrated in the 1860s, a century before many school systems in the nation. The city also advanced progressive forms of medicine. The Mount Pleasant Insane Asylum was a symbol of a new public commitment—an attempt to heal people stricken with psychiatric impairment.

Mount Pleasant has long hosted a great diversity of religious denominations. The Methodist circuit riders arrived with the earliest pioneer cabins. It did not take long for communities of Baptists, Congregationalists, Universalists, Episcopalians, Catholics, and many others to form within the city. On Washington Street, two old church buildings, St. Michael's Episcopal Church and the Congregational Church, have served the community for over a century.

The prosperity and enriching spirit found in this community and in Iowa at large was discussed in Mount Pleasant's *Weekly News* on August 23, 1893. The paper reported:

> The State of Iowa has immense natural wealth. Her resources are little short of marvelous. Her agricultural products in the year 1891 amounted at the market selling price to $468,873,000. Her annual surplus corn crop will average over a hundred million dollars annually; her wheat crop twenty-five millions; her hay crop forty millions; her butter produce thirty-three millions, and so on. Iowa has no state debt. She ranks first among the States in number of schools, teachers and pupils in proportion to population, first in grain product, first in corn product, first in butter product.

Mount Pleasant has also endured many trials. This small town sent its sons to the Civil War. Terrible fires have destroyed entire city blocks. A tornado tore through town in 1882. But the pieces were picked up, and the community moved forward.

This book will focus on the incredible progress made in Mount Pleasant's history, particularly from its formative years in the 1830s through the early decades of the 20th century. We thank you for taking the time to walk this journey.

One

PEOPLE

They came to Mount Pleasant from New England, the Appalachian Mountains, and the Ohio Valley. Many even came from Ireland and Germany. Some may have claimed a long lineage from the Puritans, while others were first-generation immigrants born in Europe. Some came for a fresh start, others for new opportunity in the land beyond the Mississippi. These pioneers shaped and formed the land. The 1888 *Portrait and Biographical Album of Henry County* noted:

> At the time of the first settlement, Iowa formed a portion of Michigan Territory. Two years afterward the Territory of Wisconsin was organized and it then became a part of Wisconsin. Two years later Iowa Territory was formed, and in 1846 it was admitted into the union of States. The first settlers of Henry County were thus citizens of Michigan, Wisconsin, and Iowa. Presley Saunders relates that he had one child born in Michigan Territory, one in Wisconsin Territory, one in the Territory of Iowa, and one in the State of Iowa, all being born on the same quarter-section of land.

The 1885 *Census of Iowa* recorded that one in ten of Mount Pleasant's citizens was born in a foreign country. Germany, Ireland, and Sweden represented the greatest immigrant populations. The 1885 *Census of Iowa* also recorded that Mount Pleasant was home to 327 African American residents. Some southerners came to Iowa because they opposed slavery, and they wanted to live in this new, "free soil" state. The presence of a sizable number of skilled pioneers is evident in the town's rapid civilization. Within a few decades, a proper city, complete with businesses, banks, churches, and schools, had sprouted from the springs that drew in the first pioneers.

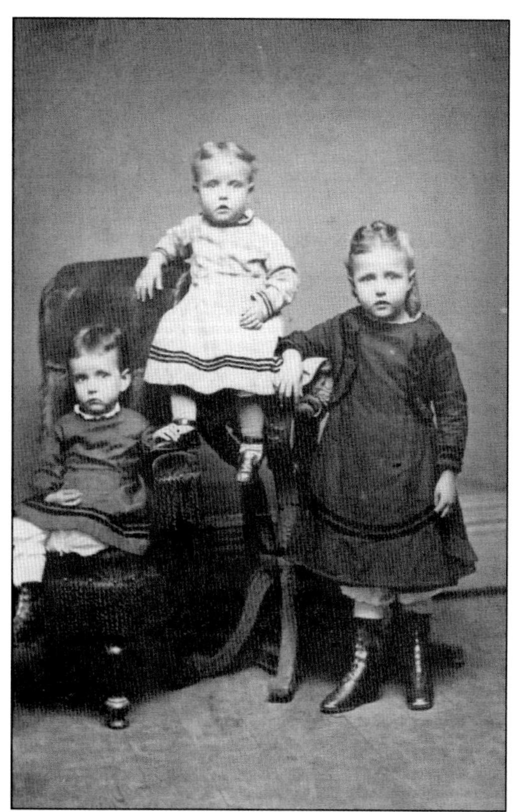

Leisenrings photography studio in Mount Pleasant was known for its excellent group portraits. It is easy to forget how many children would have been present in everyday life in previous centuries, with the families being so large. The technological changes that these children would experience in their lives were swift and dramatic, living as they did at the dawn of the electrical age. (MPPL.)

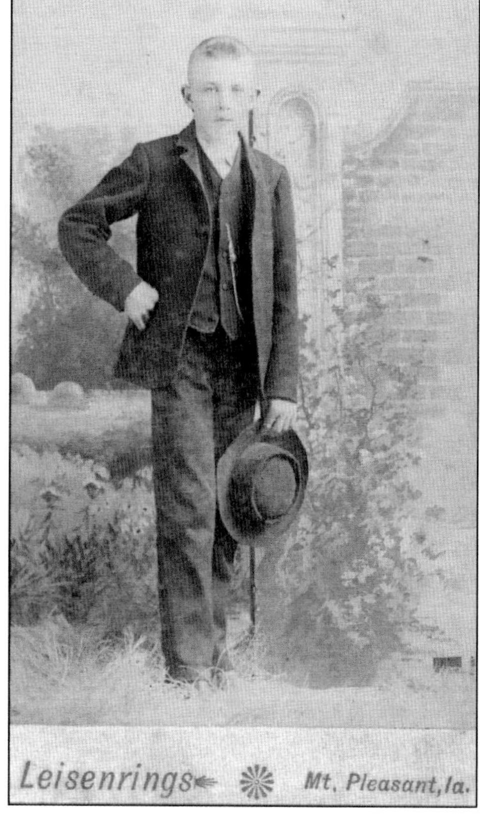

This young man poses for a picture at Mount Pleasant's Leisenrings gallery in the late 19th century. Photographic techniques were refined during the 19th century, with the world's first known surviving photograph taken in 1826 or 1827. It is possible that this young boy would grow to see the further enhancement of this new technology, including the development of motion pictures. (MPPL.)

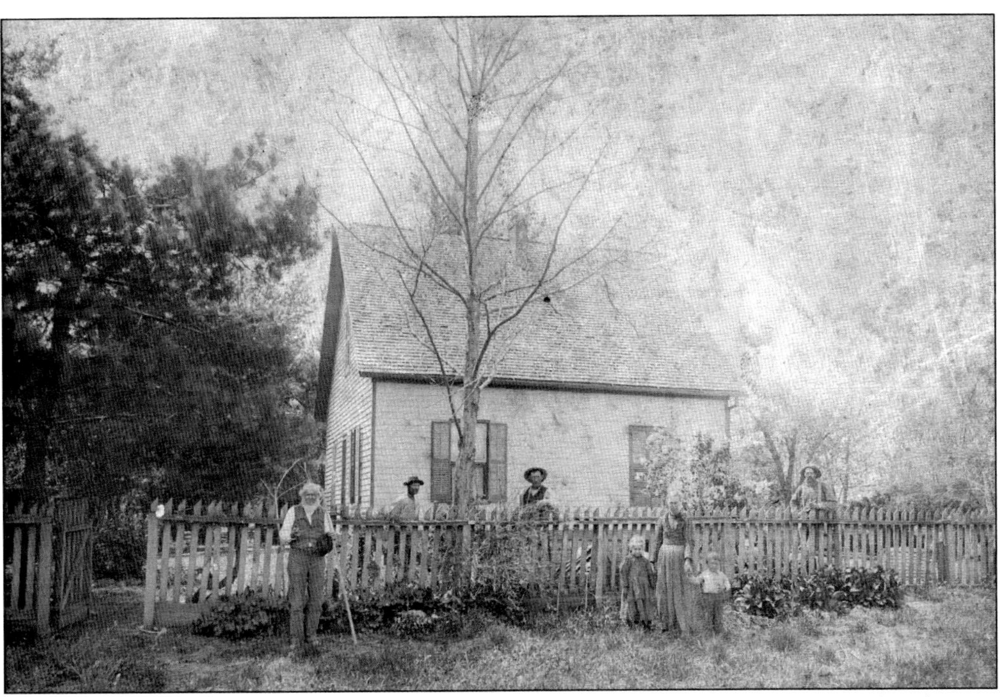

The Pickard family lived in rural Henry County during the 19th century. Notice the fine shutters on the house, the well-kept fence, and the planted rows. The 1870 *Combination Atlas Map of Henry County* recorded that local country families like the Pickards had collectively gathered 141,393 bushels of corn, 24,115 bushels of oats, and 20,098 bushels of wheat. The 1870 *Atlas* also noted that Henry County had 8,811 sheep, 3,193 hogs, and 2,096 horned cattle. (MPPL.)

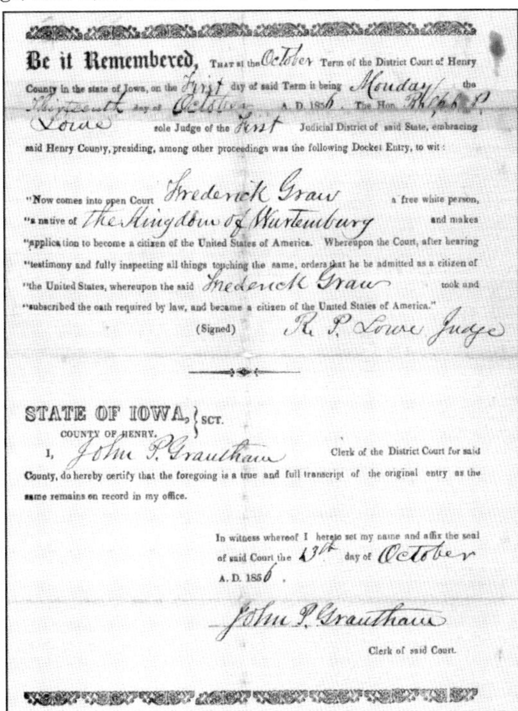

Be it Remembered, That at the October Term of the District Court of Henry County in the state of Iowa, on the First day of said Term it being Monday the Thirteenth day of October A. D. 1856. The Hon. Ralph P. Lowe sole Judge of the First Judicial District of said State, embracing said Henry County, presiding, among other proceedings was the following Docket Entry, to wit:

"Now comes into open Court Frederick Grau a free white person, "a native of The Kingdom of Wurtemburg and makes "application to become a citizen of the United States of America. Whereupon the Court, after hearing "testimony and fully inspecting all things touching the same, orders that he be admitted as a citizen of "the United States, whereupon the said Frederick Grau took and "subscribed the oath required by law, and became a citizen of the United States of America."

(Signed) R. P. Lowe Judge

STATE OF IOWA, } SCT.
COUNTY OF HENRY.

I, John P. Grautham Clerk of the District Court for said County, do hereby certify that the foregoing is a true and full transcript of the original entry as the same remains on record in my office.

In witness whereof I hereto set my name and affix the seal of said Court the 13th day of October A. D. 1856.

John P. Grautham
Clerk of said Court.

This citizenship document was composed for Frederick Grau, an immigrant from Germany. The paper reads, "Now comes into open Court Frederick Grau a free white person, a native of the Kingdom of Wurtemburg and makes application to become a citizen of the United States of America. Whereupon the Court, after hearing testimony and fully inspecting all things touching the same, orders that he be admitted as a citizen of the United States, whereupon the said Frederick Grau took and subscribed the oath required by law, and became a citizen of the United States of America." This document was prepared at the Henry County Courthouse in 1856, which was located in the center of the square at that time. (MPPL.)

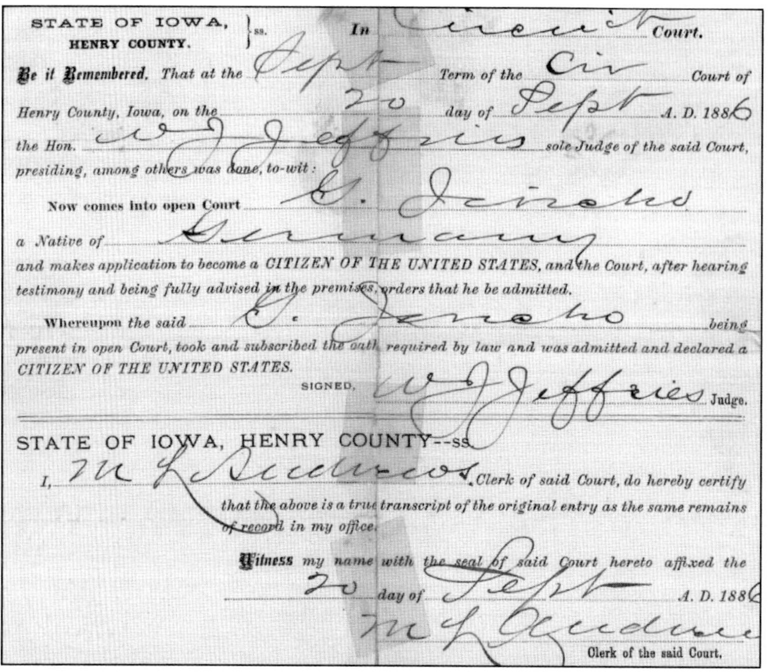

STATE OF IOWA, HENRY COUNTY. } ss. In Circuit Court.

Be it Remembered, That at the Sept Term of the Cir Court of Henry County, Iowa, on the 20 day of Sept A. D. 1886 the Hon. W. J. Jeffries sole Judge of the said Court, presiding, among others was done, to-wit:

Now comes into open Court G. Jericho a Native of Germany and makes application to become a CITIZEN OF THE UNITED STATES, and the Court, after hearing testimony and being fully advised in the premises, orders that he be admitted.

Whereupon the said G. Jericho being present in open Court, took and subscribed the oath required by law and was admitted and declared a CITIZEN OF THE UNITED STATES.

SIGNED, W. J. Jeffries Judge.

STATE OF IOWA, HENRY COUNTY--ss.

I, M. L. Andrews, Clerk of said Court, do hereby certify that the above is a true transcript of the original entry as the same remains of record in my office.

Witness my name with the seal of said Court hereto affixed the 20 day of Sept A. D. 1886

M. L. Andrews

Clerk of the said Court.

The citizenship papers for Gustaf Jericho were prepared on September 20, 1886, at the Henry County Courthouse. Jericho was a native of Germany and was admitted as an American citizen. (MPPL.)

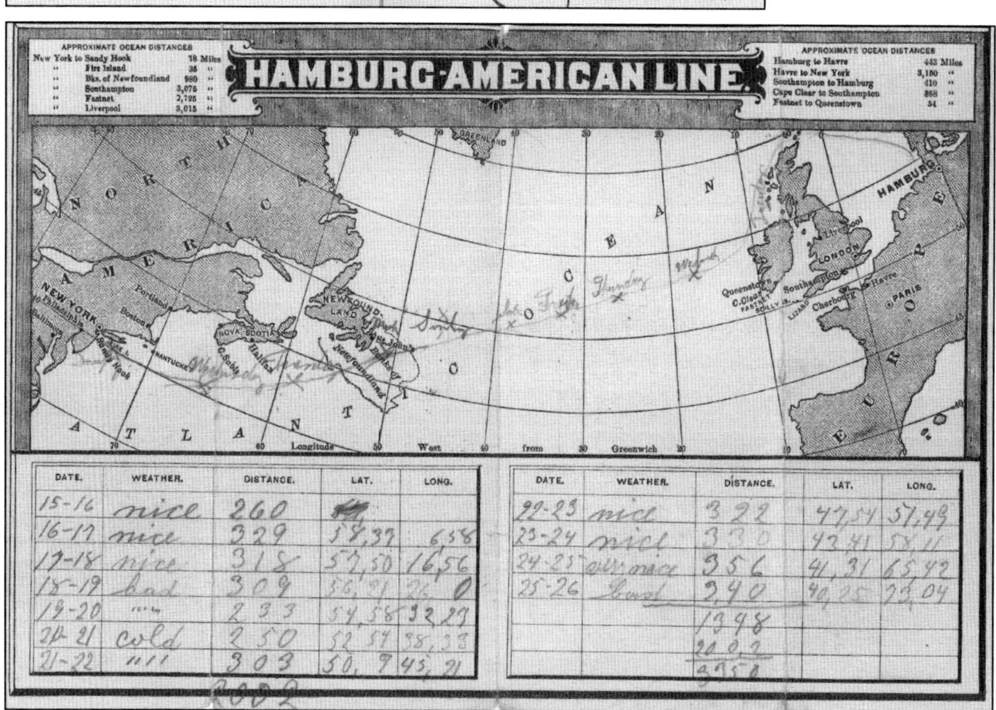

HAMBURG-AMERICAN LINE

APPROXIMATE OCEAN DISTANCES

New York to Sandy Hook	18	Miles
" Fire Island	38	"
" Bks. of Newfoundland	980	"
" Southampton	3,075	"
" Fastnet	2,725	"
" Liverpool	3,015	"

APPROXIMATE OCEAN DISTANCES

Hamburg to Havre	443	Miles
Havre to New York	3,180	"
Southampton to Hamburg	410	"
Cape Clear to Southampton	368	"
Fastnet to Queenstown	54	"

DATE.	WEATHER.	DISTANCE.	LAT.	LONG.
15-16	nice	260	[illegible]	
16-17	nice	329	58,37	6,58
17-18	nice	318	57,50	16,56
18-19	bad	309	56,21	26,0
19-20	"	233	54,58	32,27
20-21	cold	250	52,54	38,33
21-22	"	303	50,9	45,21
		2002		

DATE.	WEATHER.	DISTANCE.	LAT.	LONG.
22-23	nice	322	47,54	57,49
23-24	nice	330	42,41	58,11
24-25	[illegible] nice	356	41,31	65,42
25-26	bad	340	40,25	73,04
		1348		
		2002		
		3350		

Like many first generation immigrants, Gustaf Jericho must have missed his home and family in the old country. In 1895, he visited his native Germany. Jericho kept a log of the return voyage across the Atlantic, the route cutting across the great sea from Hamburg to New York. This log shows that the ship generally exceeded 300 miles each day. Having arrived in Germany, Jericho visited the Friedrich-Wilhelmstaedtisches Theater and the Zooligeschen Gartens in Berlin. (MPPL.)

The Hover Brothers and Company was a very early photographic studio in Mount Pleasant, listed in the 1870 *City Directory*. This portrait shows the stoic pose of a gentleman in the mid-19th century. Hover Brothers provided many photographic services, their cards advertising "Old Pictures Copied and Colored true to life, in Oil, India Ink and water colors. Negatives Preserved." (MPPL.)

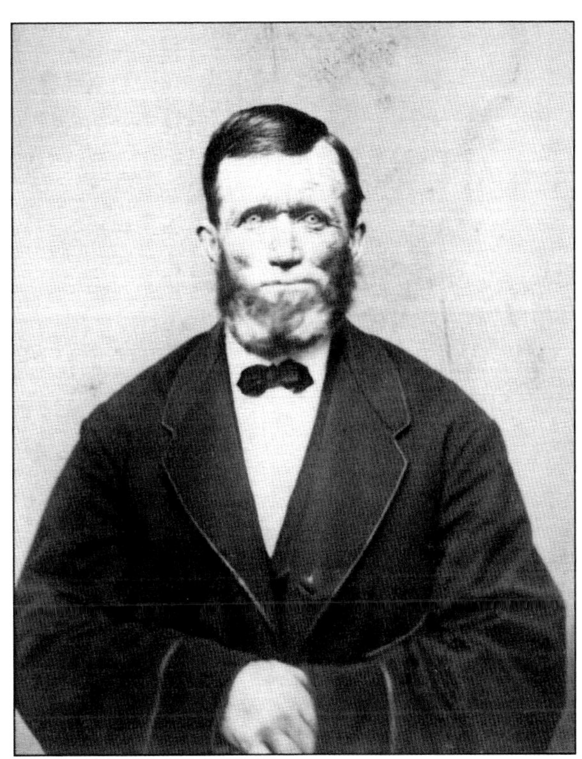

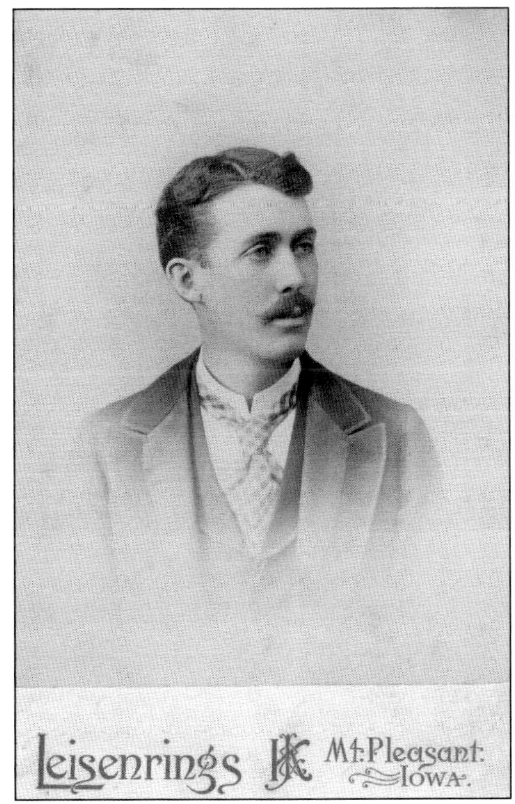

The Leisenrings photographic studio was located across from the Brazelton Hotel on North Main Street. Here, a young man poses for a portrait, exhibiting the dignified appearance of a gentleman of the 19th century. Notice the checkered tie and the parted hairstyle. (MPPL.)

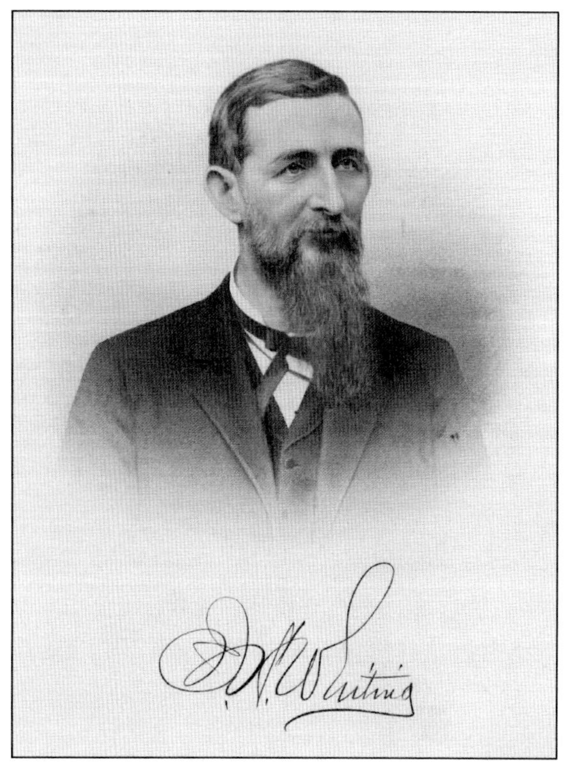

Timothy Whiting and his son John H. Whiting (pictured) were skilled bankers during Mount Pleasant's formative years. In 1865, Timothy served as the president of the National State Bank, and John served as cashier. Timothy was known for his industry and punctuality. The National State Bank was located in the building currently occupied by Miss K's Homemade Delectables at the intersection of Main and Monroe Streets. (MPPL.)

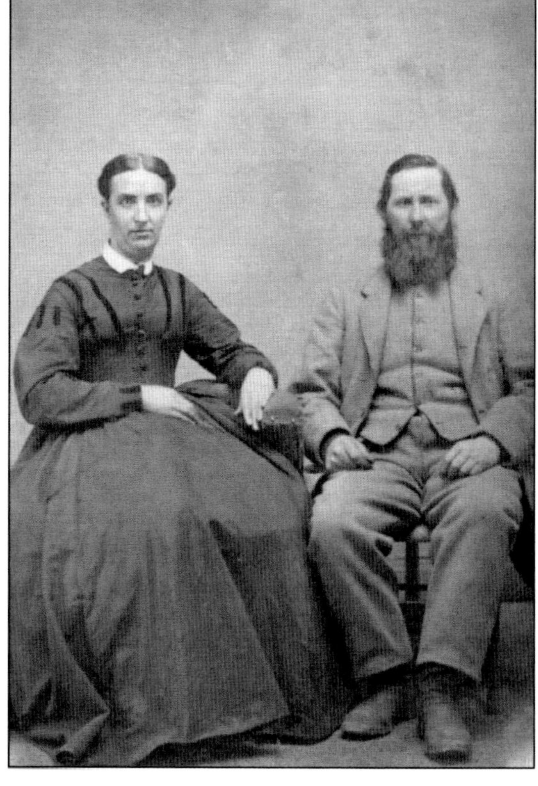

In the 19th century, Mount Pleasant residents lived in a city full of new, industrial commodities. The 1870 *City Directory* lists thirteen physicians and surgeons, nine insurance agents, four photographers, four sewing machine outlets, three hardware stores, two ice-cream saloons, one washing machine dealer, and a host of many other services and businesses. This photograph was taken at one of the local studios. (MPPL.)

Mrs. Rommel was the wife of Alexander Rommel, the director of the Mount Pleasant Conservatory of Music. The music conservatory was an important cultural center in the late 19th and early 20th centuries. The 1893 *City Directory* noted that the town felt "confident that the advantages which are offered here for the study of violin and wind instruments, are superior to any thing within the state." (Don Young Collection, HCHT.)

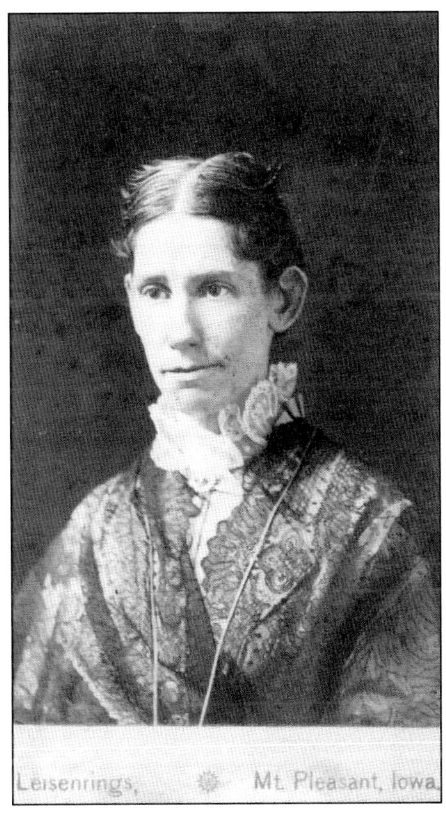

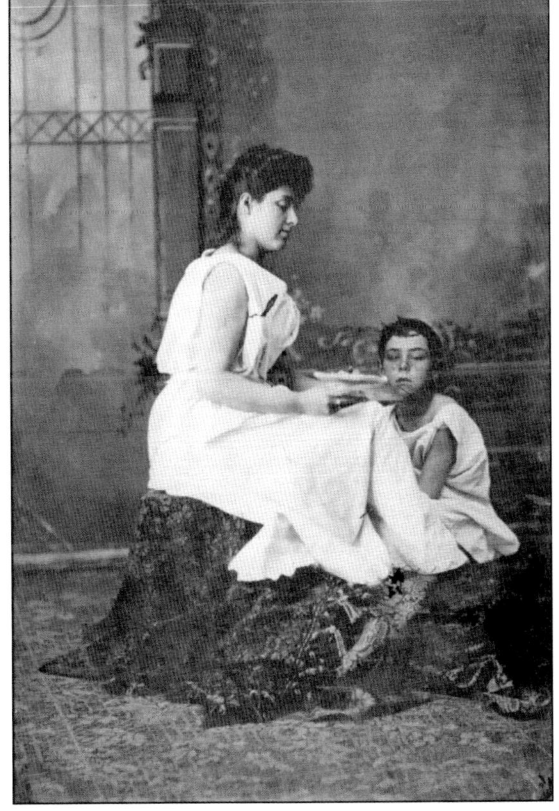

Mount Pleasant is home to acclaimed 19th century sculptor Harriet Ketchum. Ketchum graduated from Iowa Wesleyan and studied drawing and sculpture in Italy. She had the distinguished honor of developing sculptures for the Soldiers and Sailors monument in Des Moines in the 1890s. The pictured tintype shows a model for one of these sculptures. The children posing for the sculptures were also Mount Pleasant residents: J.T. Whiting (left) and Ralph Crane. The girl represents "History" and the boy "Iowa." Ketchum gave the tintypes to the children as rewards for modeling. Whiting kept these tintypes her whole life. (MPPL.)

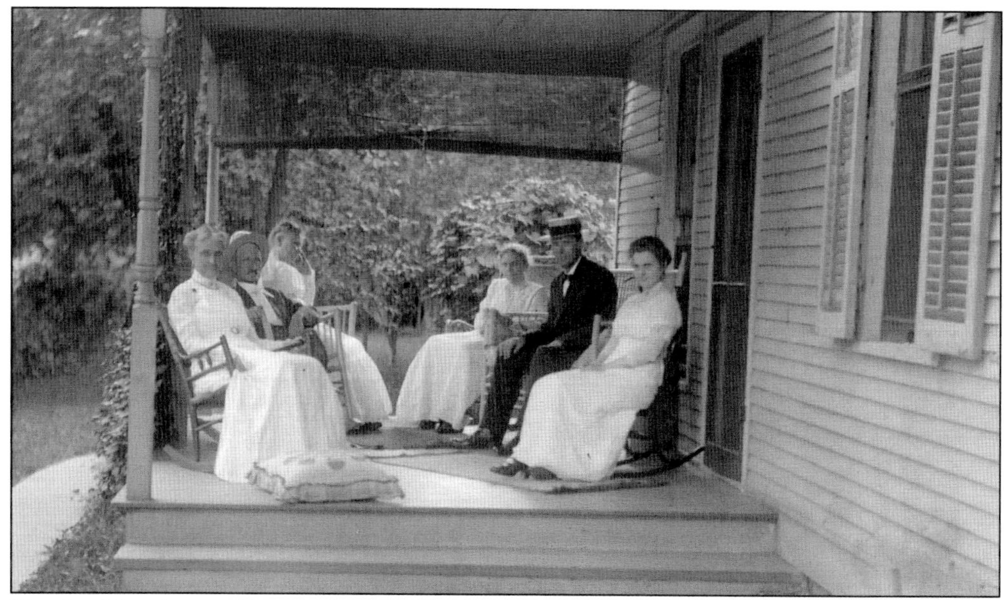

The Bird family was very prominent in Mount Pleasant in the 19th century. Dr. Wellington Bird received his education at Jefferson Medical College in his native Pennsylvania. He settled in Mount Pleasant in 1849 and served as assistant surgeon for the Fourth Iowa Cavalry during the Civil War. The Birds' home, pictured here, was located on North Main Street, at the current location of the old Carnegie Library. (MPPL.)

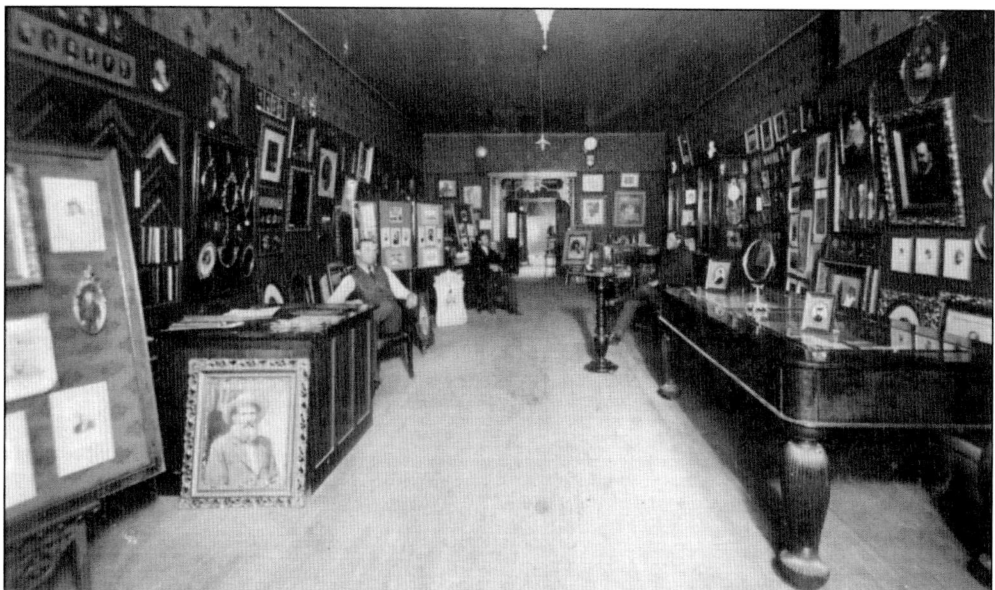

The Dyall family was active in photography in Mount Pleasant since at least the 1890s. Will and Herbert Dyall operated a studio on North Main Street. Soon, there were actually two Dyall studios on North Main Street, with the two brothers each having their own business. This photograph from about 1905 shows the various frames and selections available to customers. The 1911–1912 *Directory of Henry County* contains an advertisement for Will Dyall and Company, revealing that the Dyalls had won three medals from the Iowa Photographers' Association, including gold medals in portraits and children's classes. (Don Young Collection, HCHT.)

Prof. Lincoln Antrim was one of Mount Pleasant's many education luminaries. After receiving his master's degree at Western Normal School in Page County, Iowa, Professor Antrim taught for several years in the school system of Primrose, Iowa, where he also served as school principal. In 1897, this experienced and educated teacher came to Mount Pleasant and founded the Mount Pleasant Academy. (MPPL.)

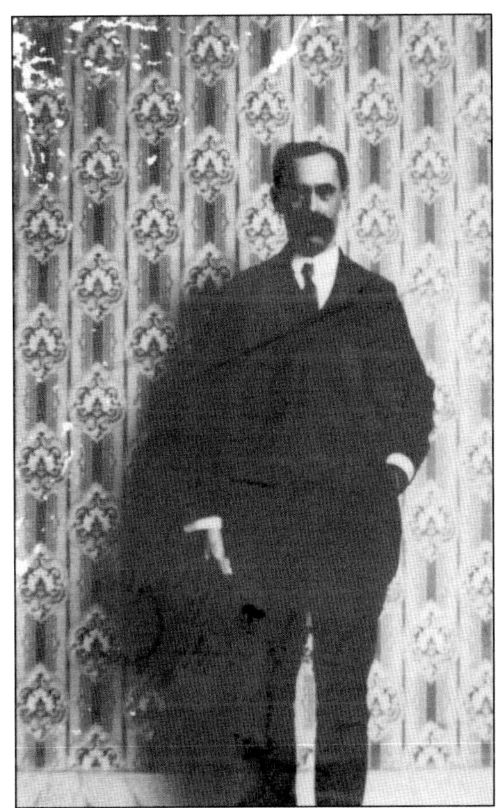

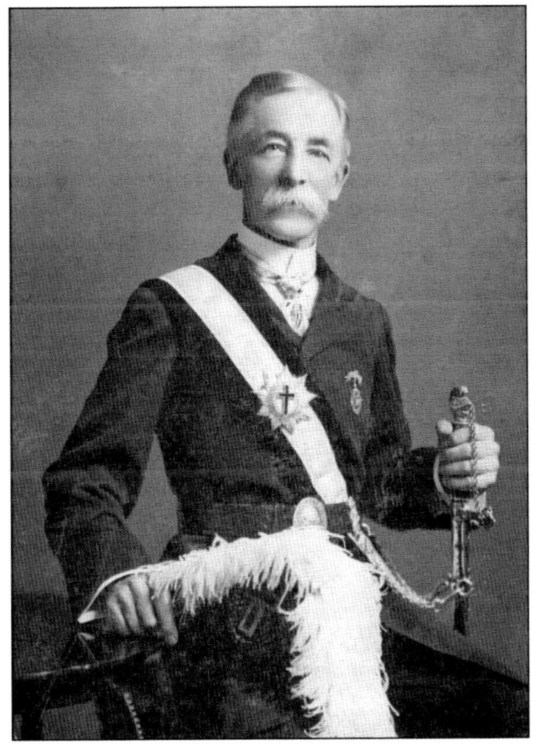

In 1855, Mr. and Mrs. William Leisenring settled in Mount Pleasant. The Leisenrings were skilled in a new art form, photography. They started a photographic gallery on the square that gained a regional reputation. Five of William Leisenring's sons committed themselves to the Union during the Civil War. Joe Leisenring, one of William's other sons, attended Iowa Wesleyan. (MPPL.)

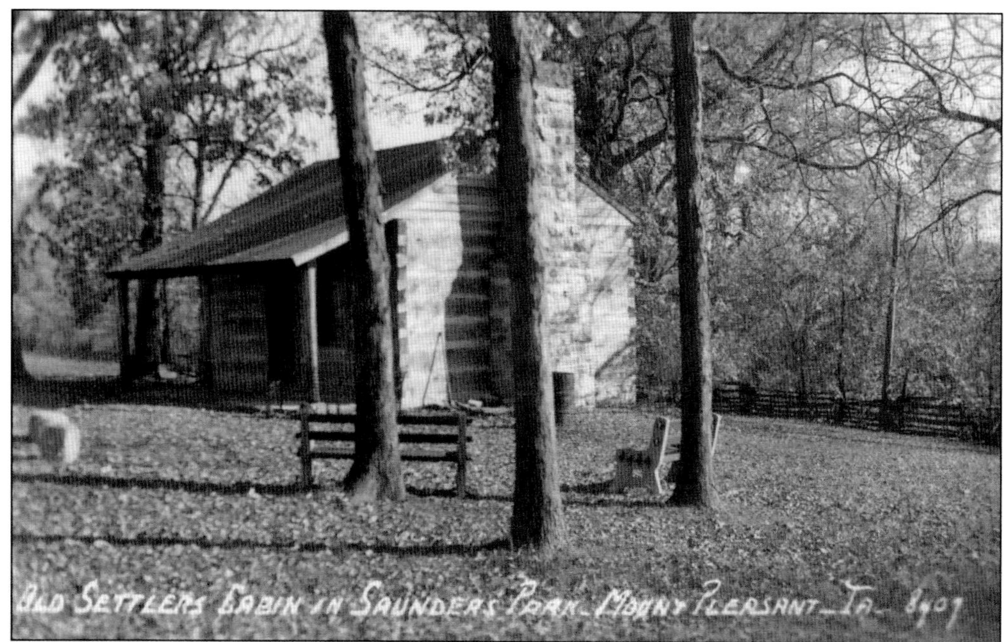

Humble cabins were the first settler lodges to appear in frontier country. These homes of wood and earth have long passed. However, organizations such as the Old Settlers Society celebrated the origins of the Mount Pleasant community, holding annual events that drew large crowds into town. (Don Young Collection, HCHT.)

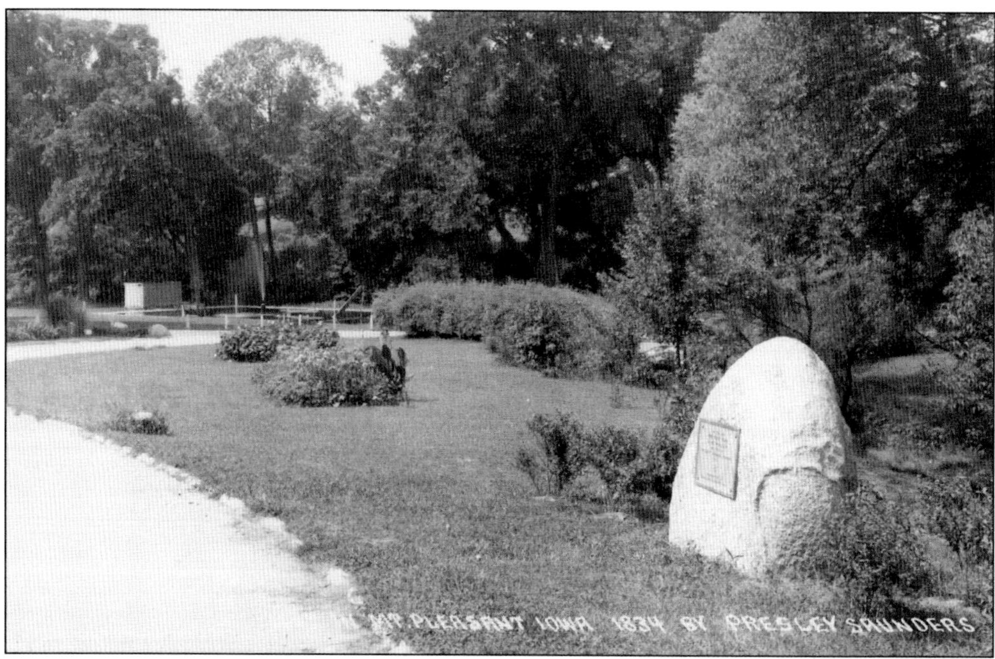

A stone in Saunders Park marks the location of Presley Saunders's frontier cabin, which he situated near spring waters in 1834. The frontier community rapidly developed over the succeeding decades. Saunders played a critical role in the town's establishment and layout. (Don Young Collection, HCHT.)

James Harlan graduated from Asbury University in Indiana, which is now DePauw University. In 1846, he was offered employment as principal of Iowa City College. Harlan was then recruited to Mount Pleasant to serve as president of the Collegiate Institute, which would become Iowa Wesleyan. As university president, Harlan provided a progressive vision for the college, working toward the establishment of a respected institution. Old Main was constructed under his leadership in 1854. (Library of Congress.)

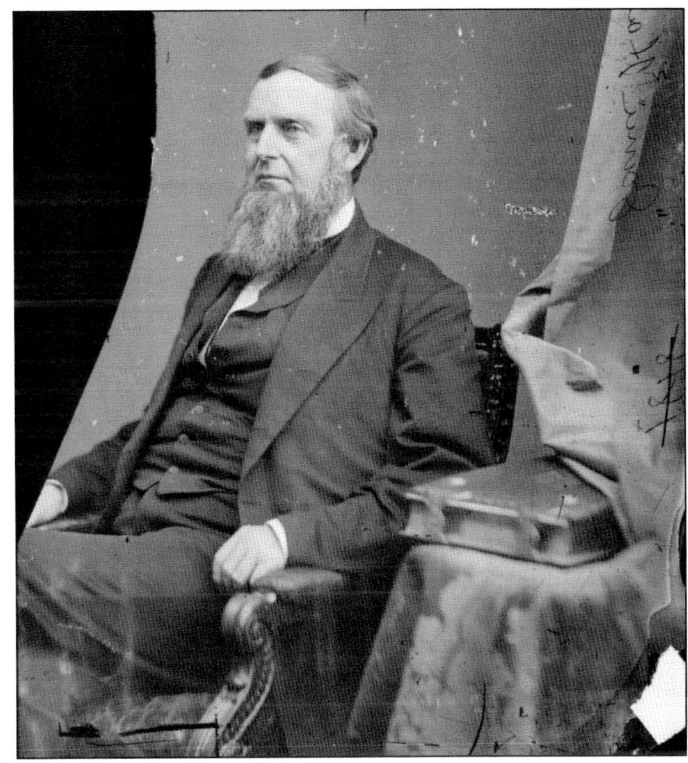

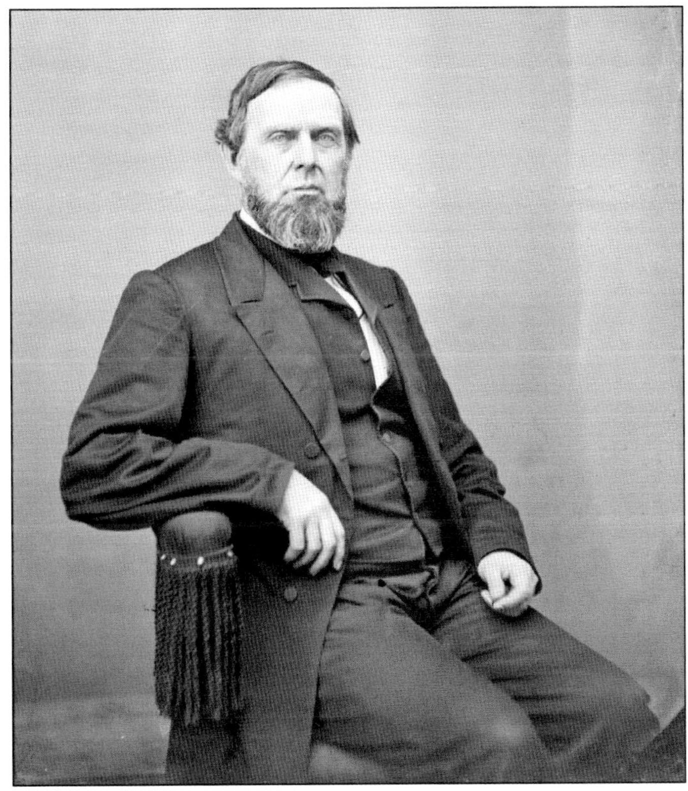

Still only in his 30s, James Harlan was elected senator for Iowa, with his term beginning in 1855. Senator Harlan very quickly emerged as a powerful opponent of slavery. On March 27, 1856, he spoke for two hours before the Senate against the expansion of slavery into Kansas. While the nervous young senator trembled in his speech, a colleague walked to his side and whispered words of encouragement into his ears. Senator Harlan's advocate that day was Sen. Charles Sumner, the Massachusetts abolitionist who was infamously beaten on the Senate floor for his antislavery views just two months later. (Library of Congress.)

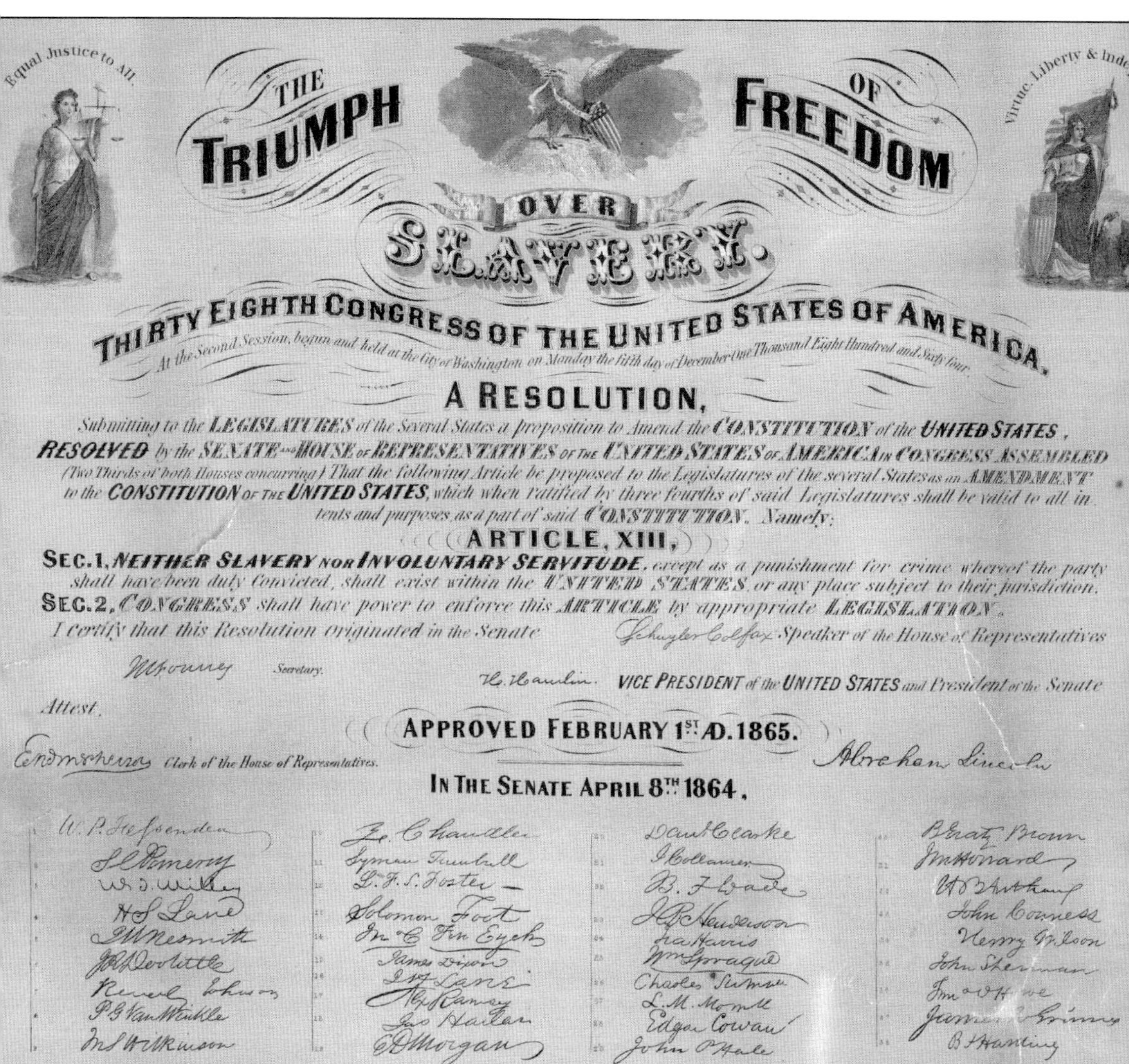

Equal Justice to All.

Virtue, Liberty & Inde

THE TRIUMPH OF FREEDOM

OVER

SLAVERY.

THIRTY EIGHTH CONGRESS OF THE UNITED STATES OF AMERICA,

At the Second Session, begun and held at the City of Washington on Monday the fifth day of December One Thousand Eight Hundred and Sixty four.

A RESOLUTION,

Submitting to the LEGISLATURES of the Several States a proposition to Amend the CONSTITUTION of the UNITED STATES.

RESOLVED by the SENATE and HOUSE of REPRESENTATIVES of the UNITED STATES of AMERICA in CONGRESS ASSEMBLED (Two Thirds of both Houses concurring) That the following Article be proposed to the Legislatures of the several States as an AMENDMENT to the CONSTITUTION of the UNITED STATES, which when ratified by three fourths of said Legislatures shall be valid to all intents and purposes, as a part of said CONSTITUTION. Namely:

ARTICLE, XIII,

SEC. 1, NEITHER SLAVERY NOR INVOLUNTARY SERVITUDE, except as a punishment for crime whereof the party shall have been duly Convicted, shall exist within the UNITED STATES, or any place subject to their jurisdiction.

SEC. 2, CONGRESS shall have power to enforce this ARTICLE by appropriate LEGISLATION.

I certify that this Resolution Originated in the Senate — Schuyler Colfax Speaker of the House of Representatives

Secretary.

H. Hamlin. VICE PRESIDENT of the UNITED STATES and President of the Senate

Attest,

APPROVED FEBRUARY 1ST AD. 1865.

Clerk of the House of Representatives. — Abraham Lincoln

IN THE SENATE APRIL 8TH 1864.

Senator Harlan played a critical role in the Senate during the trying years of the 1850s and 1860s, acting as a leading antislavery voice in Washington, DC. Mount Pleasant's senator signed the 13th Amendment, the document formally abolishing slavery in the United States. The amendment was titled, "The Triumph of Freedom over Slavery." Senator Harlan's signature ("Jas Harlan") is in the second column from the left, second from the bottom. Abraham Lincoln's signature is also on the document, to the right of the date. (Library of Congress.)

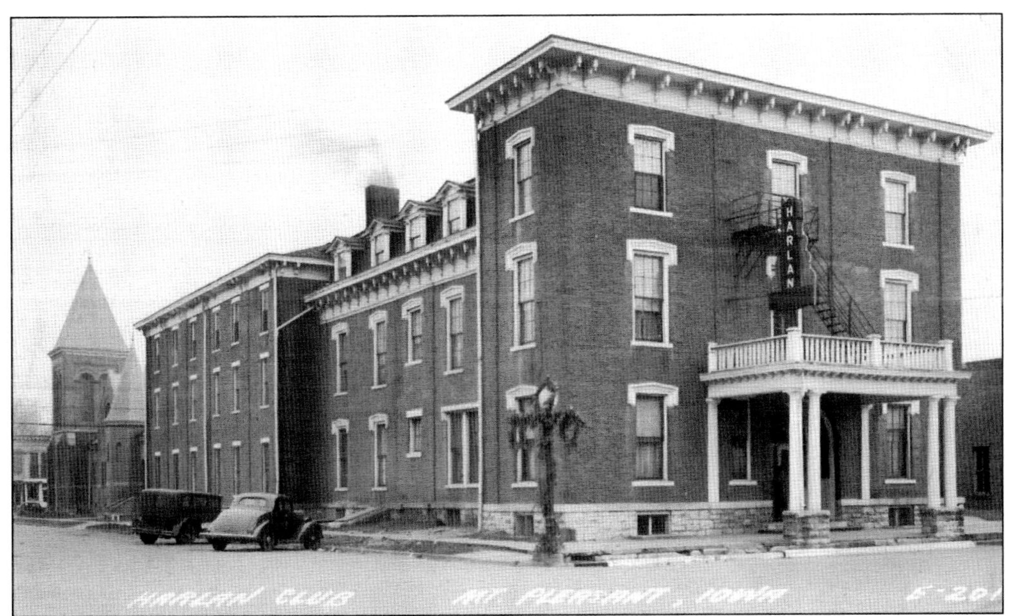

Built in 1857, the Harlan House on Jefferson Street was the residence of Sen. James Harlan during his tenure in public office. Senator Harlan became a personal friend of Pres. Abraham Lincoln, and he was present at Lincoln's bedside during the president's final hours. The old Presbyterian church is visible behind the Harlan House at left. (Don Young Collection, HCHT.)

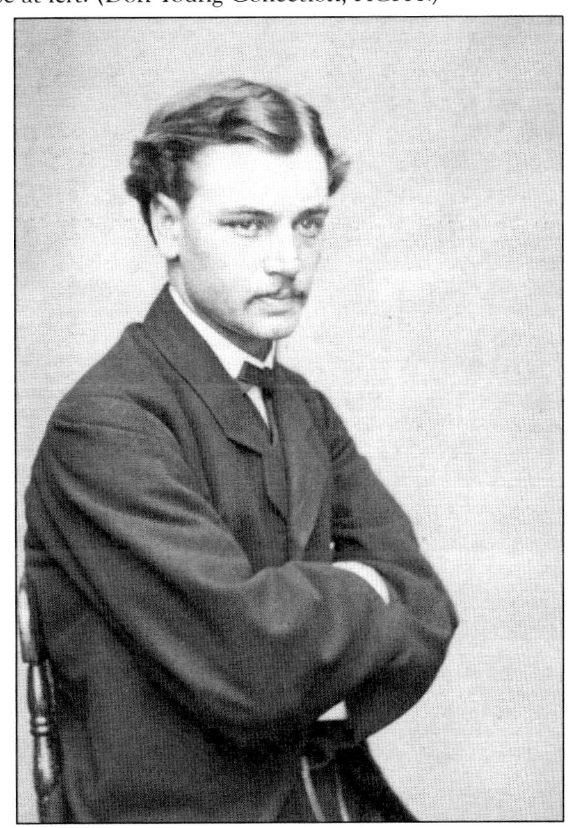

In 1868, Robert Todd Lincoln, the son of President Lincoln, wed Mary Harlan, the daughter of Senator Harlan. President Lincoln's grandchildren visited and played in Mount Pleasant. (Library of Congress.)

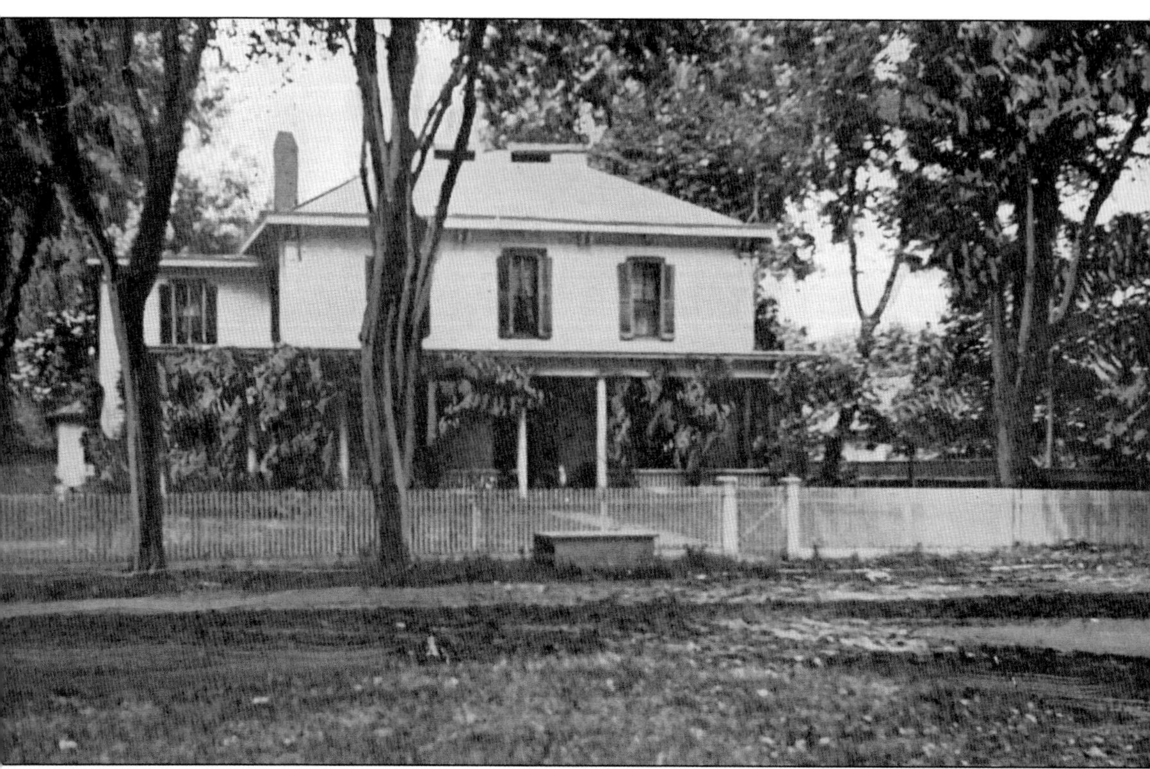

The Harlan-Lincoln home on the north part of the Iowa Wesleyan campus served as the residence of Sen. James Harlan in 1873. He retired to this location from his earlier brick home on Jefferson Street. The Senator's daughter, Mary Lincoln, and the Lincoln grandchildren—Mary, Abraham ("Jack"), and Jessie—spent their summers in this home. (Don Young Collection, HCHT.)

Two

Public School

Education in Mount Pleasant began in a frontier cabin just a few years after the arrival of the first pioneers. The development of the public school system came remarkably early, with the main "Old Central" School in operation before the Civil War. The development of the American public school system in the 19th century was nothing short of revolutionary, as society provided children with new opportunities for growth and enrichment. The 1879 *History of Henry County* remarked, "Wealth has succeeded poverty, and privation has given way to comfort. The children of the pioneers have grown up, surrounded by refining influences, and bear the stamp of training in a broader school than their parents were privileged to attend." Today, a surviving school building from the 19th century can be seen at the intersection of Lincoln and Baker Streets. The *Portrait and Biographical Album of Henry County* from 1888 recorded:

> The pioneers of the county little expected that so soon the beautiful country which they had selected for their future homes would be so abundantly supplied with the means of educating their children. To them great credit is due for inaugurating so shortly after coming the educational system which has grown to be such a powerful factor for good as the splendid schools of to-day are.

The 1885 *Census of Iowa* reported that Henry County had 3,809 pupils enrolled in public schools. These students were taught by 176 salaried teachers in 51 frame schoolhouses and 22 brick schoolhouses. The early foundation of public schools in Mount Pleasant is another hallmark of this Athens of Iowa.

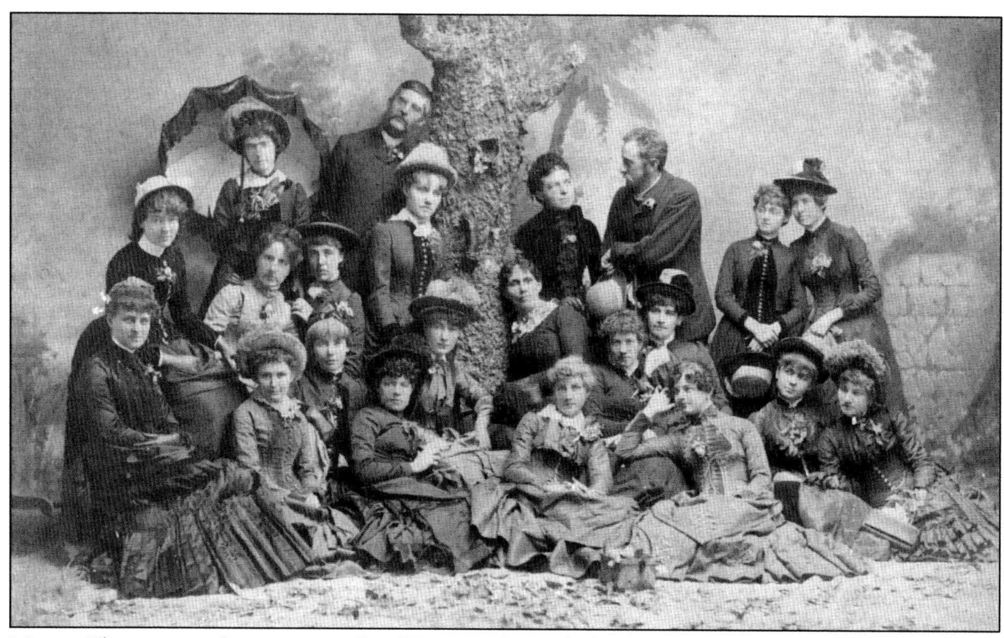

Mount Pleasant teachers pose in this Western-themed photograph from about 1885. The public school system began to form in the 1840s, and Central School, a multi-storied brick building, was erected in 1858 at the present location of the Mount Pleasant Public Library on East Monroe Street. In 1866, the Winona School, once located at the intersection of Henry and White Streets, was built to serve the western portion of the town. (MPPL.)

$ 2 72/100 State of Iowa, Henry County, ss: Oct 12 1863 No 994

Received of W. H. Campbell Two & 72/100 Dollars,

in full of the following Taxes for the year 1862, on Poll, Personal Property, and the annexed Real Estate.

	TAX. $ cts.	INT. $ cts.	PARTS OF	S.	T.	R.	A.	TOWN.	Lot.	B.
State,	25	4						Mt Pleasant	4	27
County,	50	8								
School,	12	2								
School House,	43	6								
Teachers' Fund,	31	5								
City Tax.	31	5								
County Poll,	50									
Interest,	30									

$2.72

F. White Treasurer.

Deputy.

W. Campbell of Mount Pleasant owed $2.72 for his state, county, and local taxes in 1862. School funding was considered critical in these early years, as public collections included specific line items for teachers' funds and the schoolhouse. This early commitment to public schools was remarkable, as the community emphasized children's education at an early date. (MPPL.)

Old Central was the first substantial tax-supported public school in Mount Pleasant, succeeding earlier log cabin schools. The building was constructed in 1858, and classes included reading, writing, geography, arithmetic, algebra, grammar, and spelling. It stood at the current location of the public library on East Monroe Street, adjacent to another important school in town: Howe's Academy. (MPPL.)

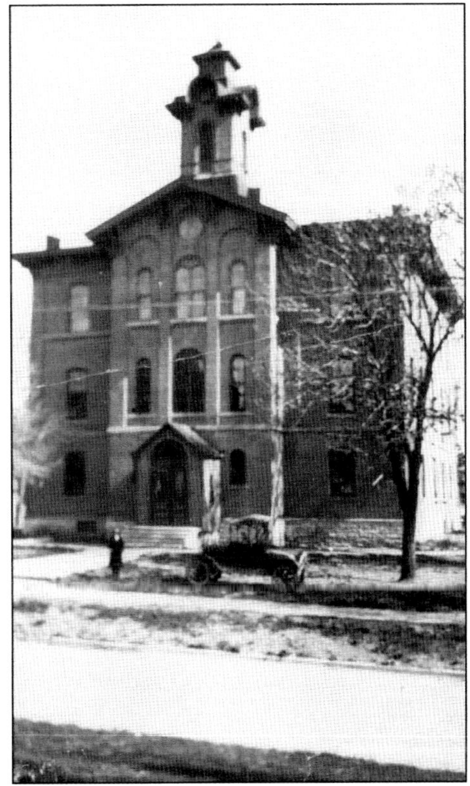

This document, dated April 26, 1878, certifies that "Grace Roberts has completed the Studies assigned to the 3rd Grade, has passed the standard examination of 80 per cent therein, and is entitled to position in the 4th Grade." Grace Roberts completed the third grade in the Old Central School. (MPPL.)

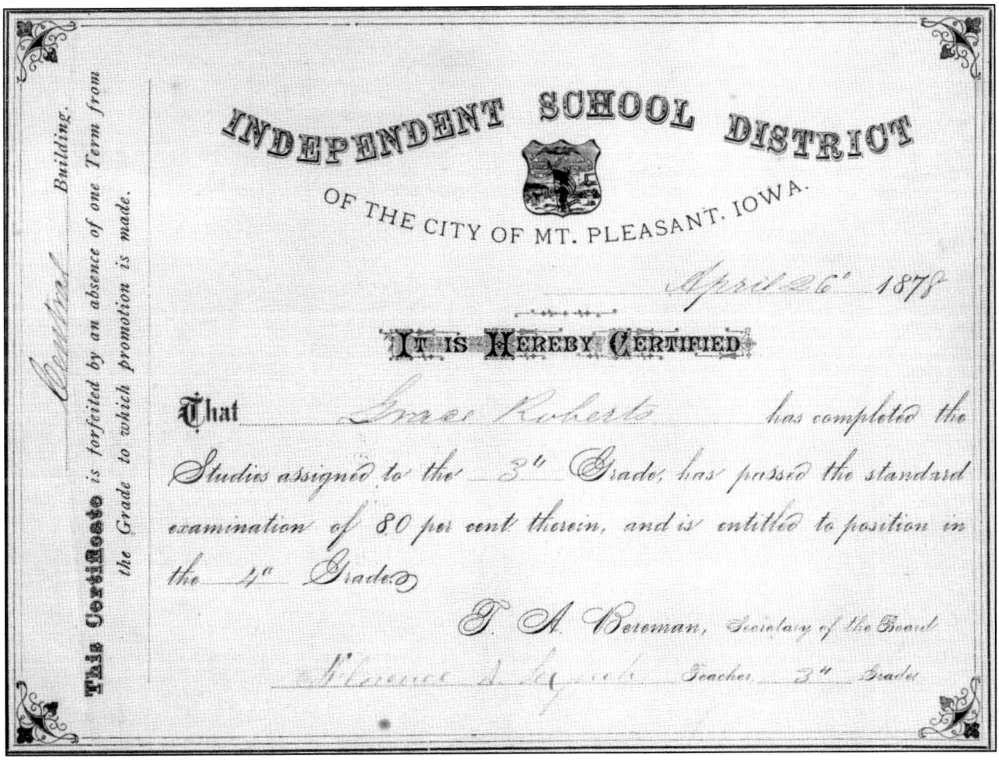

Central Building.

This Certificate is forfeited by an absence of one Term from the Grade to which promotion is made.

INDEPENDENT SCHOOL DISTRICT

OF THE CITY OF MT. PLEASANT, IOWA.

April 26' 1878

IT IS HEREBY CERTIFIED

That Grace Roberts has completed the Studies assigned to the 3d Grade, has passed the standard examination of 80 per cent therein, and is entitled to position in the 4th Grade.

T. A. Bereman, Secretary of the Board

[illegible] Teacher 3d Grade

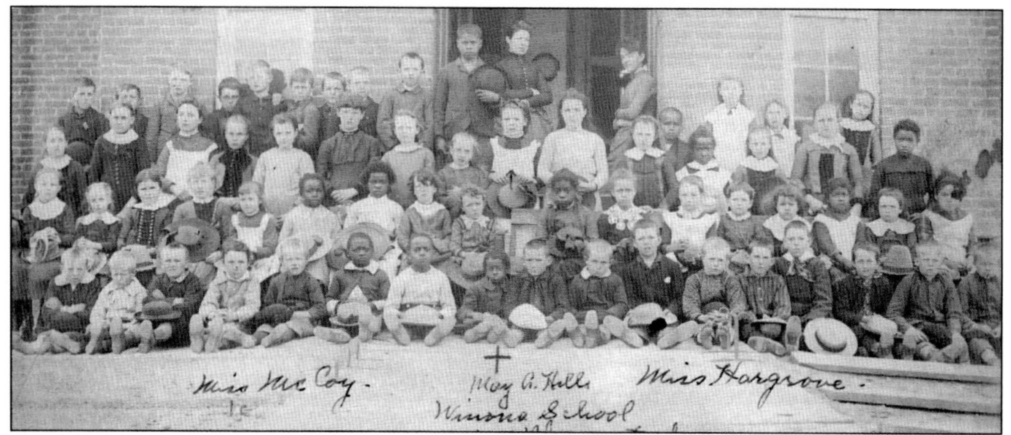

Winona School opened shortly after the Civil War. The school was located at the corner of West Henry and North White Streets, at the present location of the United Thru Play Playground near the old Saunders School. This 19th-century class photograph shows an integrated class. (MPPL.)

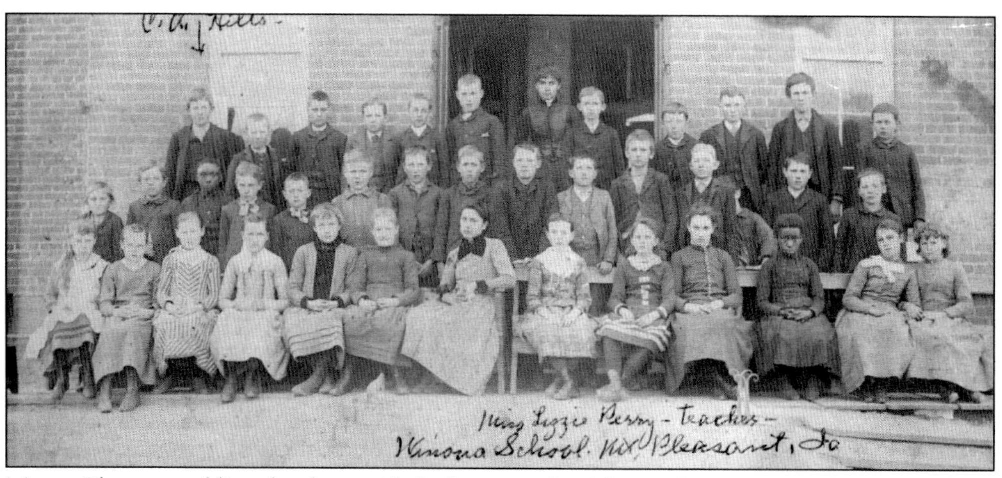

Mount Pleasant public schools provided education for African American residents as early as 1863. In that year, a frame house called the "Frog Pond" was rented by the school system to serve African American students. However, these students were integrated with white students at the Winona School when it was completed in 1867. (MPPL.)

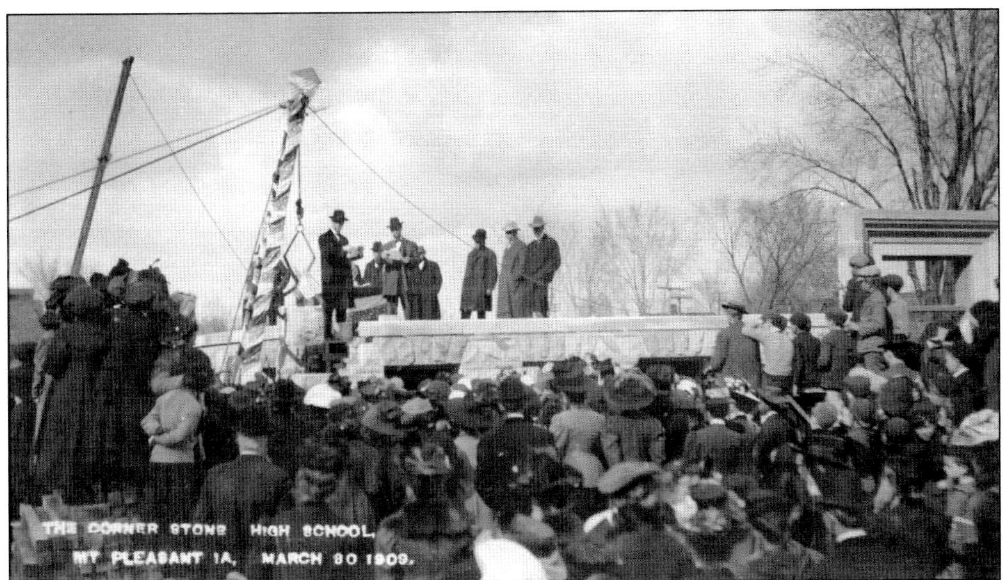

As the 20th century dawned, education became a more critical concern to the general public. In addition, a rising Mount Pleasant population rendered the spaces at Old Central inadequate. Old Central had served the community since the 1850s, but the necessity for a new high school had become evident. The class of 1909 was the last to graduate from Old Central, though the school continued to serve younger grade levels for more years. Pictured here is the cornerstone laying of the new high school in 1909. This building is the current middle school on North Adams Street. (Don Young Collection, HCHT.)

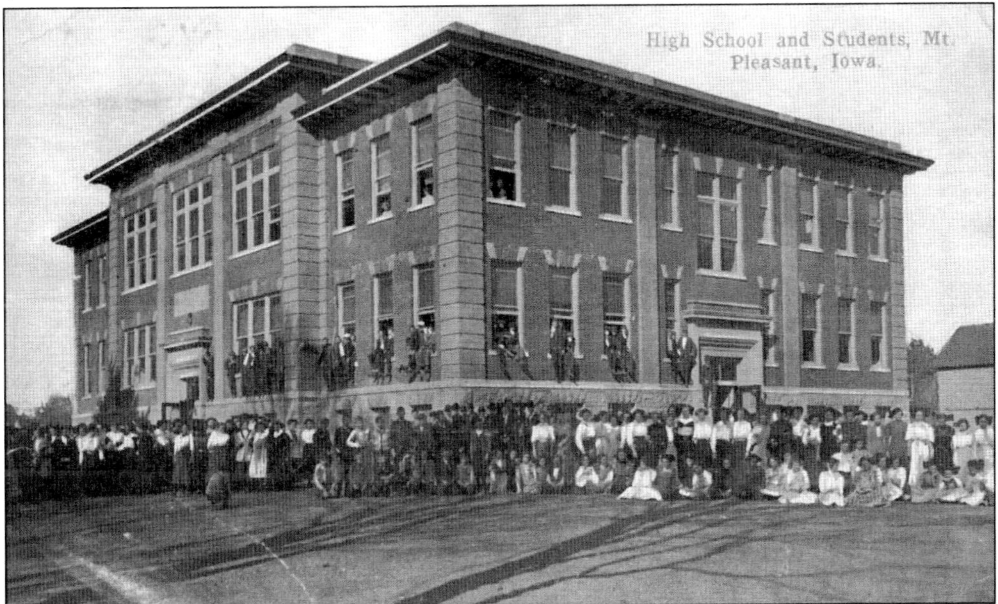

The 1909 high school on North Adams Street is seen here during its first years in operation. It was not long before the student population began to outgrow this new building. In the fall of 1920, the high school relocated to the old YMCA building at the present location of the post office. After the high school transferred to the YMCA building, the school pictured here became a junior high, as it remains today. (Don Young Collection, HCHT.)

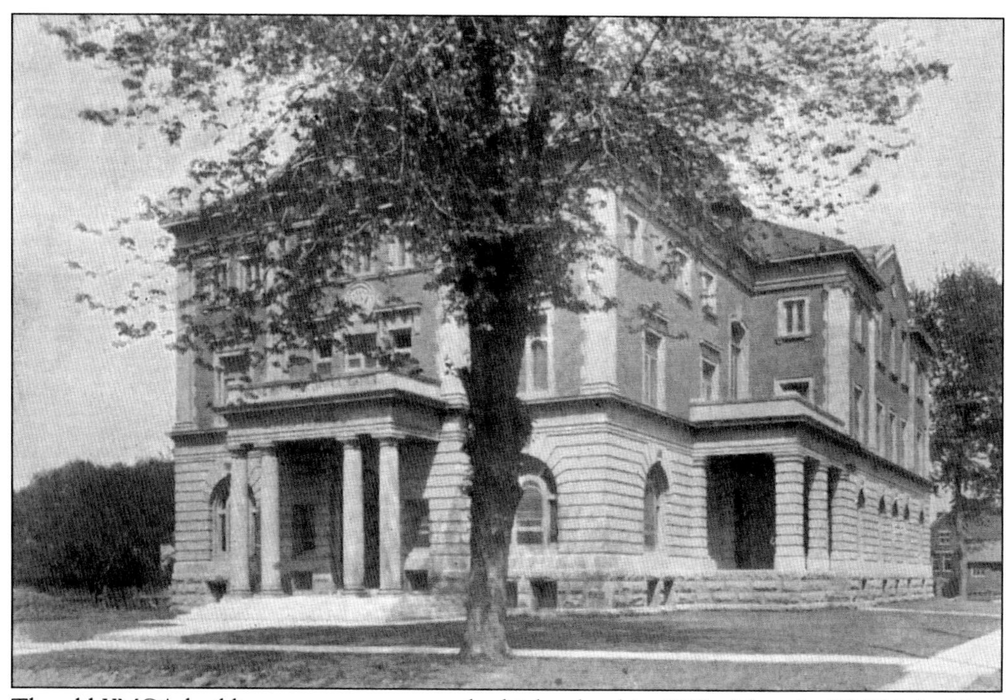

The old YMCA building came to serve as the high school in 1920. After the YMCA building burned down in 1932, classes were arranged in various places, including the public library, empty stores, churches, and the courthouse. The next high school was built on East Monroe Street; that structure serves as the public library today. (Don Young Collection, HCHT.)

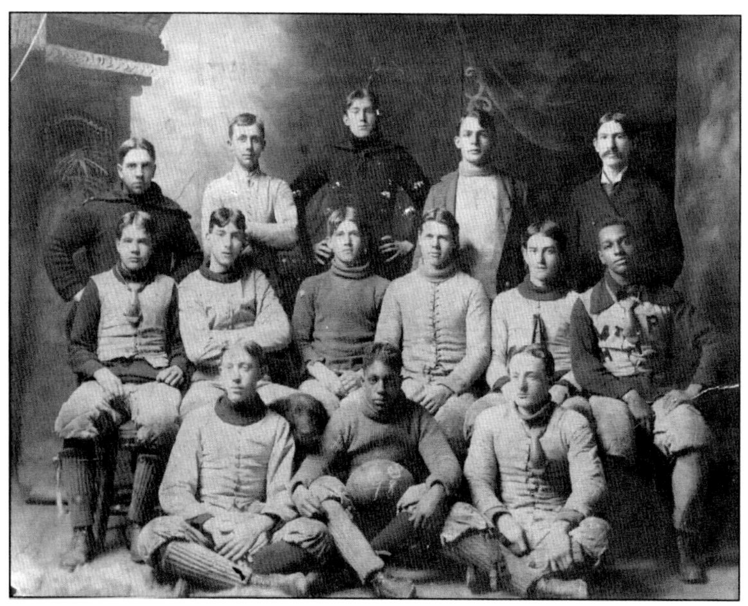

The 1898 Mount Pleasant football squad poses in gear. The team was racially integrated. Notice the large size of the football in the lap of the player at center in the first row. Three of the players sport nose guards around their necks, and a dog pokes his head between two teammates in the first row. (MPPL.)

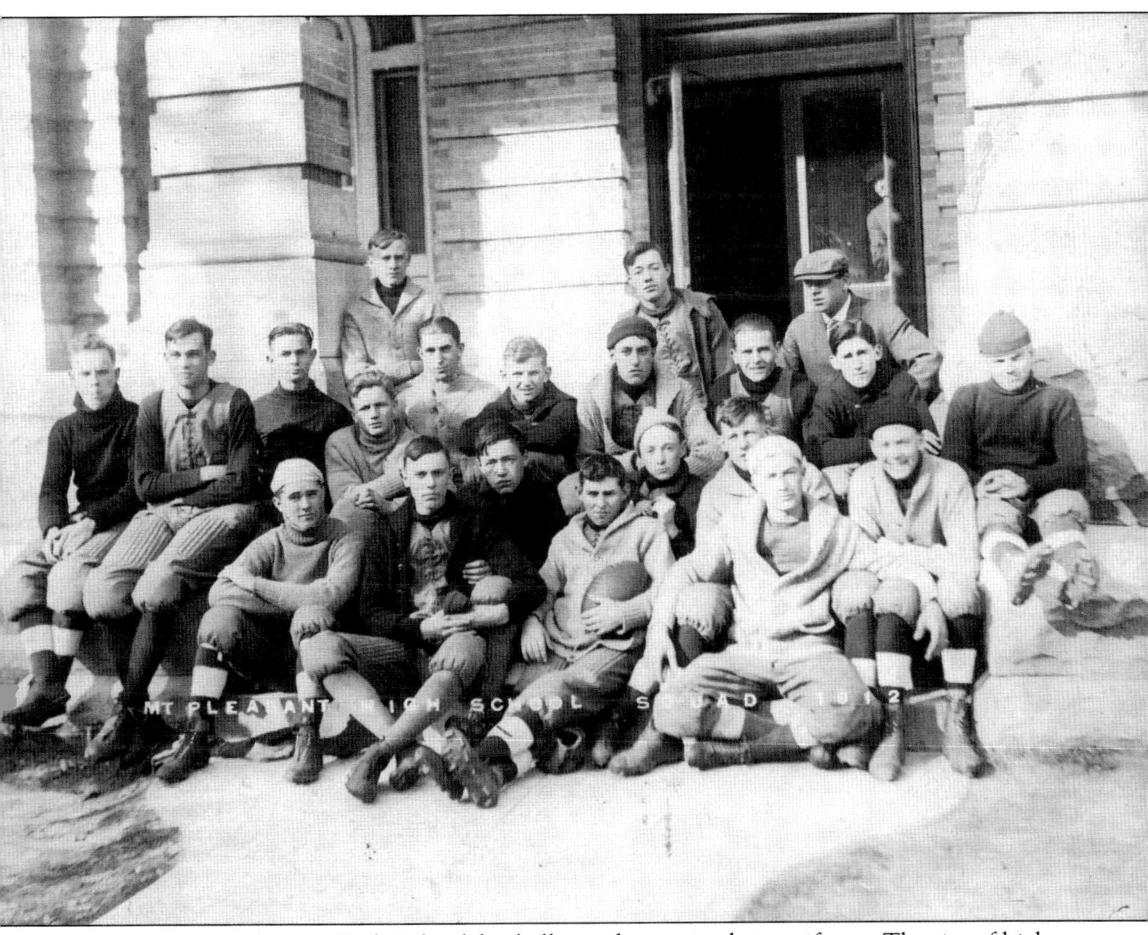

The 1912 Mount Pleasant High School football squad poses in their uniforms. The size of high school football players has changed rather dramatically in a century. In 1914, Rilea Doe, Mount Pleasant's red-headed quarterback, nicknamed "Runt," led the team to a 5-2 record. The able quarterback weighed 120 pounds. The biggest guy on the team was Elmer Litzenberg, or "Litz" for short. His teammates called him "Baby Elephant," as he was not only the biggest guy on the team, but also the youngest. The powerhouse Baby Elephant weighed 168 pounds. (MPPL.)

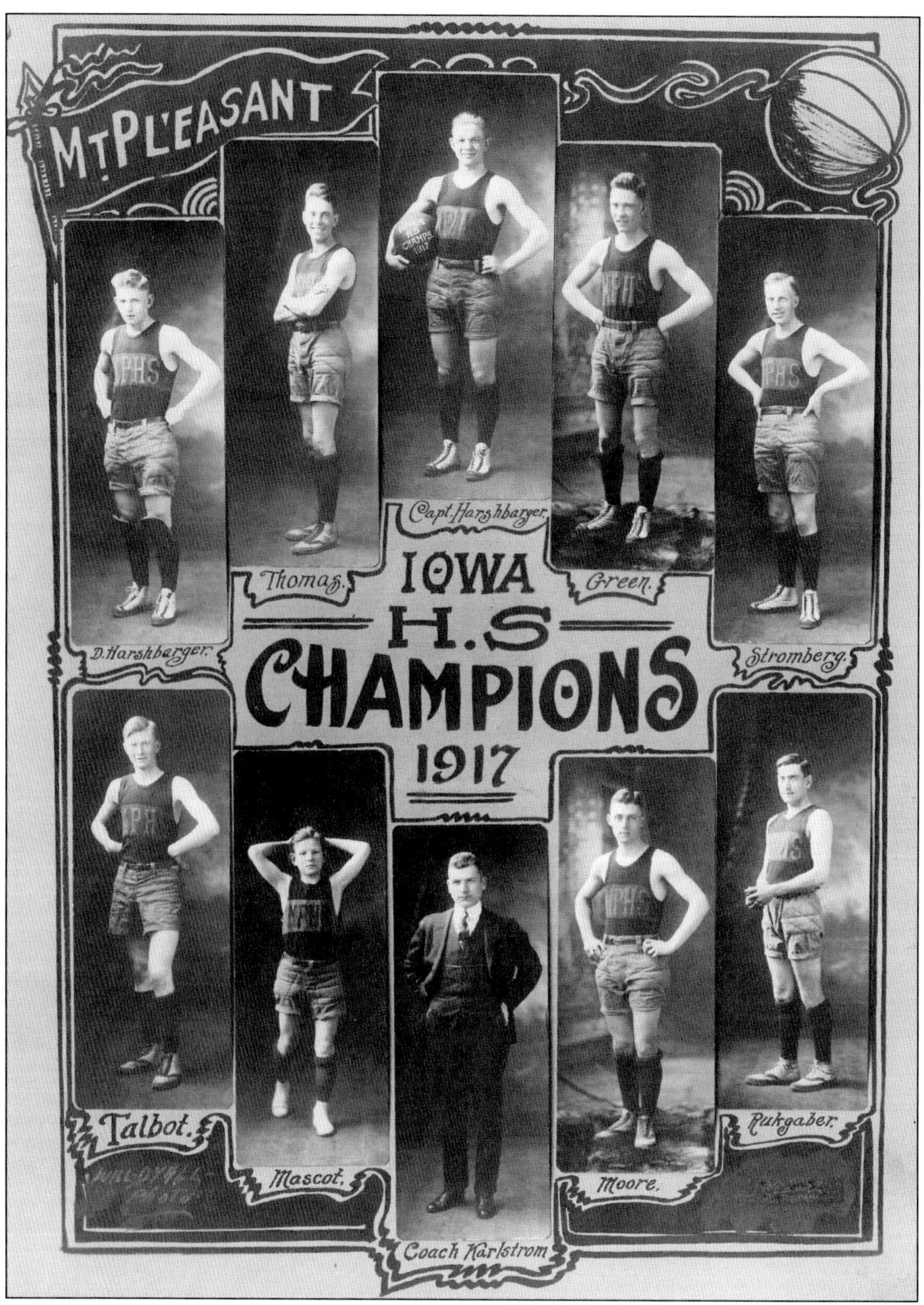

The 1918 Mount Pleasant High School *Tattler* boasted about the school's successful basketball team: "For two years in succession Mt. Pleasant High School has walked off with the Iowa State Championship, showing our brilliant-playing quintette second to none in the state. . . . The past season will be long remembered in Mt. Pleasant and especially by those who witnessed some of the thrilling games, such as the one with Iowa City." (MPPL.)

Three

Academies

Education has always served as a central hallmark to Mount Pleasant. The first private academy began in a cabin less than 10 years after the first pioneers settled here. This early institution, Samuel Howe's Academy, began a long tradition of progressive education that prepared generations of residents for professional fields. Samuel Howe's passion for learning and progress was critical to the community's early development. Howe applied his learning to the public good, serving as the editor of the *Iowa True Democrat*, Mount Pleasant's abolitionist paper.

Howe's Academy was one of many educational institutions in the 19th century that cultivated young minds. The Mount Pleasant Female Seminary, once located on Washington Street, and the Mount Pleasant Academy, begun under the leadership of Lincoln Antrim, also played critical roles in earning Mount Pleasant's reputation as the Athens of Iowa. In a 1978 issue of the *Annals of Iowa*, Robert E. Belding noted, "It is a tribute to Iowa's adaptable, frontier climate that a town the size of Mount Pleasant, with a population a hundred years ago of less than 4,300, was able to support two such different academies as Howe's and the Female Seminary."

It is astonishing that a college was in the works in Mount Pleasant hardly 10 years after the first cabins appeared. The *Portrait and Biographical Album of Henry County* reported in 1888 that "Mount Pleasant is called the Athens of Iowa, and here is located one of the best known educational institutions of the Mississippi Valley, the Iowa Wesleyan University." Iowa Wesleyan, originally the Mount Pleasant Collegiate Institute, was the result of a cultural crossroads, the meeting point of this community's early Methodist heritage and its commitment to education. Iowa Wesleyan has a long tradition of producing distinguished graduates. Belle A. Mansfield, class of 1866, became the first woman admitted to the bar in the United States. In the 1950s, James Van Allen discovered the cosmic radiation belts that now bear his name. Dr. Peggy Whitson, class of 1981, is a highly experienced NASA astronaut, serving as a space flight commander.

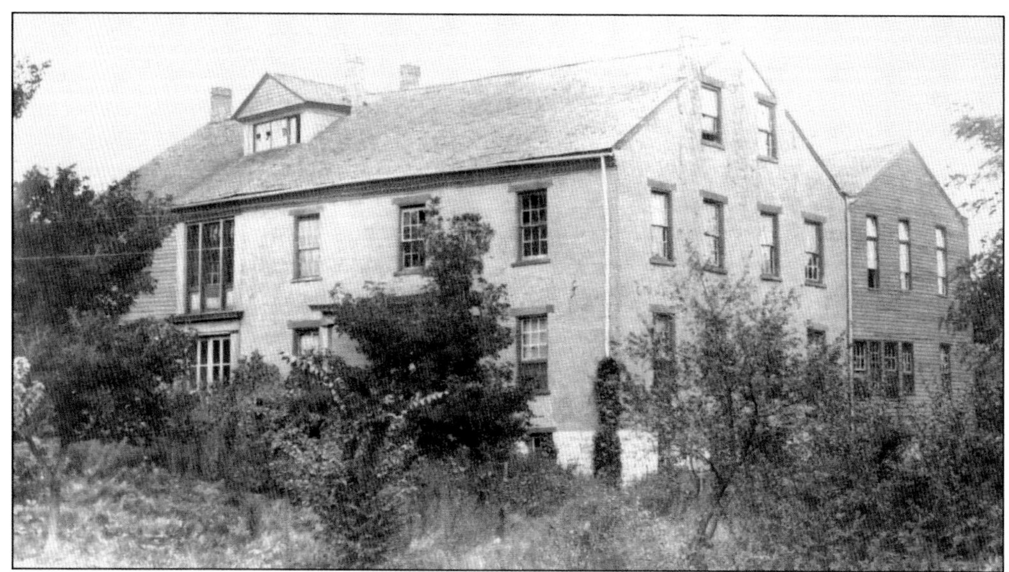

Howe's "Old Mill" school was built in 1845. The academy was located on East Monroe Street, at the present location of WisdomQuest Alternative High School. It remained there for several decades before relocating to South Jefferson Street around the turn of the 20th century. Prof. Samuel Howe, the academy's founder, had taught in Ohio before he came to Iowa in 1841. Among his students in Ohio were two boys who would later become important Civil War generals, William Tecumseh Sherman and Philip Sheridan. (MPPL.)

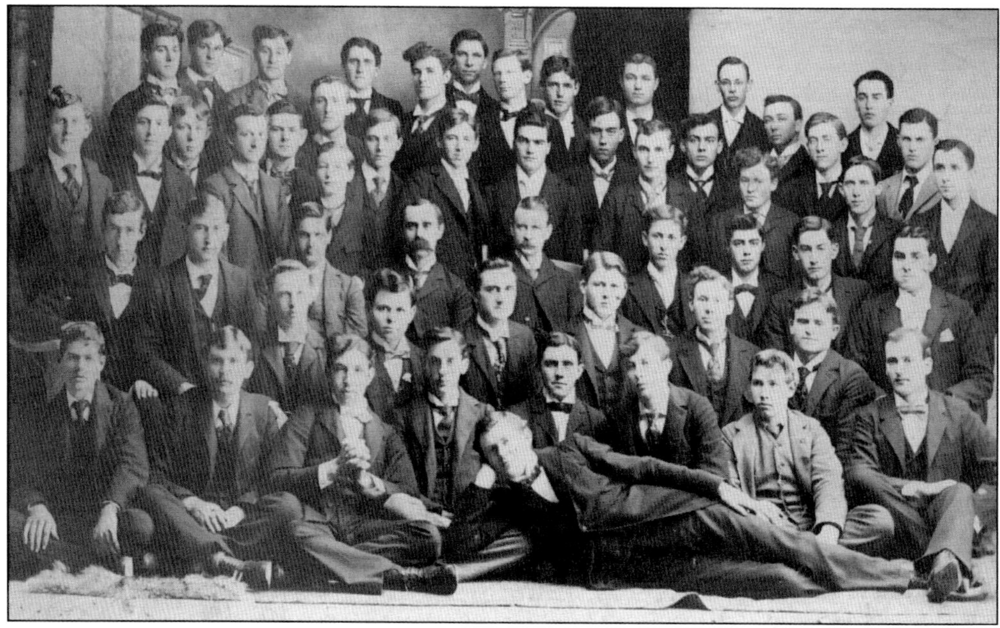

Prof. Lincoln Antrim (third row, fourth from left) and Prof. Seward Howe (third row, fifth from left) pose with their students at Howe's Academy in 1896 or 1897. The 1879 *History of Henry County* revealed the expectations of the Academy's students: "Every student, in every science, is trained individually and in concert to do his own work, give his own reasons for so doing, and exhibit before the class how, in the best possible manner, he would impart his acquisitions to others." (MPPL.)

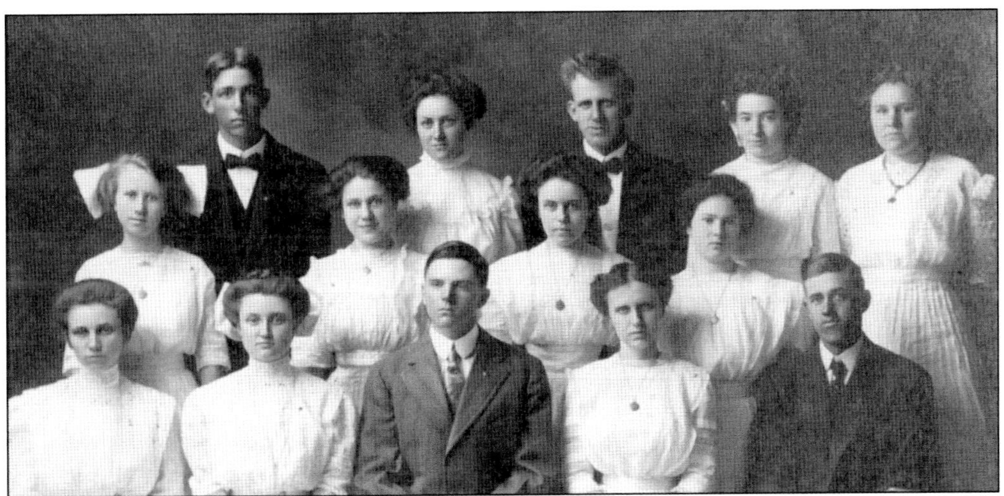

Prof. W.P. Howe, the son of Samuel Howe, reminisced about his late father in the Mount Pleasant *Dial of Progress* on June 15, 1899. Though his father was well established in Ohio, W.P. Howe noted that his father "could not resist the fascination presented by the beautiful Eden beyond the great Father of Waters. And so, at a great loss of money, and putting aside the most flattering prospects, he turned his face toward the western world." The academy's class of 1911 poses in this photograph. (MPPL.)

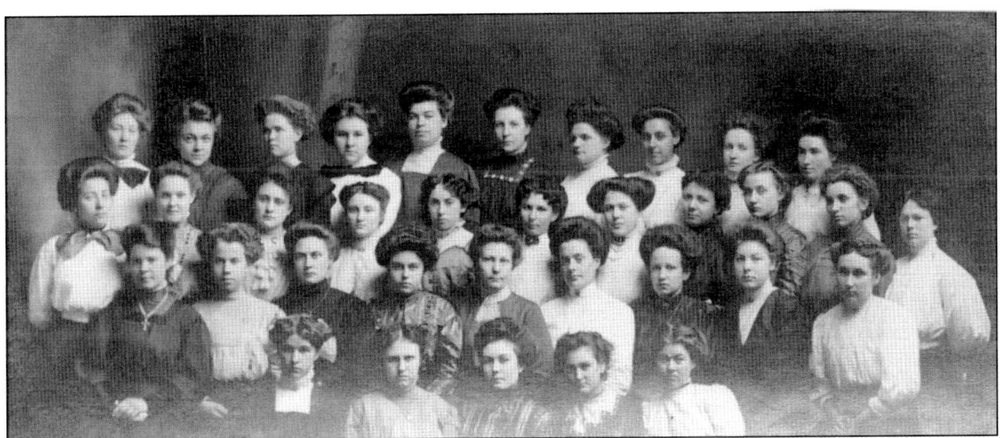

The women of Howe's Academy pose for a picture in 1910. The school's annual catalogue in 1900 described the institution's purpose, a focus "not merely to send out graduates to fill positions as book-keepers, clerks and teachers, but rather to prepare young men and women to meet the demands of the times. This is a school where young men and women of all ages and degrees of advancement may enter at any time during the year and find classes corresponding to their attainments." (MPPL.)

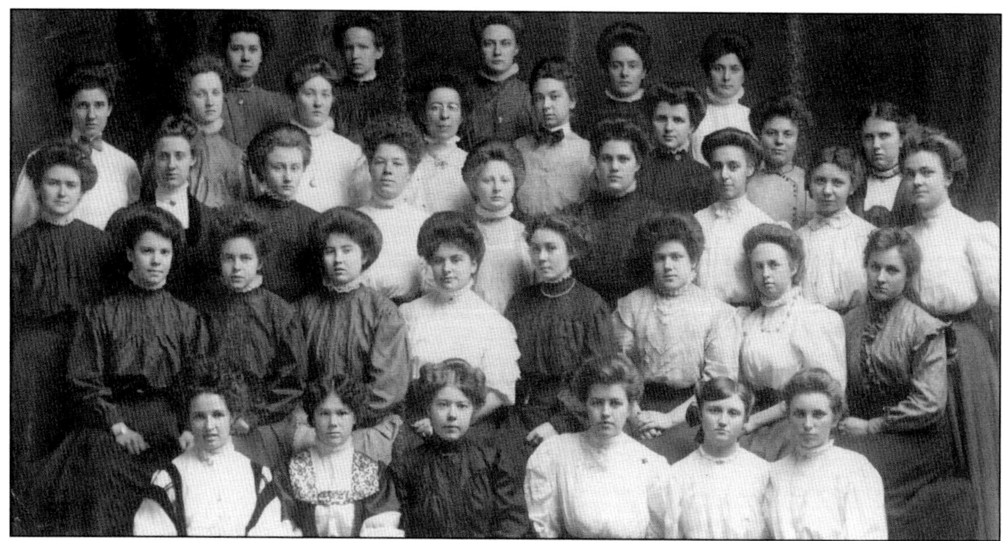

Notice the formal dress in this Howe's Academy photograph from 1908–1909. Many female graduates moved into professional work. Clara S. Foltz became an able lawyer in San Francisco. Emily Porter and Lizzie Snider were bright scholars and provided inspiration to fellow classmates. Some women received local employment, including Minnie Newton of the class of 1892, who served as a teacher in Mount Pleasant. Others traveled far, including Ethel Gardner of the class of 1899, who worked as a teacher in Tennessee. (MPPL.)

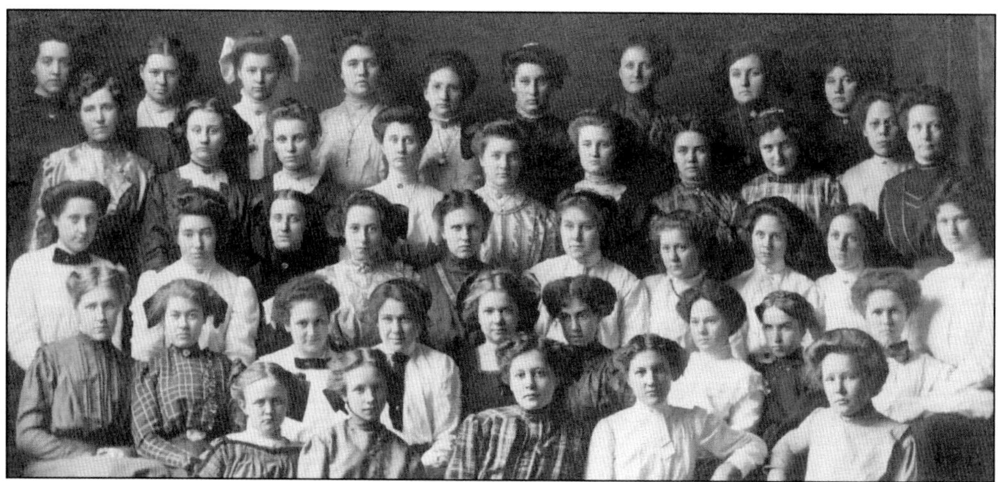

Howe's Academy promoted education for many women. The August 18, 1893, *Weekly News* provided Minnie Bartlett's testimony, a graduate who received employment as a bookkeeper at the Mount Pleasant Insane Asylum: "I was a student in Howe's Academy some years ago, taking with other branches, a course in book-keeping. The instruction there received has been of great value and service to me since in teaching school and in my present occupation as book-keeper; and I herewith gratefully acknowledge my indebtedness to Prof. Howe." (MPPL.)

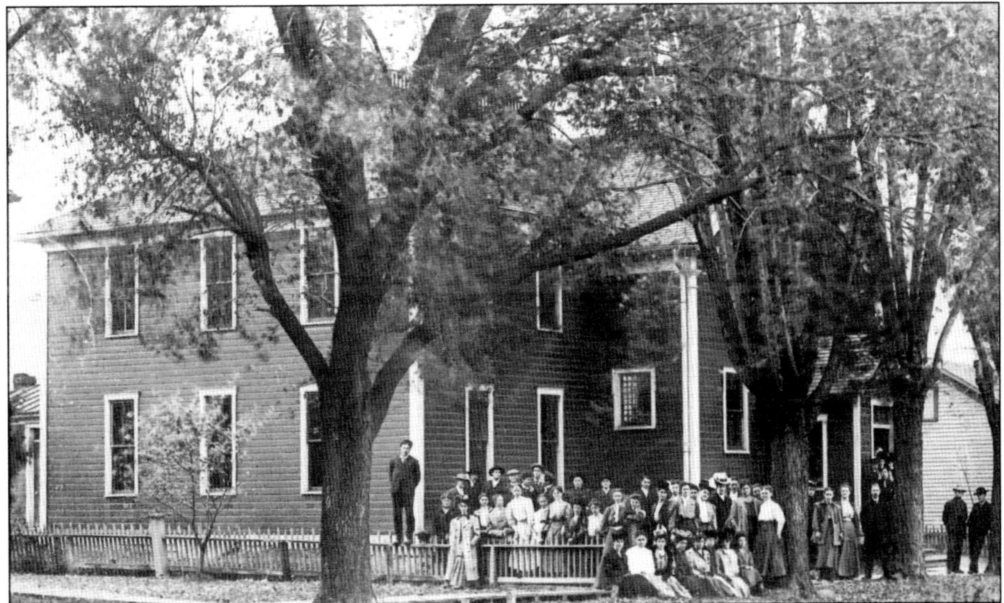

Howe's Academy remained an important center of learning in town through the greater part of a century. The Old Mill school on East Monroe Street, at the present location of WisdomQuest Alternative High School, was a two-story school, which was very different from the academy's humble beginnings in a log cabin in the 1840s. The school is pictured here at its final location on South Jefferson Street. (Pat White.)

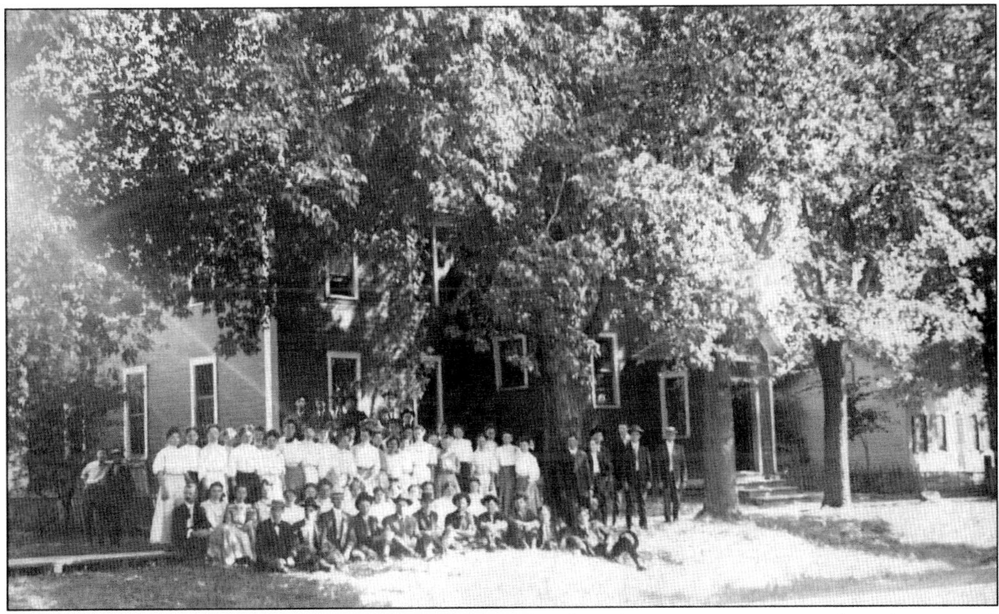

Prof. Samuel Howe and his son Prof. Seward Howe developed a progressive curriculum that earned accolades around the region, especially with respect to producing teachers and other skilled professionals. The 1893 *City Directory* noted, "No particular course is required of any pupil, but to those who graduate, a diploma is given." (Don Young Collection, HCHT.)

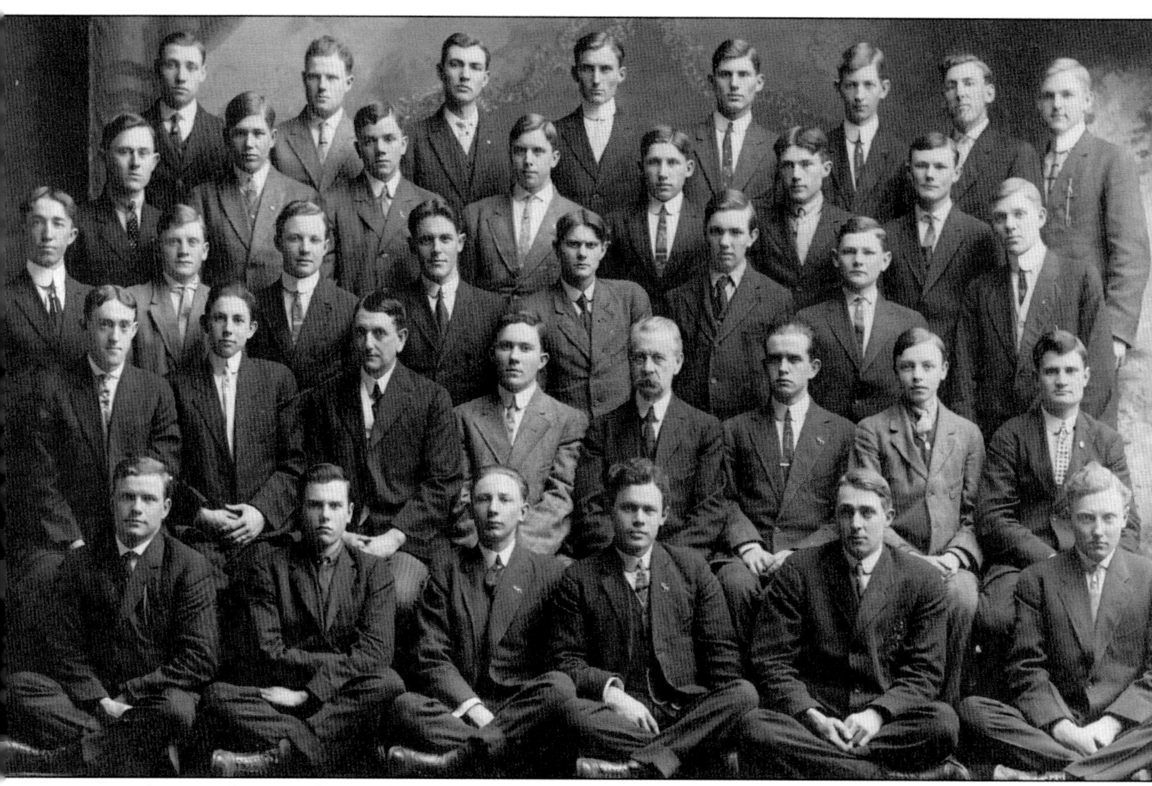

Prof. Seward Howe (second row, fourth from right) and Prof. David Barton (second row, third from left) appear with their students in this turn of the 20th century image. Prof. Seward Howe took up the torch lit by his father, Prof. Samuel Howe, and continued the operation of Howe's Academy. (MPPL.)

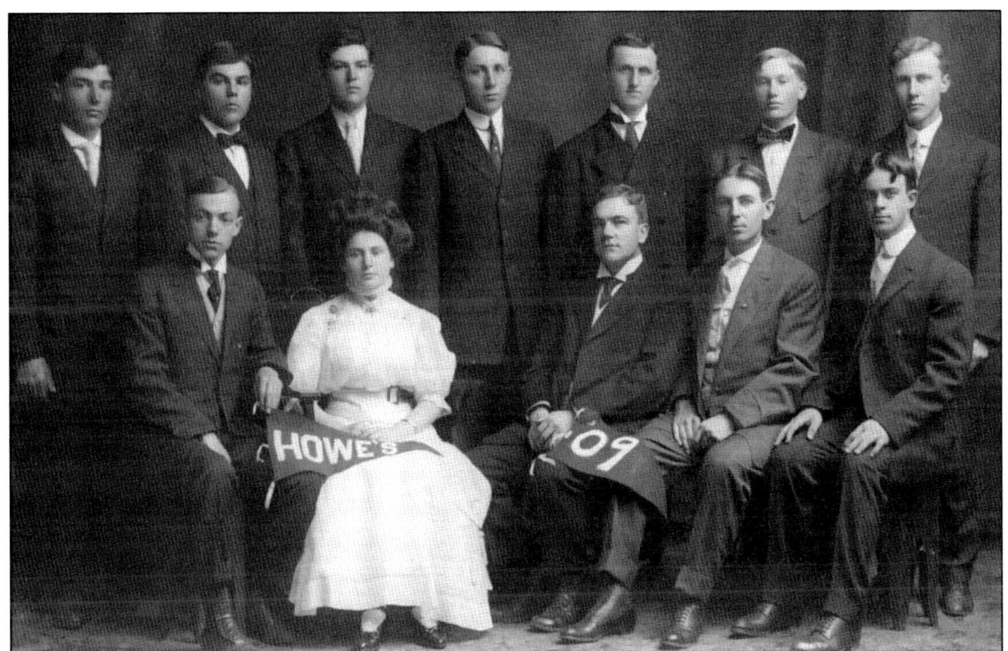

The 1909 class from Howe's Academy poses in this picture. The 1893 *City Directory* stated that "the aim of the institution is to fit young men to fill positions as book-keepers, clerks and teachers as well as to prepare them to meet the demands of the times. The school is non-sectarian in religion, but is Christian in its tone and influence." One can see that women were also represented among the graduates. (MPPL.)

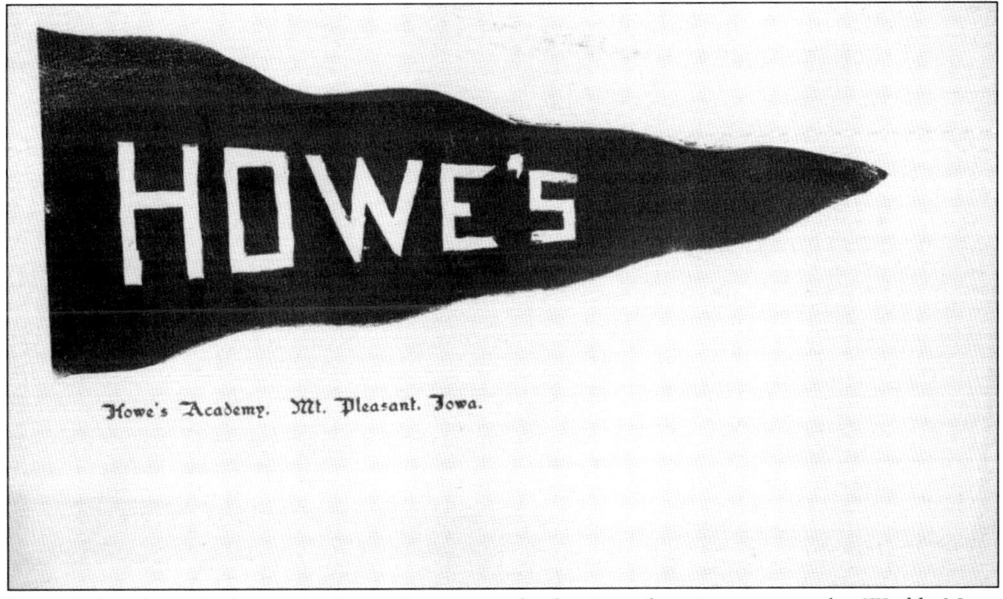

Howe's Academy had very high academic standards. An advertisement in the *Weekly News* from August 18, 1893, stated, "Howe's Academy is the best school to patronize, because it has no temptations whatever to divert from students. . . . The afternoons are devoted to recitations and study instead of Foot ball, Base ball, Tennis, etc. No Athletics but mental Athletics." (Don Young Collection, HCHT.)

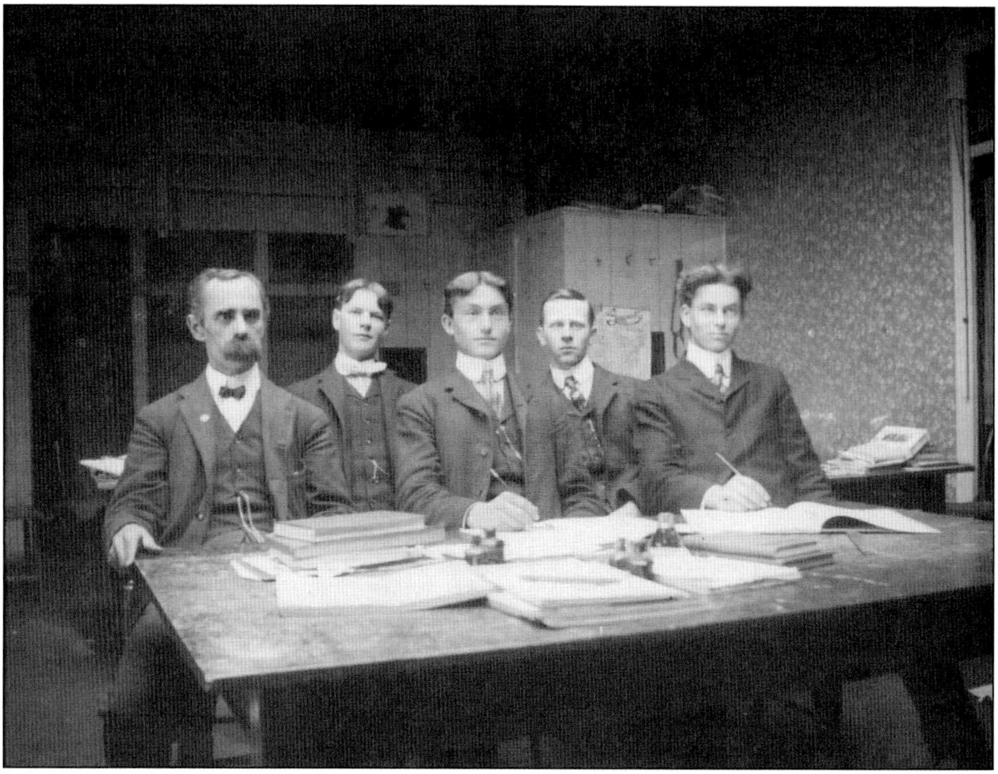

Prof. Lincoln Antrim (far left) sits with four of his bookkeeping students at the Mount Pleasant Academy. Professor Antrim, like Prof. Samuel Howe of Howe's Academy, originally hailed from Ohio. He settled in Iowa with his parents in 1877. He received a bachelor's degree in didactics at the State Normal School in Cedar Falls and a master's degree from Western Normal School in Page County. (MPPL.)

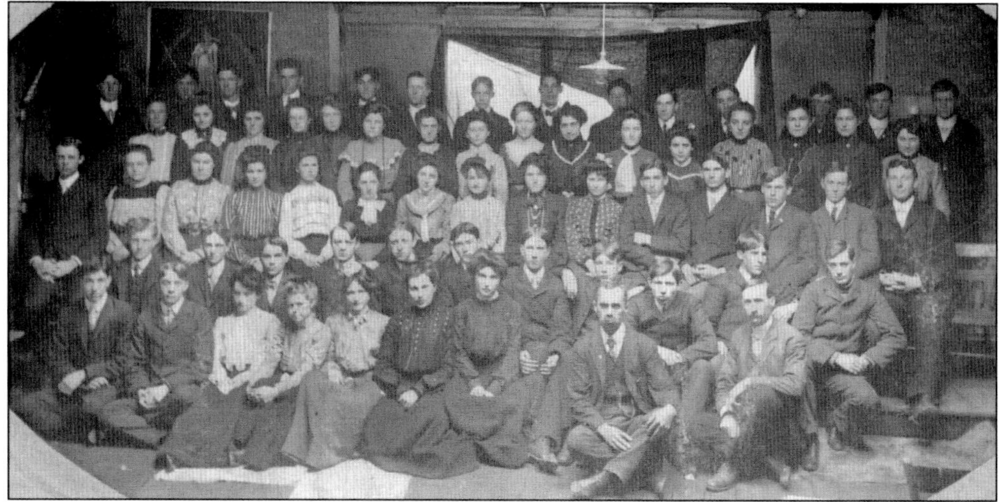

Prof. Lincoln Antrim is seated in front of the first row of students at the Mount Pleasant Academy. The class of 1898 was the first to graduate from the academy. Among these first graduates were rising professionals including Edward C. Lynn, who later became superintendent of Lee County. (MPPL.)

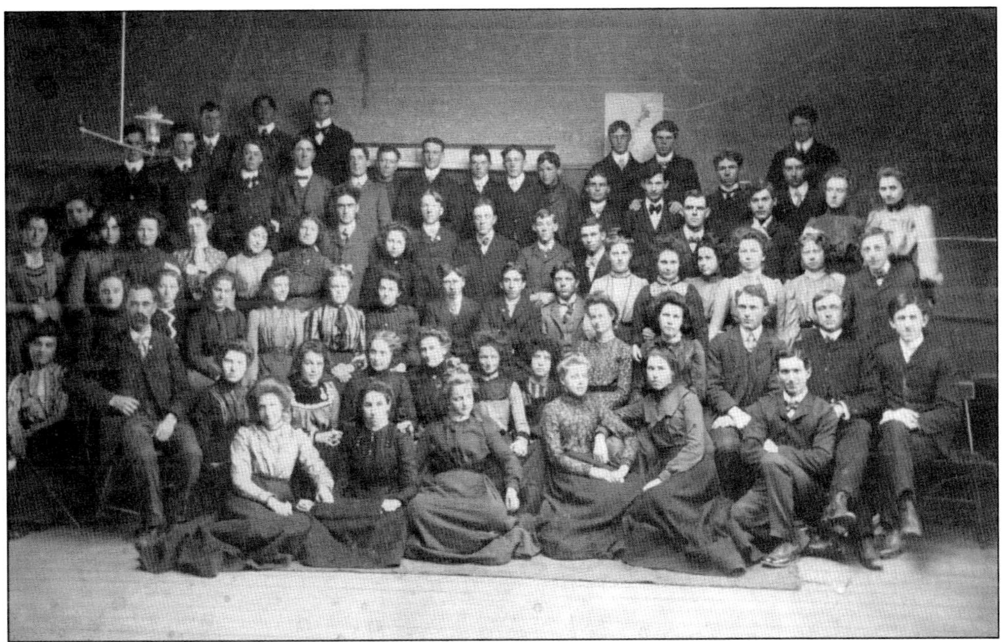

The Lincoln Literacy Society began at the Mount Pleasant Academy during the 1897–1898 school year. Prof. Lincoln Antrim is visible in the second row at far left, identified by his distinctive mustache. The Mount Pleasant Academy was located on the north side of the square, operating between 1897 and 1906. The academy prepared students for careers in teaching, banking, and clerical positions. (MPPL.)

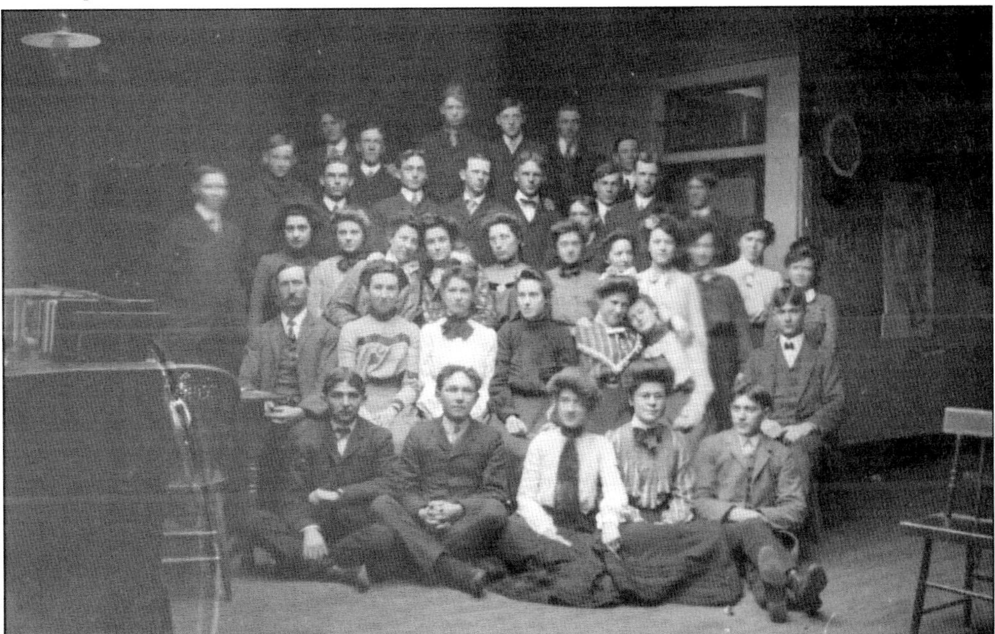

Prof. Lincoln Antrim, in the second row at far left, is pictured with his coeducational class at the Mount Pleasant Academy in 1904. This was one of multiple local schools providing women with professional futures. The Mount Pleasant Academy offered a four-year course to prepare students for college. (MPPL.)

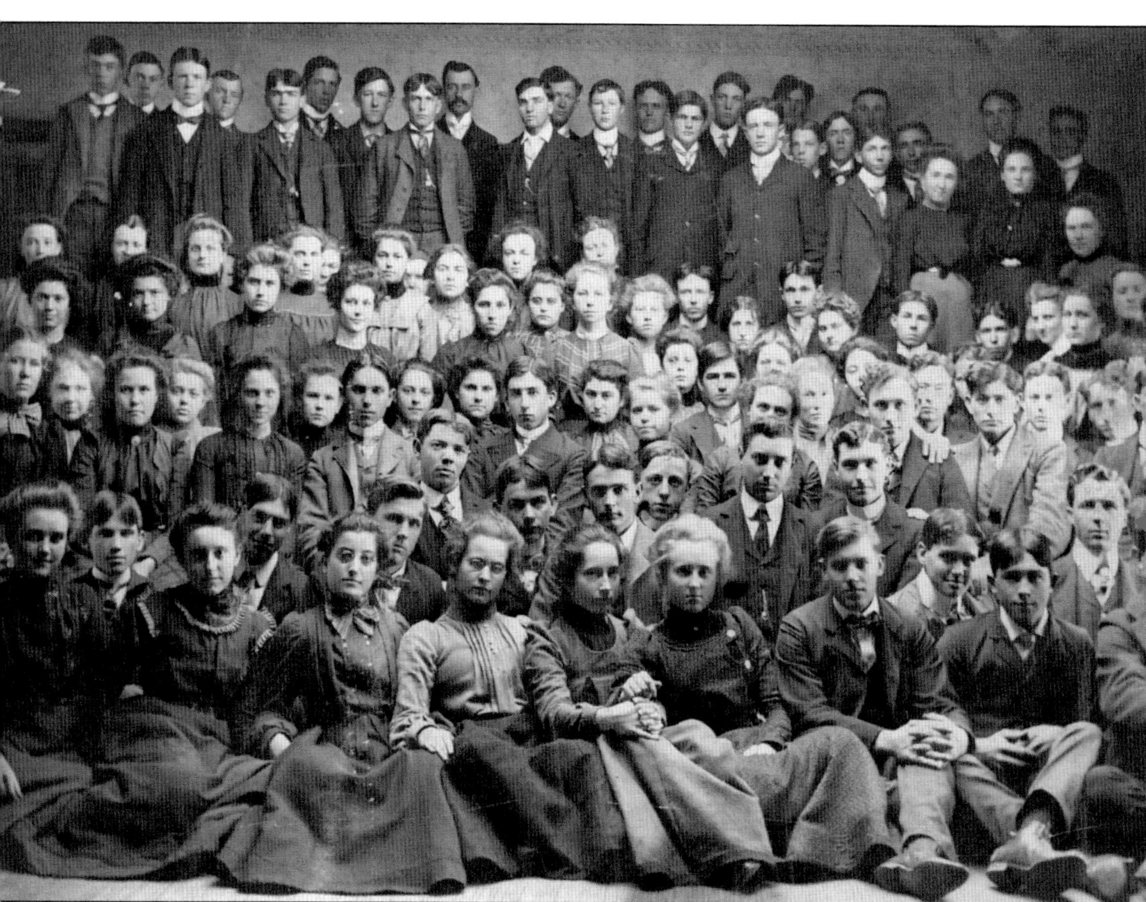

The pupils of the Mount Pleasant Academy exemplify the community's early commitment to education. It is striking how many women were present at this preparatory school, as evidenced by this image from around the turn of the 20th century. The school moved locations; its final location was on the north side of the square before it closed in 1907. (MPPL.)

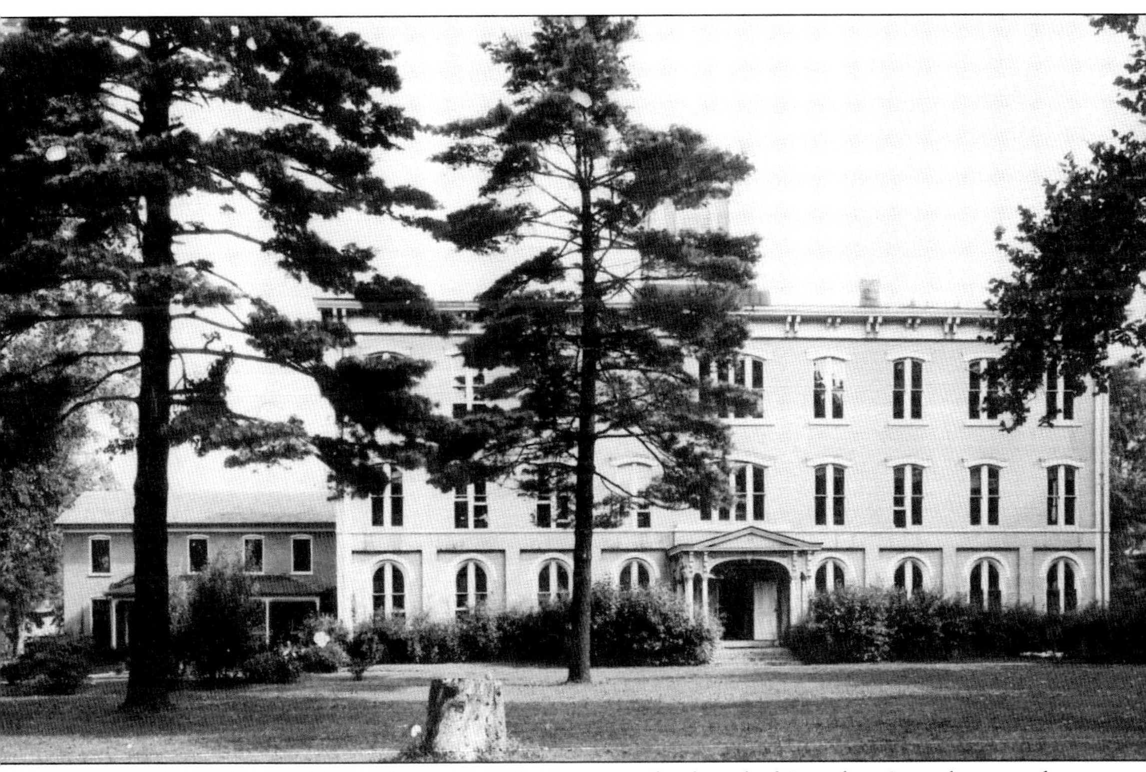

James Harlan, who would later become a US senator and a friend of President Lincoln, served as president of Iowa Wesleyan. Harlan's progressive vision came to fruition on July 4, 1854, with the cornerstone laying of the Old Main building. Pioneer Hall, predating Old Main by 10 years, is seen on the left. The P.E.O. Sisterhood was founded in Old Main in 1869. (MPPL.)

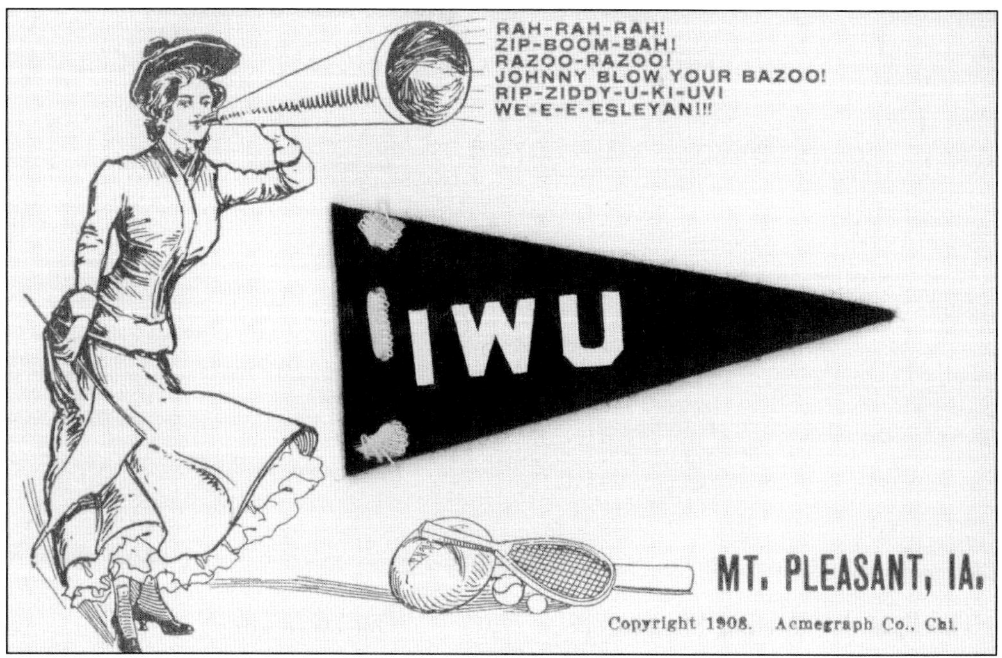

This 1908 Iowa Wesleyan University pennant postcard encouraged school spirit. The 1893 *City Directory* noted, "The University has several courses open to students. The classical course leading to the degree of Master of Arts and the scientific course leading to the degree of Master of Science, the normal course and the preparatory departments." (Don Young Collection, HCHT.)

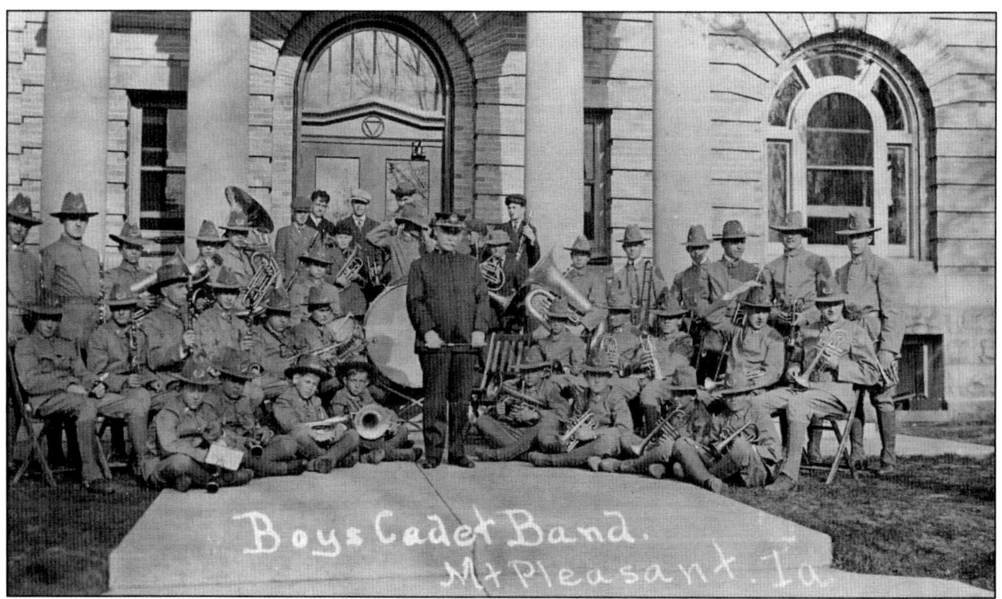

Iowa Wesleyan maintained a student Cadet Corps during the late 19th century. The corps began in 1887, and for some years, drill was mandatory for male freshmen and sophomores. The students performed patriotic celebrations in Mount Pleasant and surrounding communities. The cadet program ended in 1899. (MPPL.)

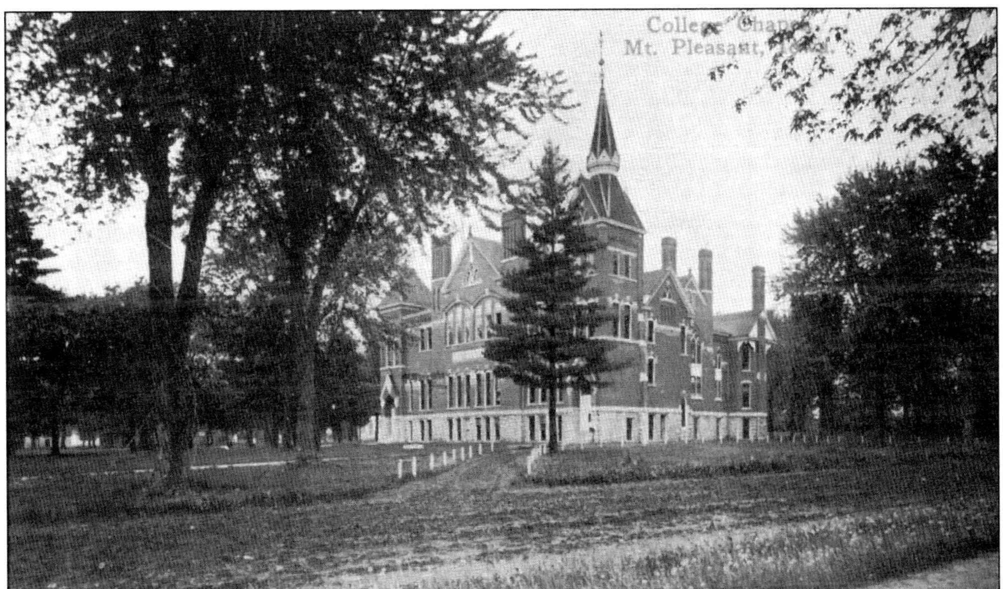

The college chapel took years to plan and build. Some four years before its completion, the 1888 *Portrait and Biographical Album of Henry County* recorded, "Contracts have been let for the erection of a new building at a cost of $35,000, and for remodeling the old one at a cost of $3,000. The new building will be erected just east of the old one. It will contain a chemical and physical laboratory, a number of recitation rooms, and a chapel with a seating capacity of 1,400." (Don Young Collection, HCHT.)

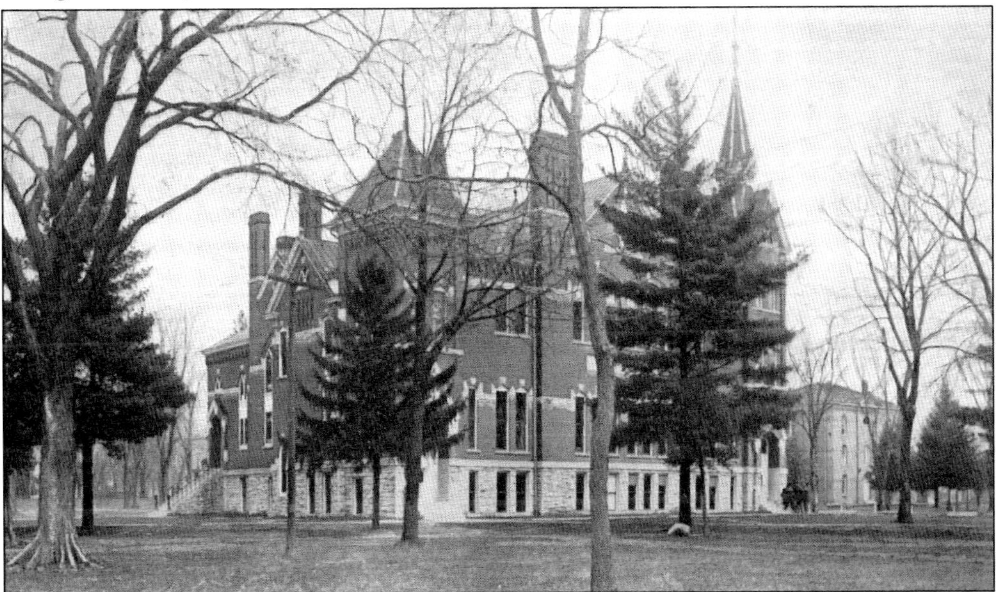

The Chapel and Science Hall opened for classes in fall of 1892. Laboratories were located in the basement. The 1893 *City Directory* noted that the "beautiful building which is the pride of every citizen of Mt. Pleasant was begun over 5 years ago under the administration of Dr. J.T. McFarland and the foundation including the basement story was then built and the work rested for quite a while for lack of funds." Notice the old German College behind the chapel at right. (Don Young Collection, HCHT.)

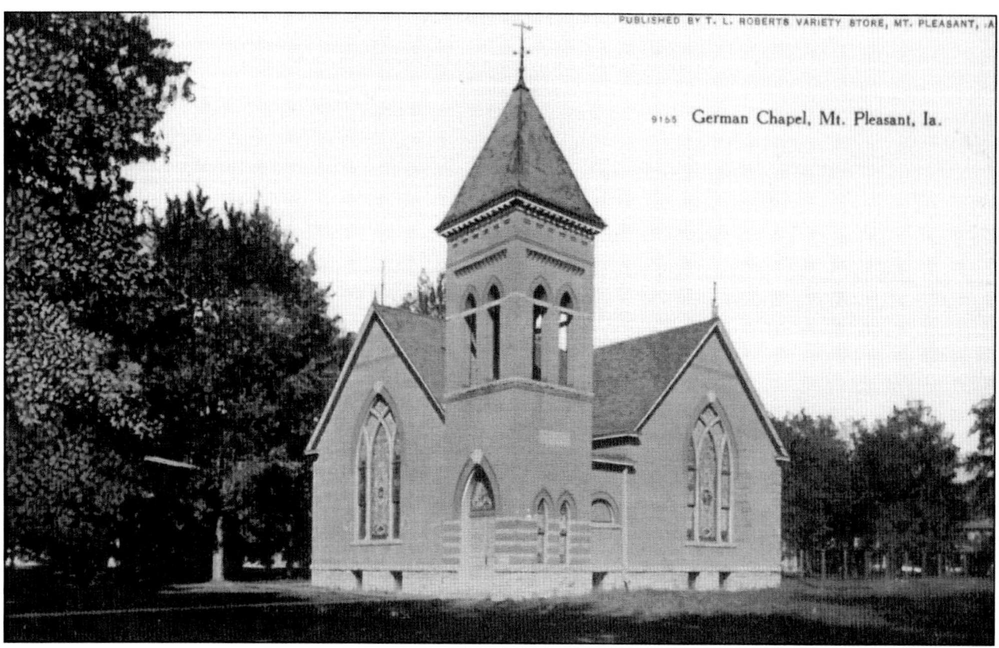

The German Methodist Chapel was built in 1901. It once stood near the German College at the present location of the Science Hall on the Iowa Wesleyan campus. This church was actually the second German-language congregation in town, the first being the German Presbyterian Church. The German Presbyterian Church was built in 1869 on Jefferson Street, between Clay and Warren Streets. (Don Young Collection, HCHT.)

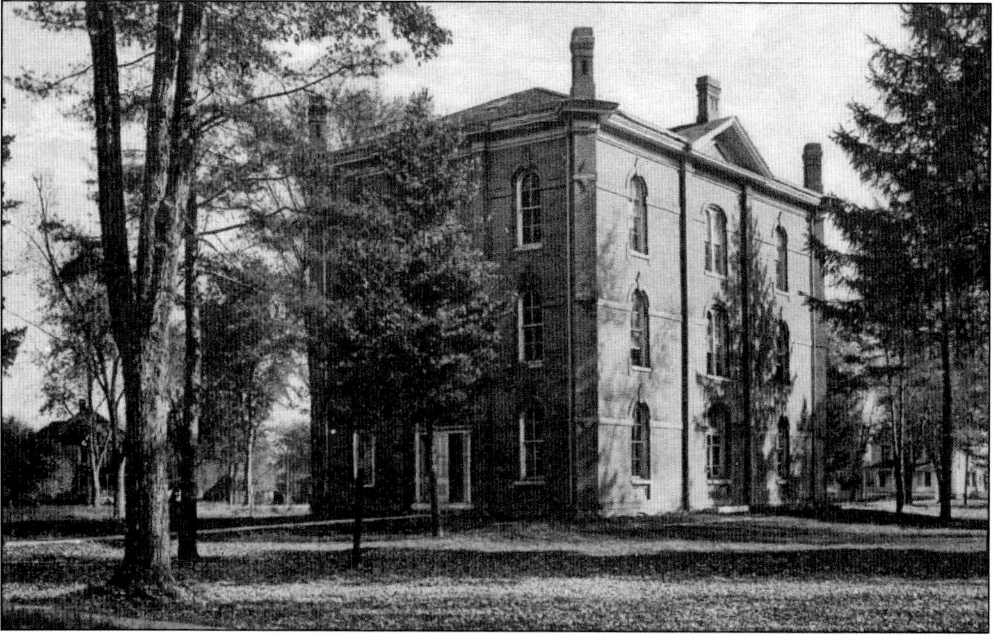

The German College once stood prominently on the Iowa Wesleyan campus for nearly a century. This building, constructed in 1874, was established by the Southwest German Conference of the Methodist Episcopal Church. This college served German-speaking students until 1909. The building remained until 1961, when it was replaced by Adam Trieschmann Hall. (HCHT.)

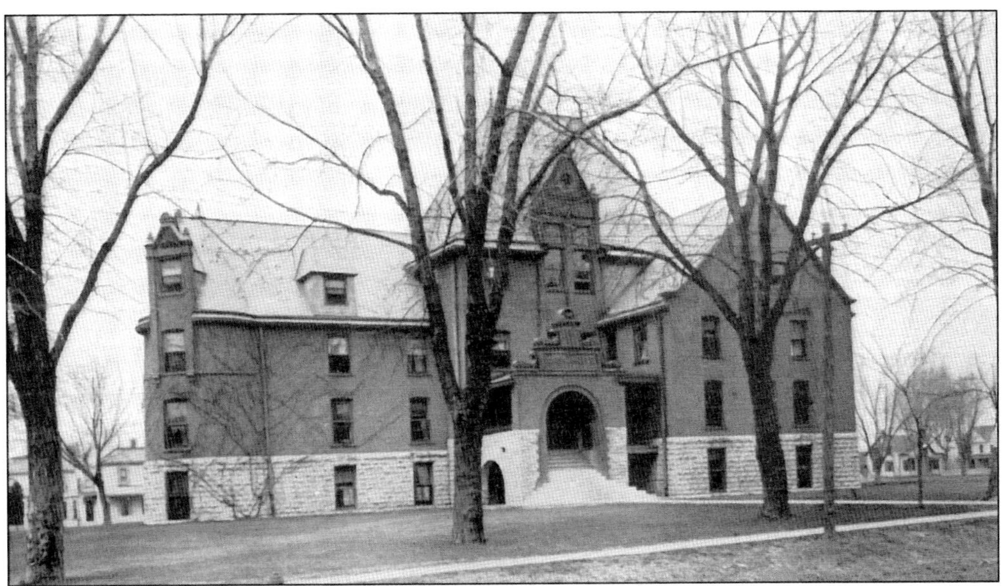

Hershey Hall was completed in 1897. The building was named after its primary financier, Elizabeth Hershey from Muscatine, Iowa. Hershey Hall functioned as a female dormitory, and also contained a lounge and women's gymnasium. (Don Young Collection, HCHT.)

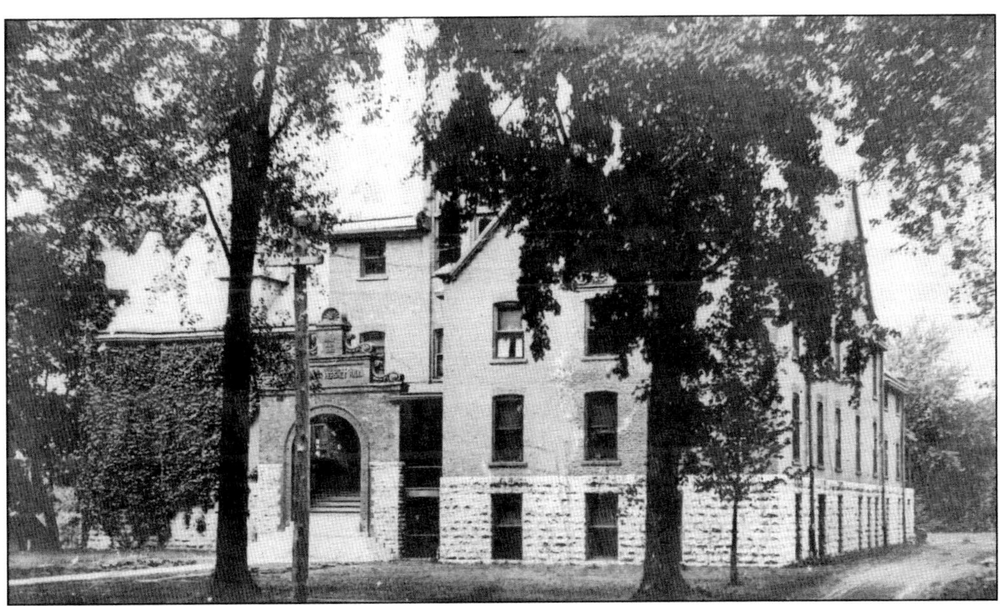

Hershey Hall provided new accommodations for female students, encouraging recruitment of young women from a larger region. Iowa Wesleyan's first women's basketball team formed in this building in 1902. Hershey Hall also served as the campus's dining hall until the construction of the Student Union in 1957. (Don Young Collection, HCHT.)

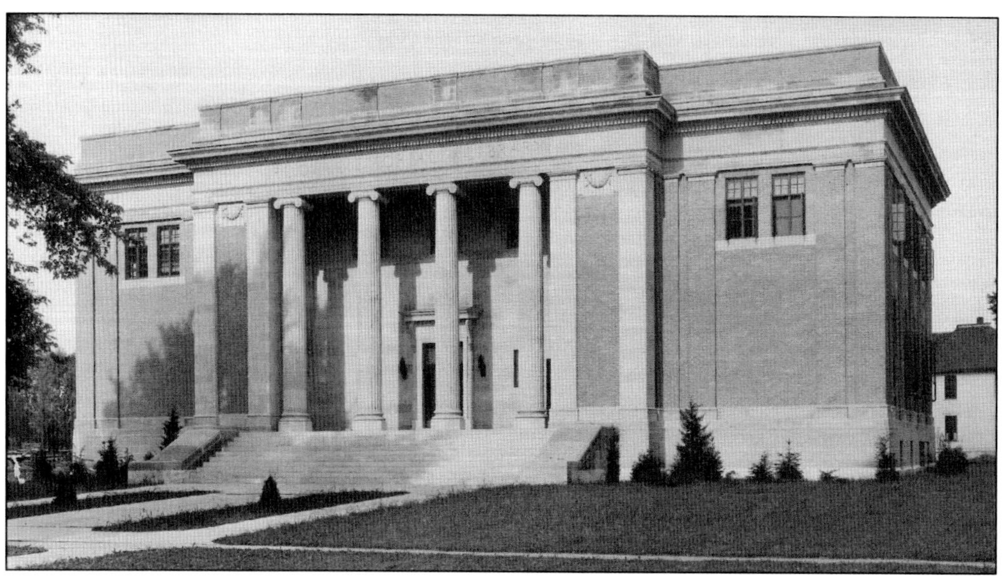

In January 1869, the P.E.O. Sisterhood was organized on the Iowa Wesleyan campus. P.E.O. was originally a sorority at Iowa Wesleyan, but later, the organization grew to national and international scales. In 1927, the P.E.O. raised money to construct the P.E.O. Memorial Building, which served as both the headquarters for the organization and as the college library. Today, the P.E.O. Memorial Building is home to Iowa Wesleyan's college administration. Visitors can often find various art exhibits on display on the main floor. (MPPL.)

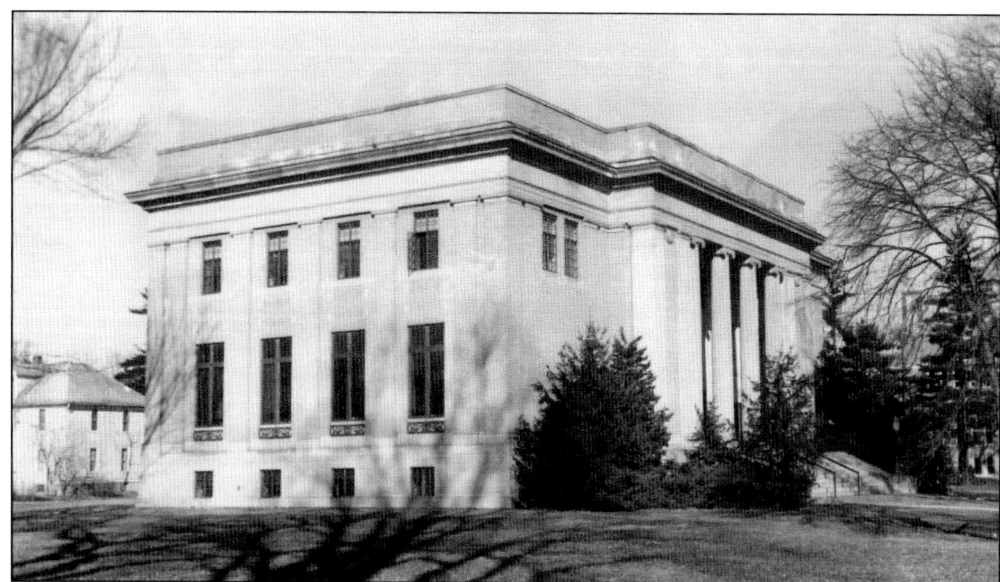

The 1928 P.E.O. Memorial Library provided the school with its first dedicated library. The library was built in honor of the P.E.O. founders. This library provided greatly improved book space and reading room for students. (Don Young Collection, HCHT.)

Four

The Library

The story of the public library goes back to the town's formative years. In the 1840s, Dr. W.B. Chamberlain donated 800 books to the Universalist Society. Sunday schools shared these books, as churches began to develop their own library collections. Literary societies formed. The Ladies Library Association began in the 1870s, and the steady resolve for a public library took shape.

The Ladies Library Association began a library on the east side of the square, and donated books began to accrue. The library held some 2,200 books when it first opened in 1876. In 1882, the library moved to North Jefferson Street, where its collection grew to 5,000 volumes. Museum pieces were added, including specimens of petrified wood, shell, and coral. Native American artifacts were added to the library's museum displays, as was a giant stuffed buffalo. In addition to reading books, magazines, and newspapers or viewing museum pieces, library patrons could also play chess, checkers, and dominoes at the library.

The step toward a proper city library was underway at the dawn of the 20th century. In 1902, the Ladies Library Association succeeded in gaining the necessary votes to establish a city library. A grant from Andrew Carnegie in Pittsburgh, Pennsylvania, provided the funds for a library building in 1905. The Carnegie Library still stands on North Main Street, functioning as a branch of Southeastern Community College. The public library is now located in the old high school on East Monroe Street. Citizens from Mount Pleasant and the surrounding area check out about 100,000 items from the library each year. The Mount Pleasant Public Library is another temple in the Athens of Iowa.

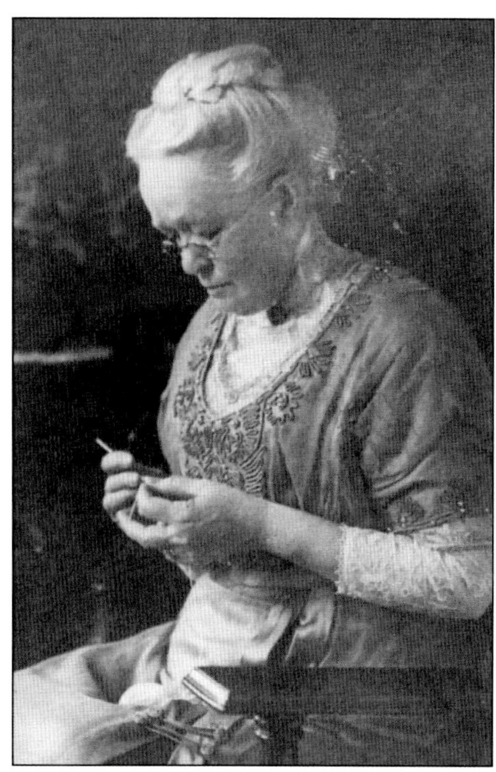

Sarah Beckwith (left) was president of the Ladies Library Association in 1901. Cordelia Throop Cole (below) was a founding member of the Ladies Library Association. Her obituary, printed in the Mount Pleasant *Dial of Progress* on May 10, 1900, stated that Cole was one of the association's "most devoted workers and liberal supporters." (Both, MPPL.)

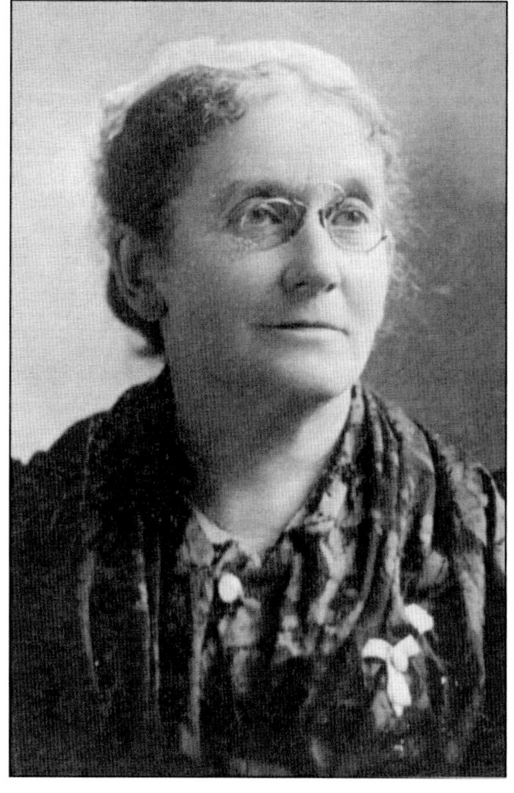

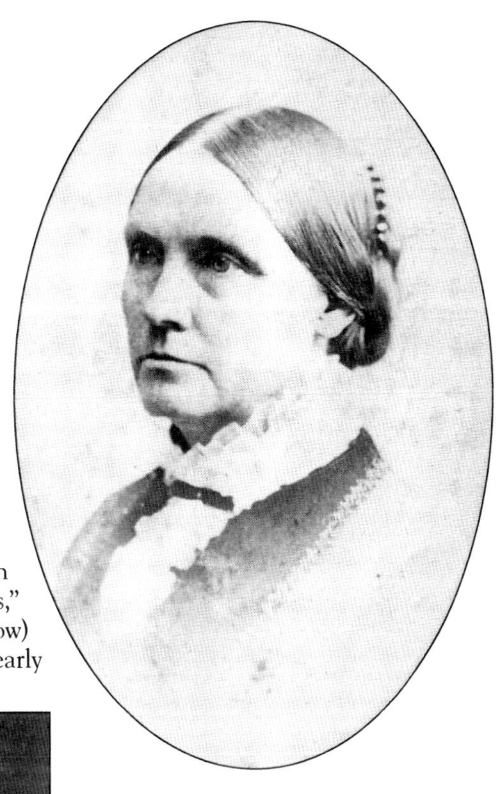

A.C. Woolson (right) served on the executive committee of the Ladies Library Association in the 1880s. During the association's 1886–1887 lecture series, speakers presented on a wide range of topics, including "The Utilitarian Element in Modern Civilization," "Pasteur and His Theories," and "The Gospel of Science." R.A. Van Tress (below) served in the Ladies Library Association in the early 20th century. (Both, MPPL.)

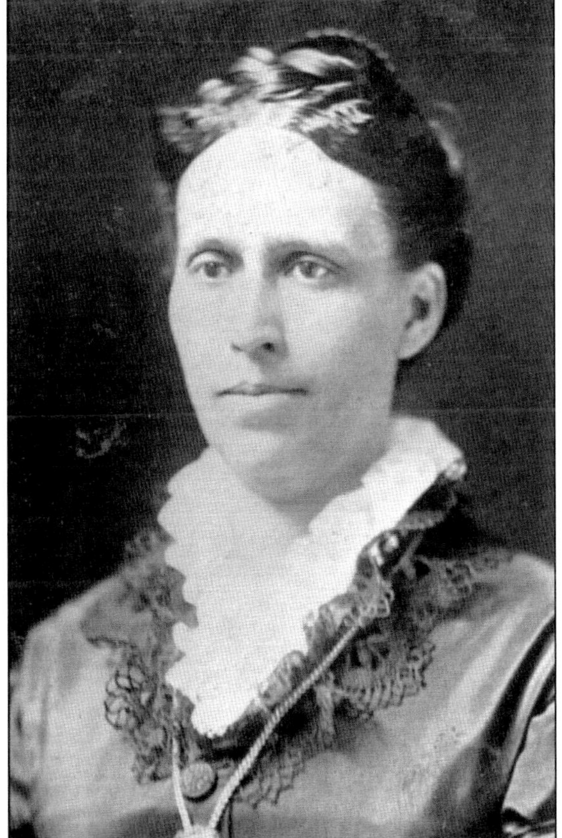

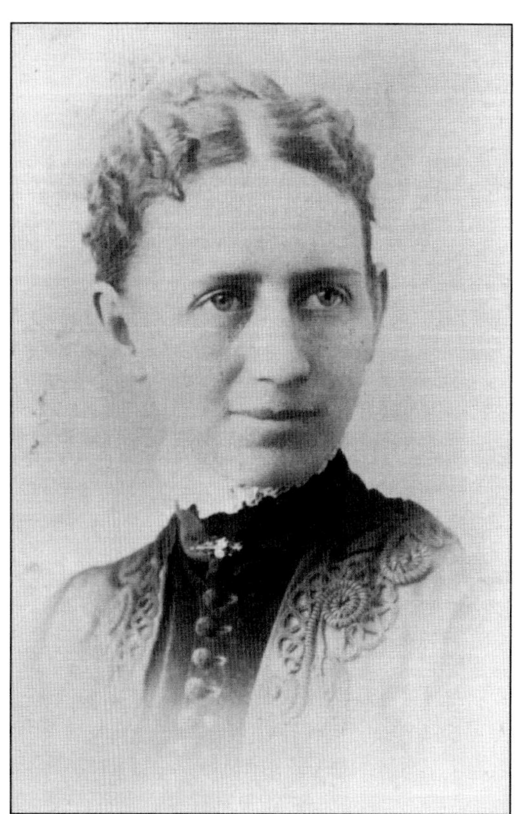

Emma Schwenker was the vice president of the Ladies Library Association around the turn of the 20th century. She helped develop the various and sophisticated programs during the lecture season of 1899–1900. On November 27, 1899, Schwenker served as program hostess, with S.L. Walker lecturing on German art. Music was provided before and after the lecture. The library lectures were conducted at the old Baptist church at the intersection of Main and Madison Streets. (MPPL.)

A.S. Marsh served as treasurer in the early years of the Ladies Library Association, and was very active in the development of the public library. Marsh was originally from Maine and served as a teacher there before settling in Iowa. (MPPL.)

L. L. A.

Life Membership Ticket.

This is to Certify that Hon J. L. Gillis

Having paid the requisite fee, is a LIFE MEMBER of the Ladies Library Association of Mt. Pleasant Iowa.

E. L. Schwenker Sec. A. S. Marsh Pres.

This Ladies Library Association membership ticket certified that J.L. Gillis paid the requisite fee to hold a lifetime membership. This forerunner of the modern library card was signed by officers Emma Schwenker, secretary, and A.S. Marsh, president. (MPPL.)

BORROWER'S AGREEMENT.

Paul McCoid No. 1737

FREE PUBLIC LIBRARY

Mt, Pleasant, Iowa, DEC 1 1905

I, the undersigned, a resident of Mt. Pleasant, hereby apply for a reader's card in the Free Public Library. I promise to observe all rules, pay promptly all fines and make good any loss or injury to the library incurred by me.

Name Paul McCoid

Age 9 (If a minor)

Read this pledge carefully before signing
Fill out with ink

SEE OTHER SIDE

Library cards were given out to patrons over 100 years ago. This card, issued to nine-year-old Paul McCoid on December 1, 1905, states, "I, the undersigned, a resident of Mt. Pleasant, hereby apply for a reader's card in the Free Public Library. I promise to observe all rules, pay promptly all fines and make good any loss or injury to the library incurred by me." The Carnegie Library on North Main Street was a new building when this card was issued. (MPPL.)

75

Record of L. L. A. Literary Meeting
May 29 1905.

The president Mrs. Beckwith called the meeting to order by calling for quotations from various authors which were responded to by those present.

The leading topic for the day was "Comparison of Russian and Japanese Civilization most ably presented by Prof. Lucy Booth giving principally the economic and socialistic conditions of the present but also giving the conditions of religion, science and the national military forces which represents the present civilization of the two countries.

Miss Lucrode read the last paper of the year on Present Japan.

Misses Schwinker, Snyder and Lucrode were appointed to interview the trustees of the B.C. in regard to some missing chairs.

The May 29, 1905, minutes of the Ladies Library Association recorded, "The leading topic for the day was 'Comparison of Russian and Japanese Civilization' most ably presented by Prof. Lucy Booth giving principally the economic and socialistic conditions of the present but also giving the conditions of religion, science and the national military forces which represents the present civilization of the two countries." (MPPL.)

The Ladies Library Association penny-pinched, working tirelessly and methodically from its founding in 1875 to its successful establishment of a city library in 1901. This treasurer's note from May 10, 1902, records that a Miss Twinting provided $25 for the library carpet. (MPPL.)

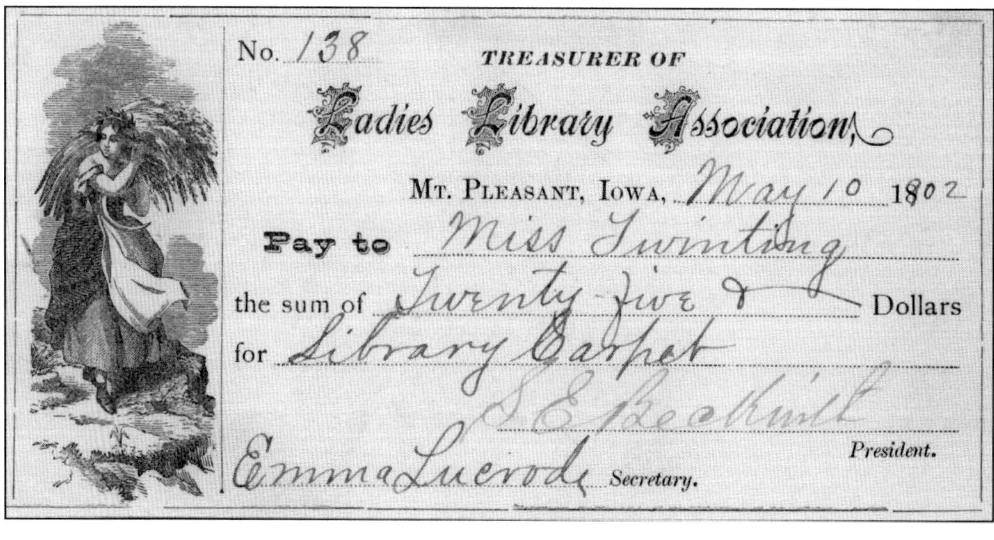

No. 138 TREASURER OF

Ladies Library Association,

MT. PLEASANT, IOWA, May 10 1902

Pay to Miss Twinting

the sum of Twenty-five & — Dollars

for Library Carpet

S E Beckwith President.

Emma Lucrode Secretary.

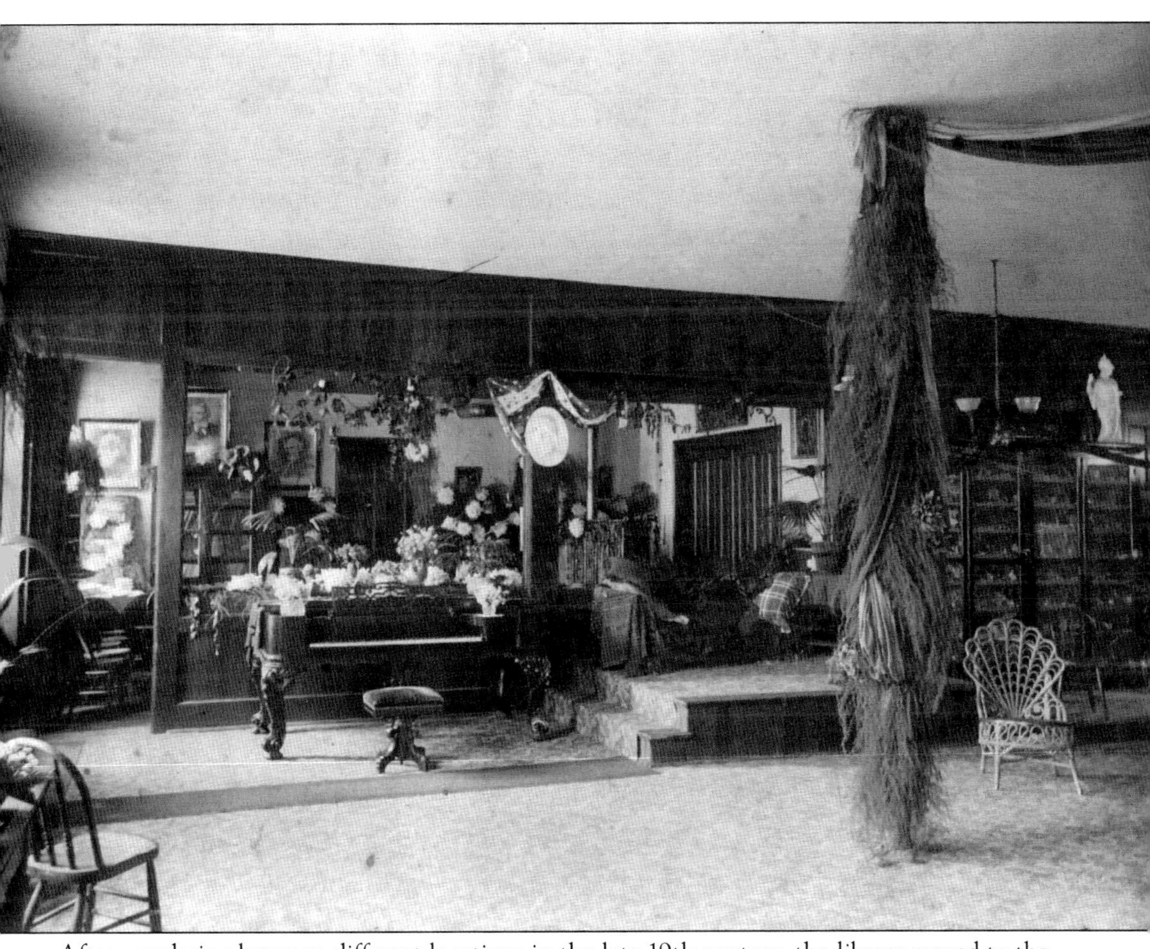

After wandering between different locations in the late 19th century, the library moved to the basement of the old Baptist church at the intersection of North Main and Madison Streets. The library was fitted out in fine décor, as evidenced in this 1903 or 1904 photograph. In addition to books, the library included an art gallery, museum exhibits, and reading spaces. (MPPL.)

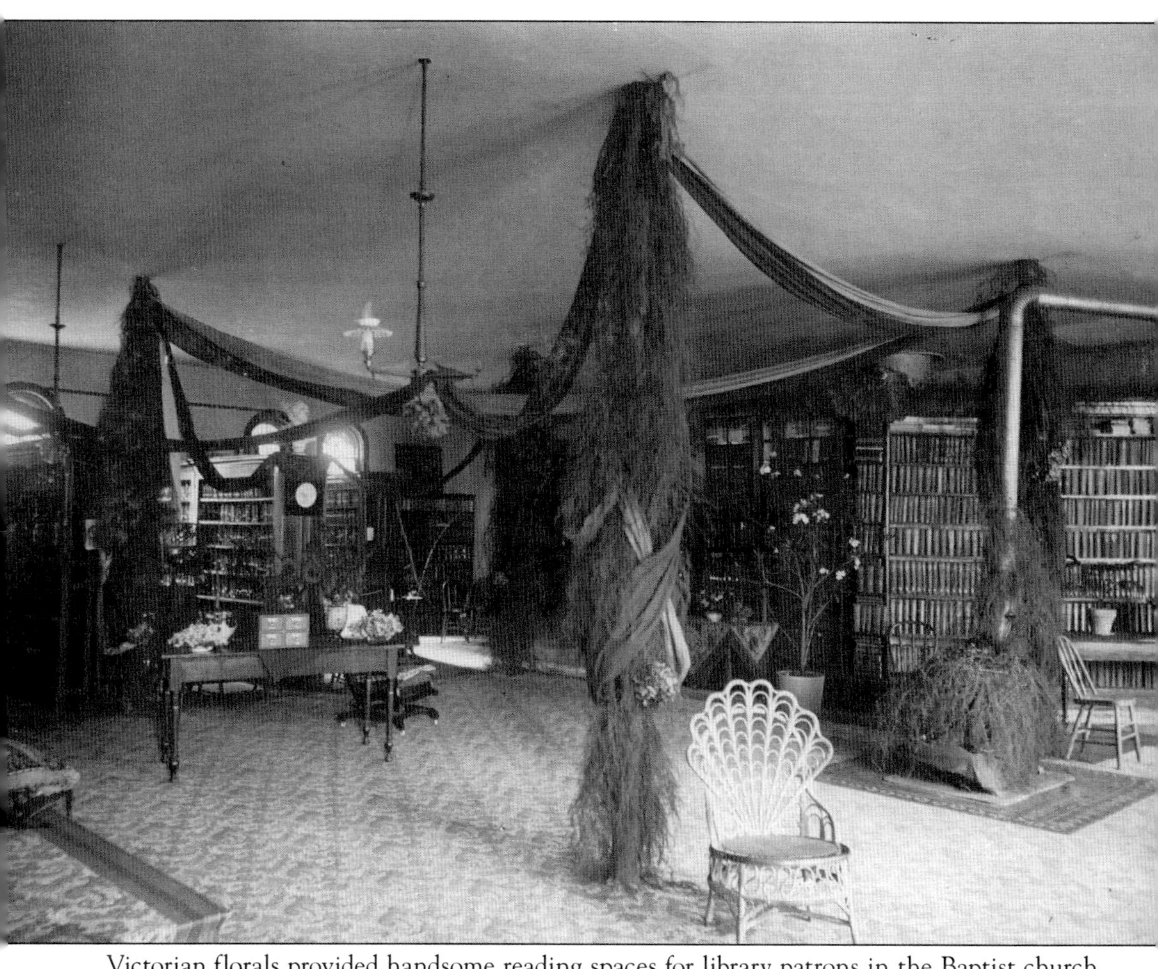

Victorian florals provided handsome reading spaces for library patrons in the Baptist church basement. The Baptist church was the final location for the library before it became an official city department. Andrew Carnegie provided funding for the library at just the right time, for very shortly after the library relocated into the Carnegie building in 1905, the old Baptist church burned down. (MPPL.)

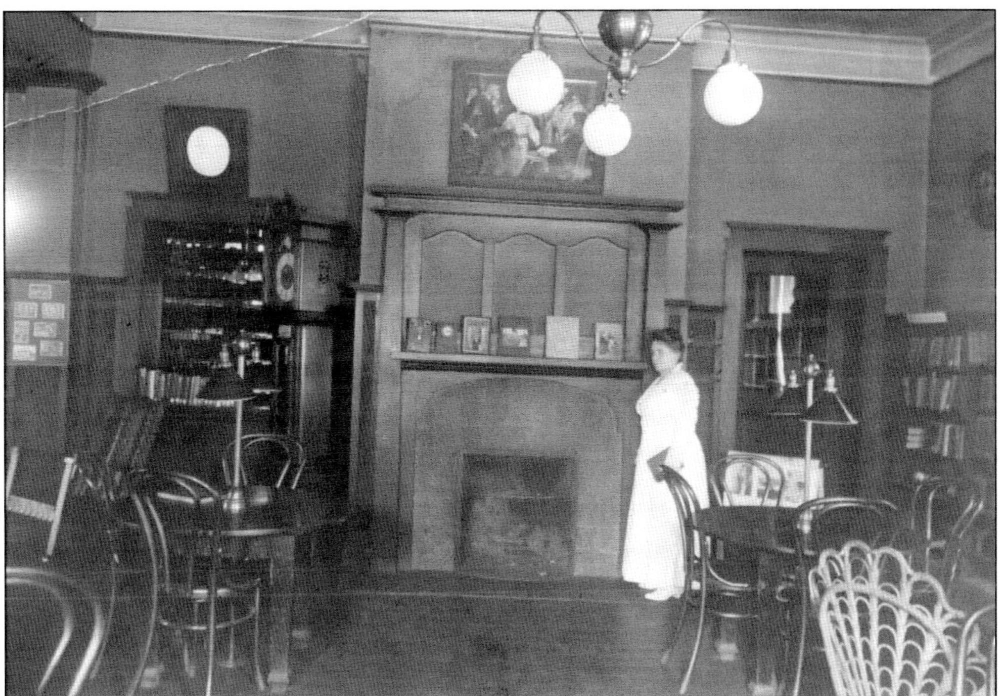

Today, people use the Mount Pleasant Public Library for many of the same reasons they did a century ago. Library patrons were encouraged to sit at chairs and spread their materials over the tables. The library brought citizens the latest information from the arts and sciences, and readers also had the option to find light fiction, domestic magazines, and newspapers. (MPPL.)

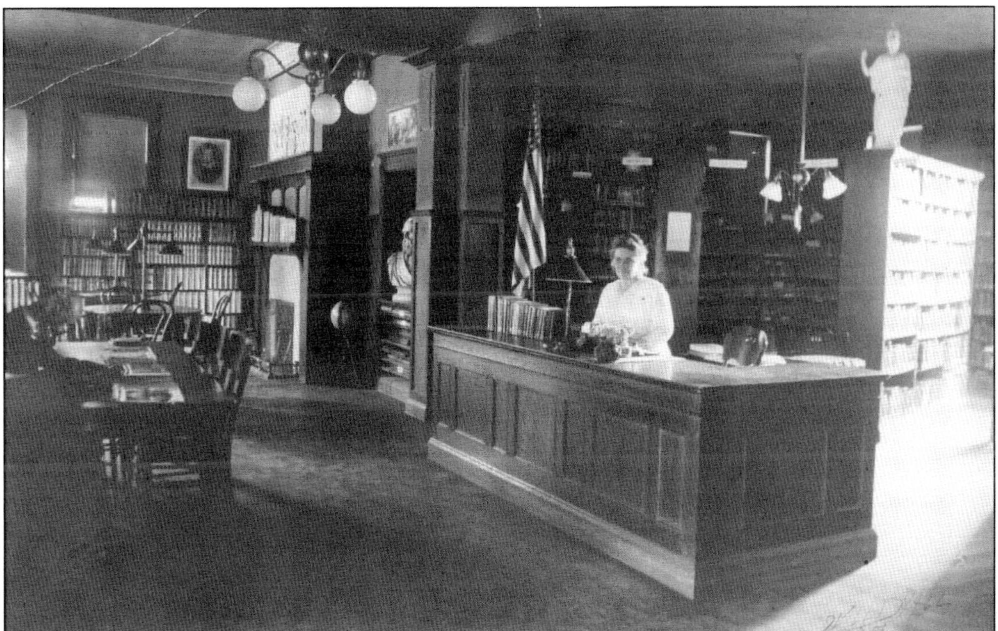

The librarian is ready to serve patrons at the main desk in this 1917 photograph. Notice the classical statue at upper right and the paintings hanging from the walls. From its earliest beginnings, the library also functioned as a museum and art gallery. (MPPL.)

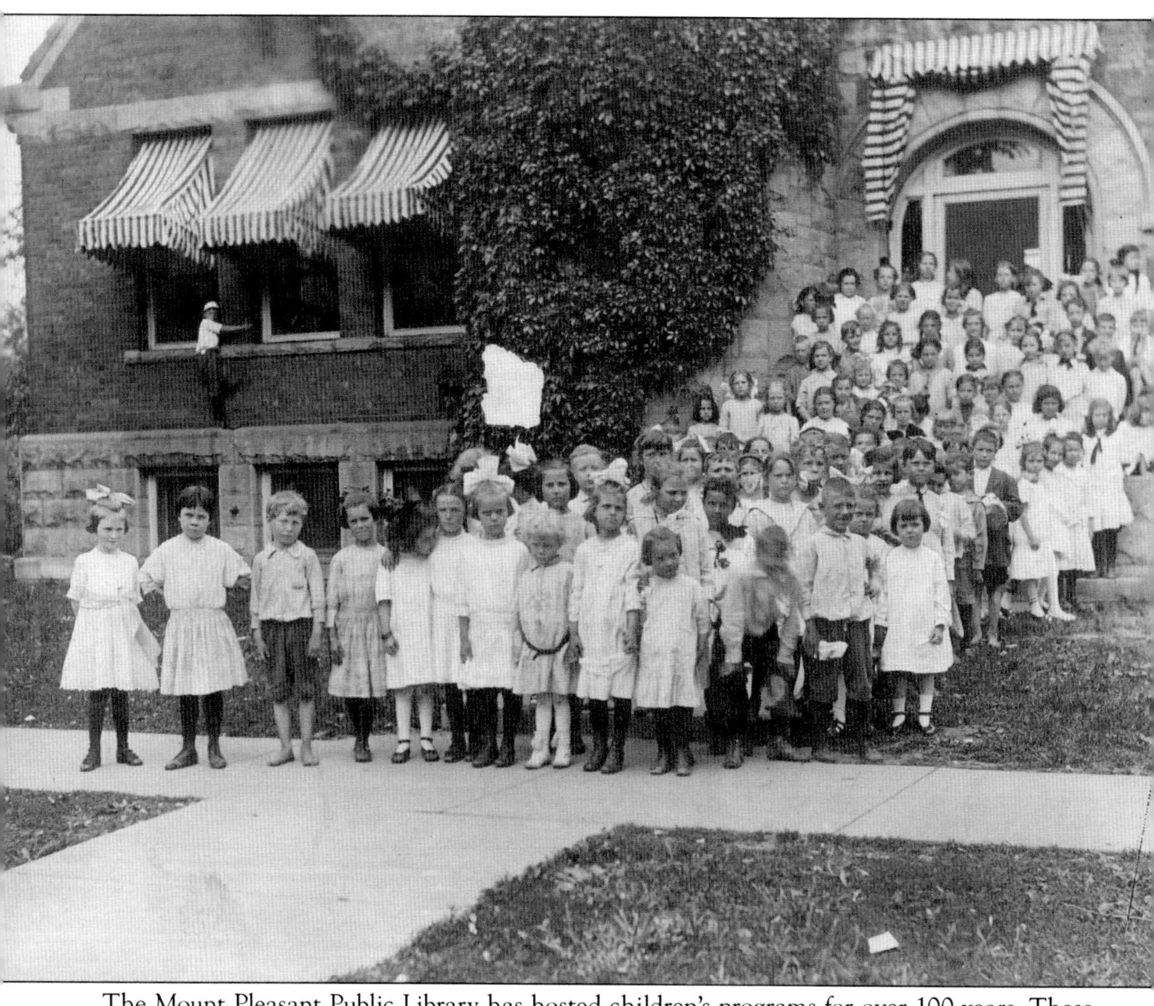

The Mount Pleasant Public Library has hosted children's programs for over 100 years. These children's clothing hints that all economic stations used the library, as some children have clean, fresh outfits, while others have no shoes. Notice the youngster clowning on the window. (MPPL).

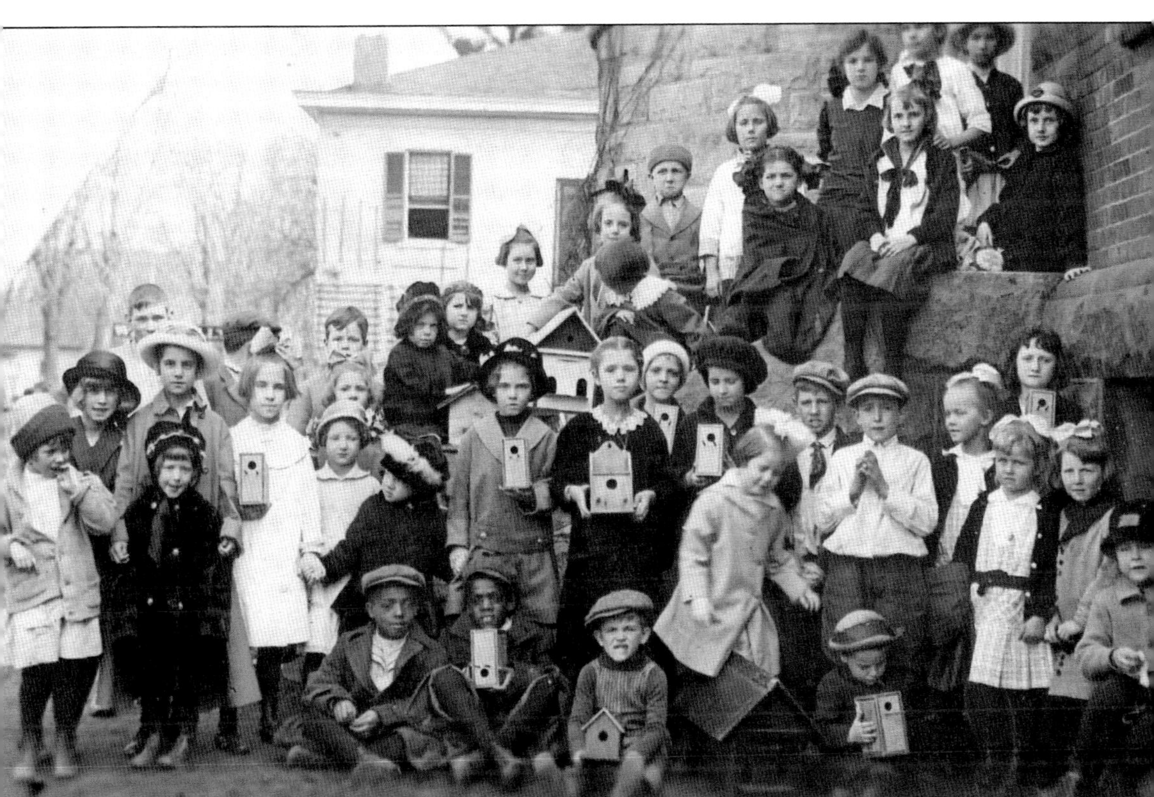

Children successfully constructed birdhouses at the library. Some of them seem quite proud of their creations. The racially integrated library programs show that all Mount Pleasant children were welcome to participate in library programs. Notice the amusing faces on many of the children. (MPPL.)

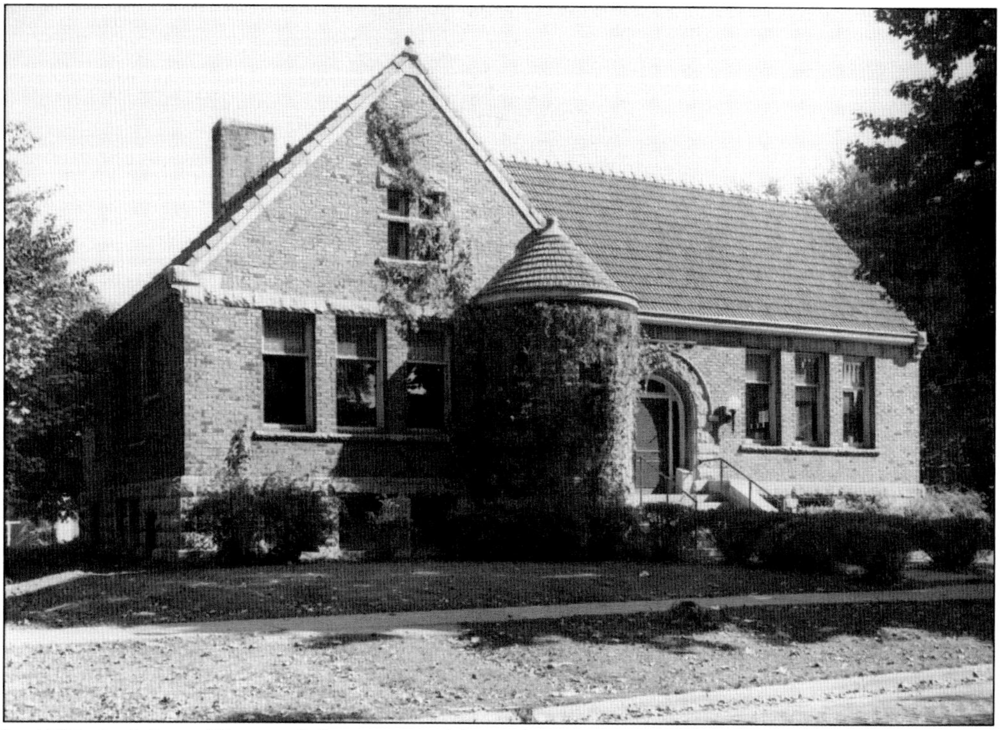

In 1905, the Mount Pleasant Library moved from the Baptist church to the Carnegie building at the intersection of Main and Madison Streets. The library stayed in the Carnegie building for an entire century before moving to the former Mount Pleasant High School on East Monroe Street. The old Carnegie building is now occupied by Southeastern Community College. (MPPL.)

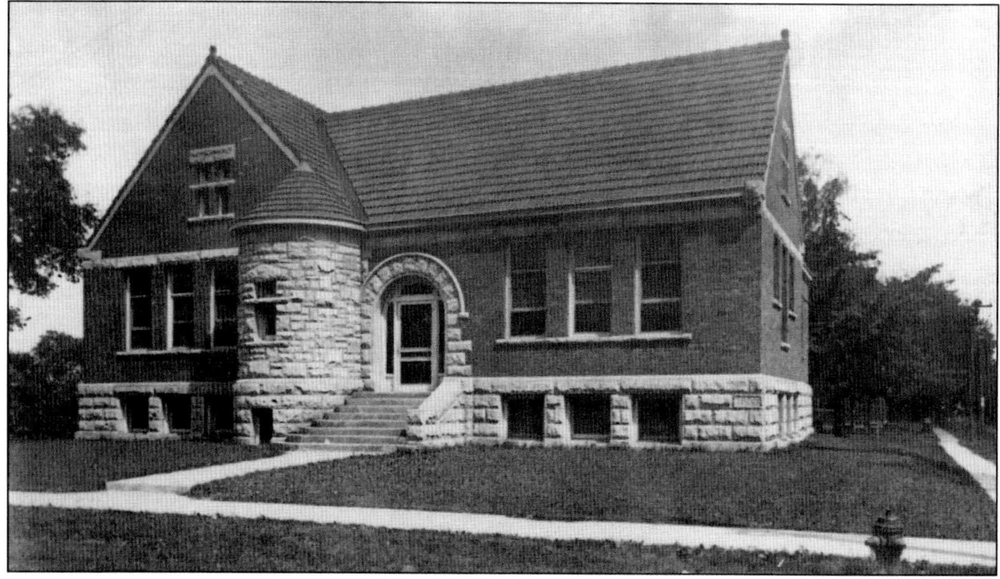

The process leading to the completion of the Carnegie Library was years in the making. After the Ladies Library Association worked selflessly for decades toward this end, W.F. Kopp secured a $12,000 grant from Andrew Carnegie for the construction of the library. Mount Pleasant's Carnegie Library was dedicated in 1905. (MPPL.)

Five

Work

The industrial revolution transformed people's lives in fundamental ways, even in small towns like Mount Pleasant. A great many storefronts and businesses lined the square by the mid-19th century. Commerce spread along North Jefferson and North Main Streets. Industry and manufacture also came to Mount Pleasant. The railroad arrived in 1856, and the pace of commerce increased to an industrial clip. Banks, wagon makers, brick manufacturers, cigar makers, and all manner of trades were established in the town, and the community provided various work and material opportunities for its citizens. In 1870, there was so much business in Mount Pleasant that a customer could find wall paper on West Monroe Street, a horse saddle on Washington Street, a musical instrument on West Monroe Street, and a suitable hat on North Jefferson Street, or shop for groceries on North Main Street.

Professions diversified at an accelerated rate during the industrial revolution. The 1885 *Census of Iowa* reported that the state was home to a diverse range of professionals, including machinists, marble cutters, saw repairers, carriage-trimmers, and boiler makers. In 1885, a total of 108 blacksmiths reported to the Iowa Census that their average annual wage was $683.44, and their average annual cost of living was $419.30. The fantastic growth of Mount Pleasant in the 19th century mirrored the explosion of material and capital growth in the nation as a whole.

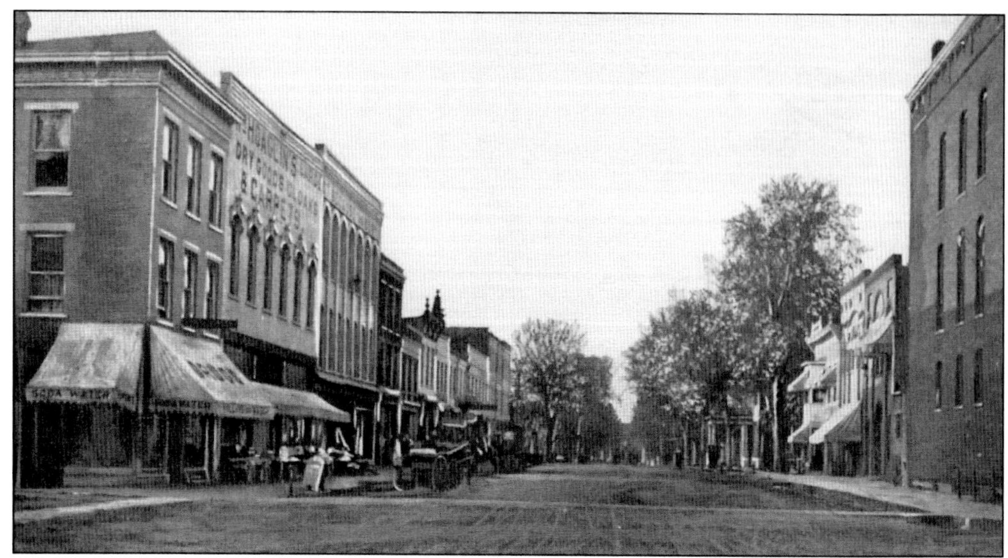

William Hoaglin's Dry Goods store stands prominently on the west side of North Jefferson Street in this late 19th century photograph. Trees on the right side of the street mark the lawn of the Harlan House. The Harlan House, at the time of this picture, had recently been sold by the Harlin-Lincoln family to George Smith. (Don Young Collection, HCHT.)

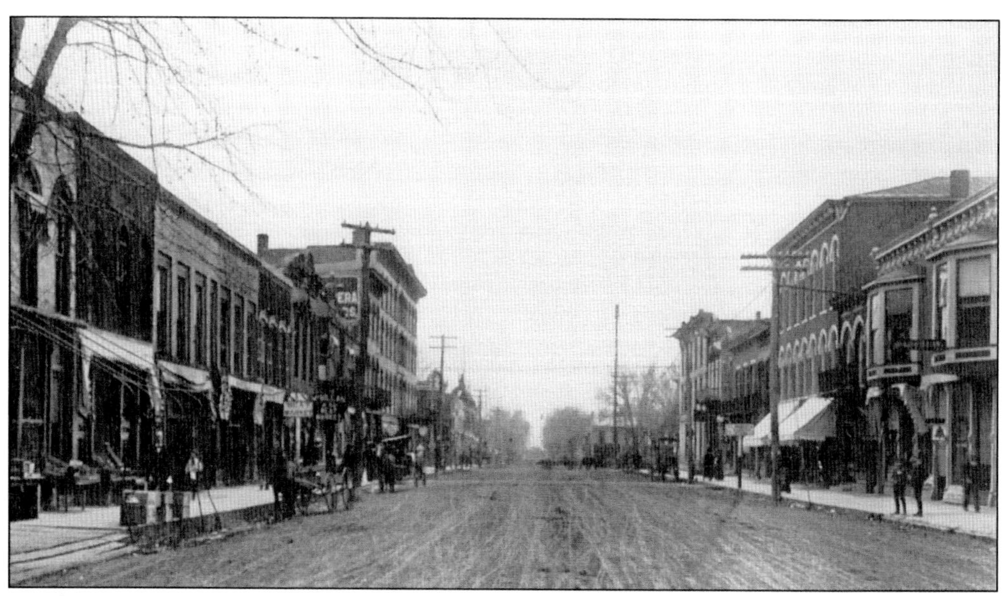

North Main Street is lined with shops in this early 20th-century photograph. On the left side of the street, the last three letters of the word "Opera" are visible on the building adjacent to the Brazelton Hotel, marking the location of the G.A. Grau Opera Cigar Factory, a local cigar manufacturer. (Don Young Collection, HCHT.)

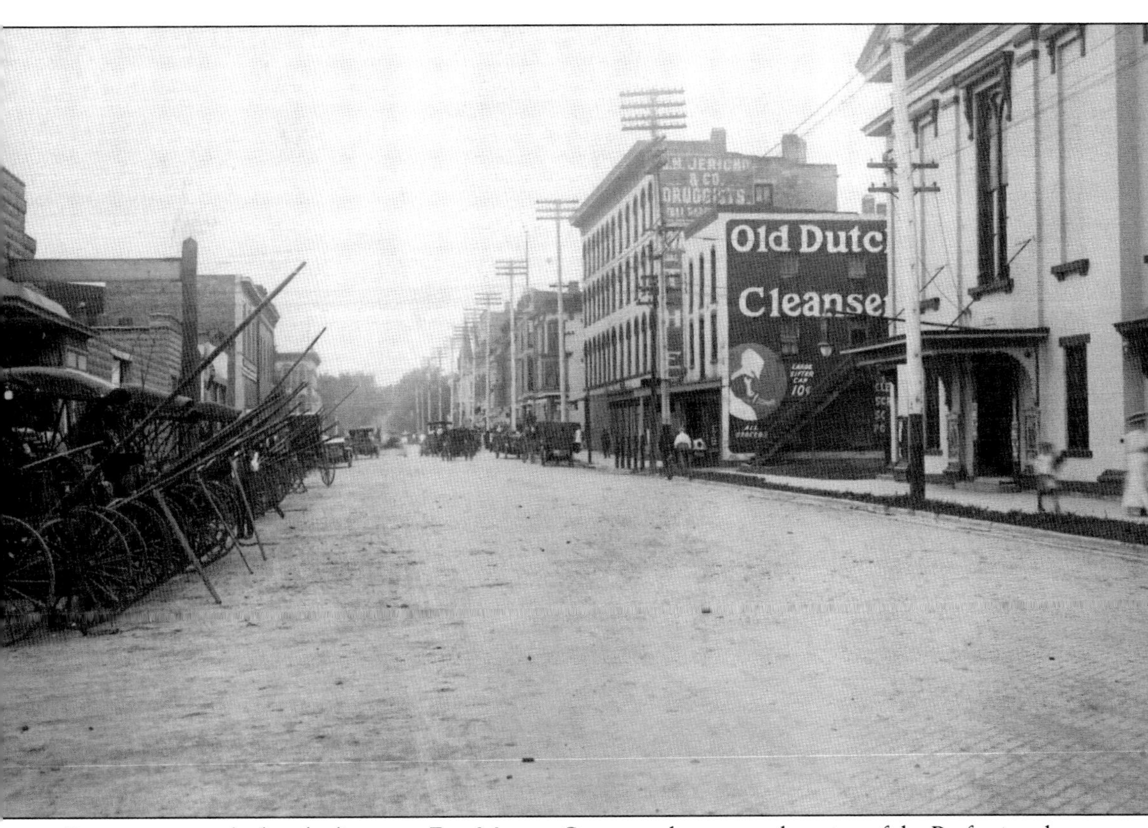

Carriages are parked at the livery on East Monroe Street, at the current location of the Professional Office Building. Across the street from the livery stands the Asbury Methodist Episcopal Church, presently Colonial Apartments. The road bricking is discernible at bottom right. This photograph was taken from the corner of Adams and Monroe Streets, where the REC Center is located today. (Don Young Collection, HCHT.)

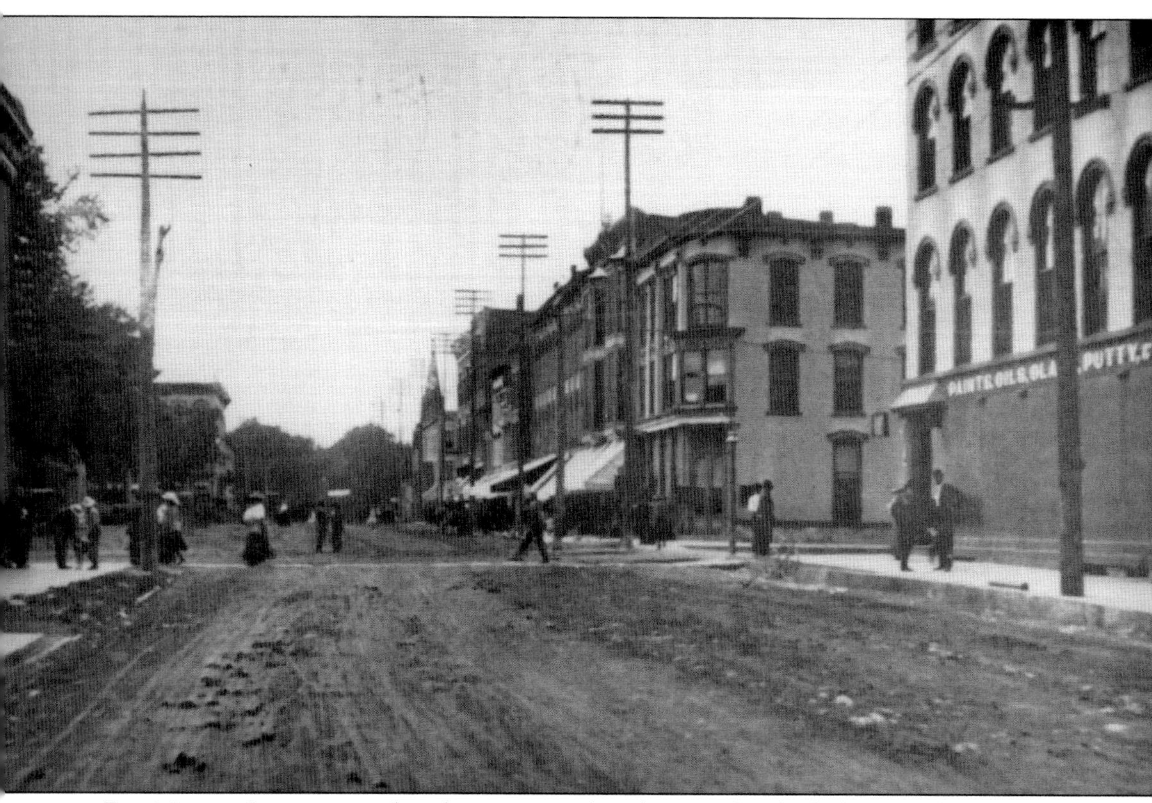

East Monroe Street approaches the square in this photograph, which dates to about 1909. The J.H. Jericho drugstore stands to the right, on the ground floor of the Brazelton Hotel. Though a few blocks distant, the steeple of the Christian church pokes above the other buildings on the north side of Monroe Street. (Don Young Collection, HCHT.)

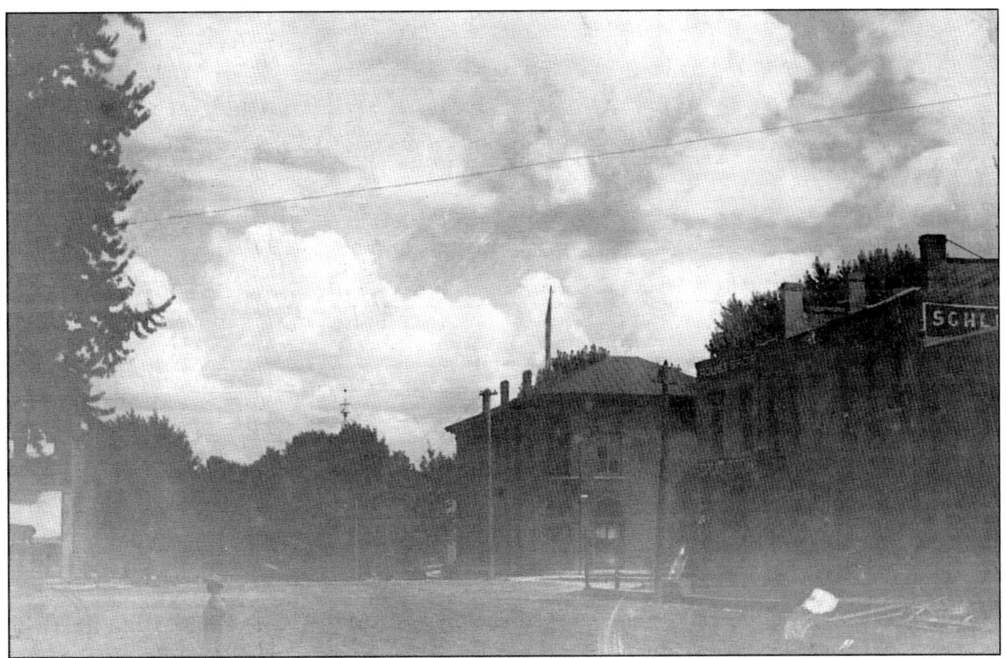

This c. 1900 photograph was taken on the south side of the plaza. The 1872 courthouse is seen at the intersection of North Main and Washington Streets, where the veterans' monument stands today. (Don Young Collection, HCHT.)

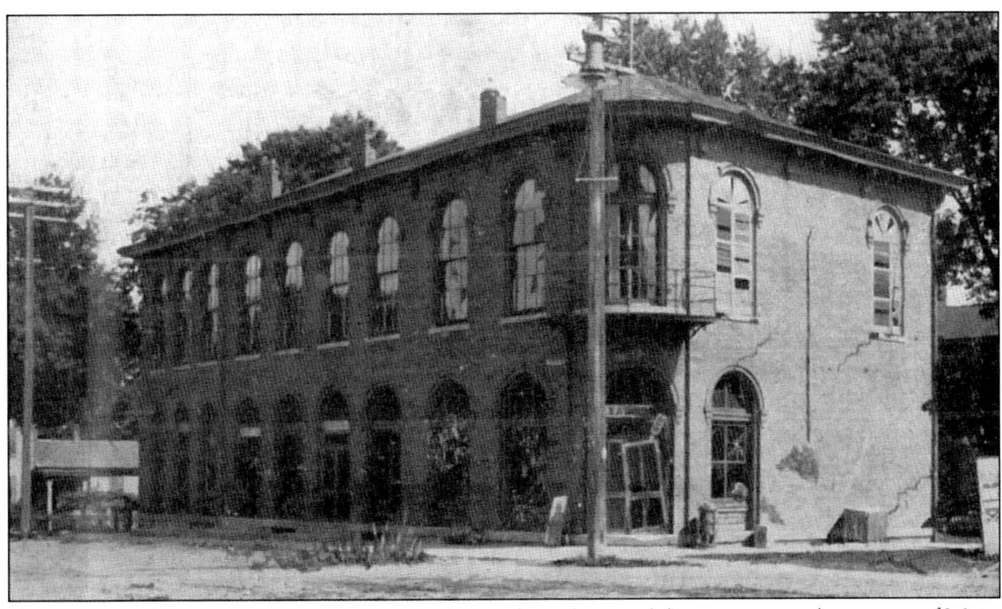

The old courthouse in Henry County was located southeast of the square, on the corner of Main and Washington Streets. This courthouse was in operation from 1872 to 1914. It replaced the original courthouse, which was located in the middle of the square. (MPPL.)

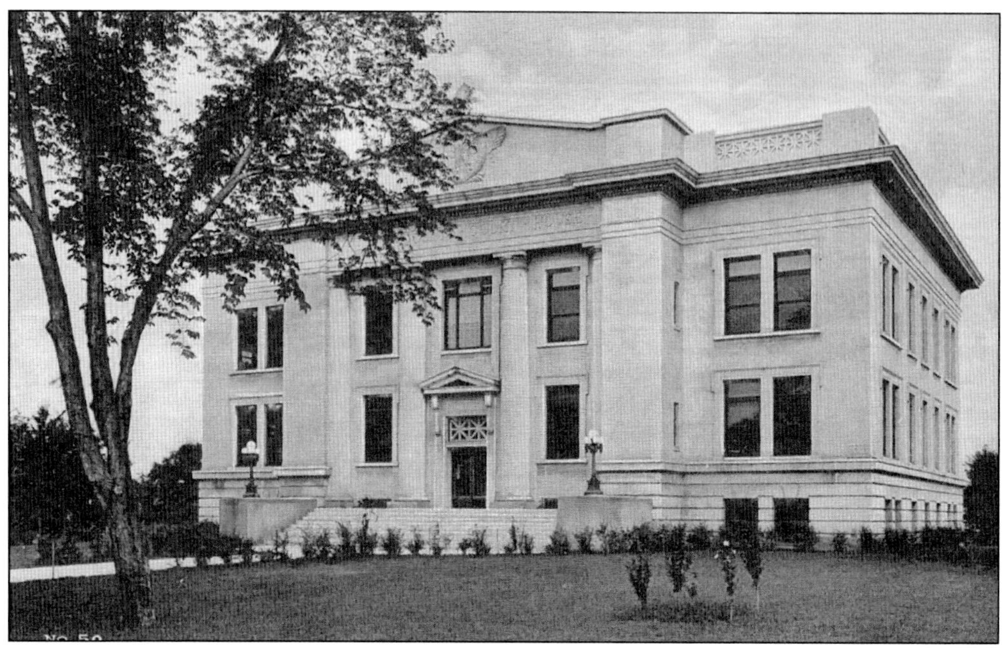

Mount Pleasant serves as the county seat for Henry County. The first courthouse was constructed in 1839. In August 1914, the current Henry County Courthouse officially opened. The courthouse has undergone some changes since its completion in 1914, but the same building still serves the residents of Henry County. (MPPL.)

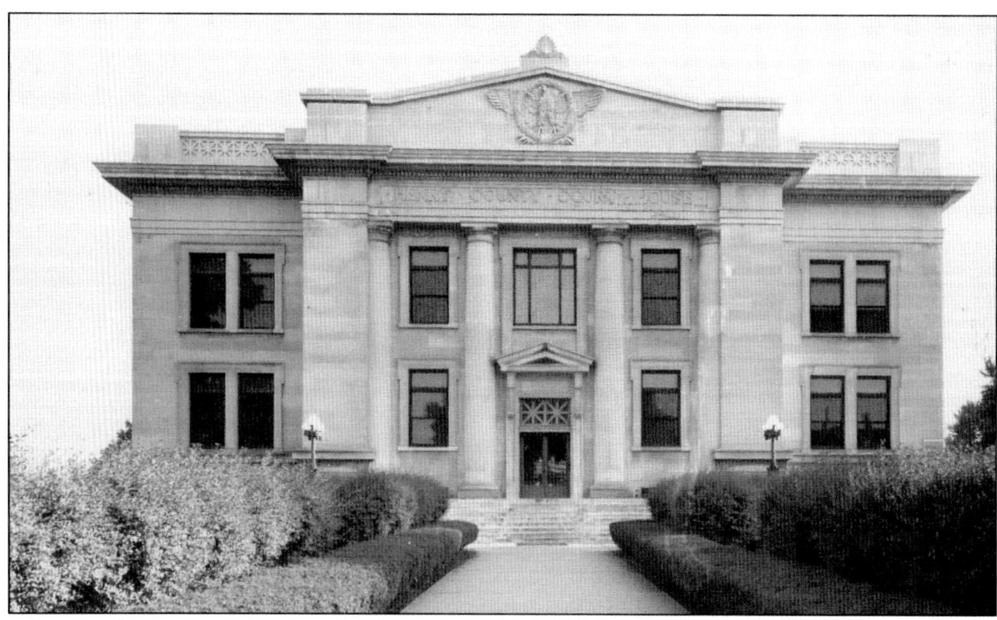

The courthouse's architecture is classical in style, with columns and a highly symmetrical structure. An eagle was once set in relief within the main pediment. The construction of this courthouse occurred 75 years after the completion of the original courthouse in 1839. (Don Young Collection, HCHT.)

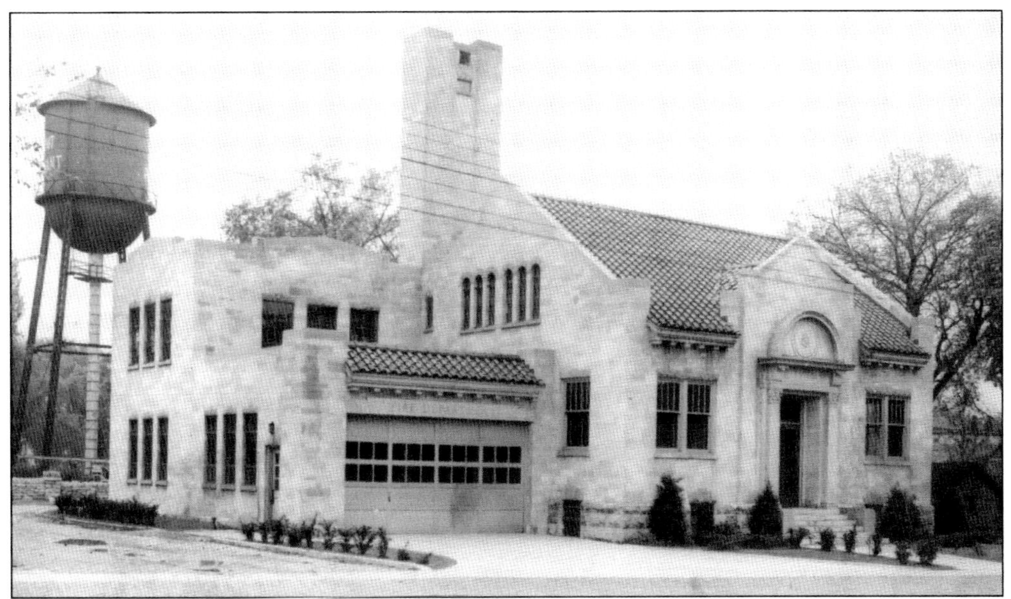

In August 1935, the Public Works Administration, a key program of Pres. Franklin D. Roosevelt's New Deal, provided over $24,000 in funds to build a new city hall and fire station on West Monroe Street. Material from the YMCA building, which burned in 1932, was salvaged for the construction of city hall. Mount Peasant's old water tower is visible in the background. This building is still used by the city government, but the fire station has moved. The city council chambers are now located in the old fire station. (MPPL.)

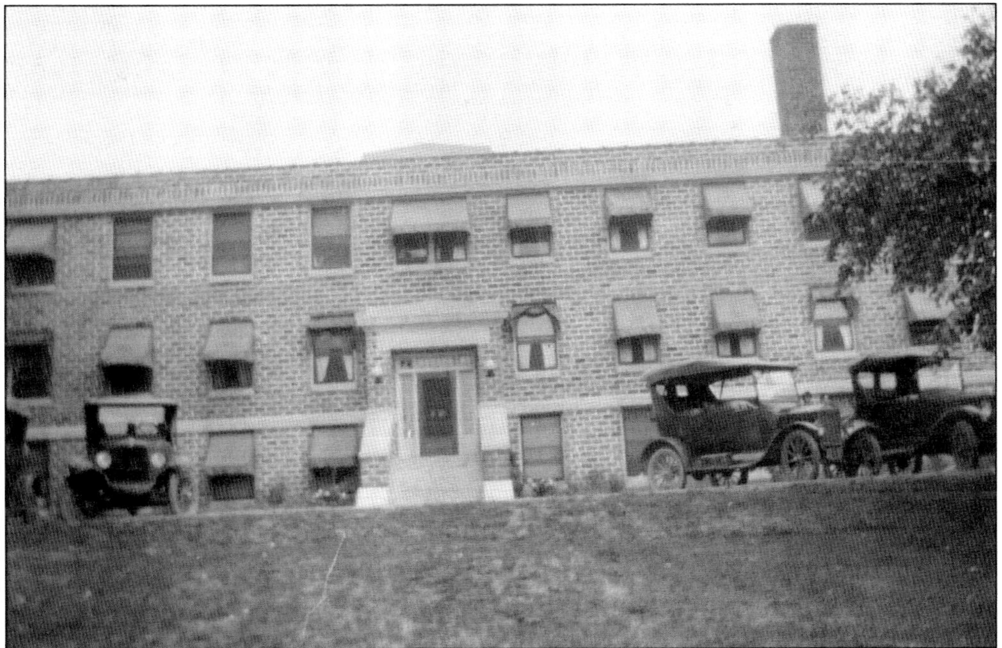

A supervisory board met in 1920 to plan a county hospital. By 1921, the hospital was receiving patients. This photograph is from the hospital's first years. This original building still operates within the current Henry County Health Center, now a much larger facility. (Don Young Collection, HCHT.)

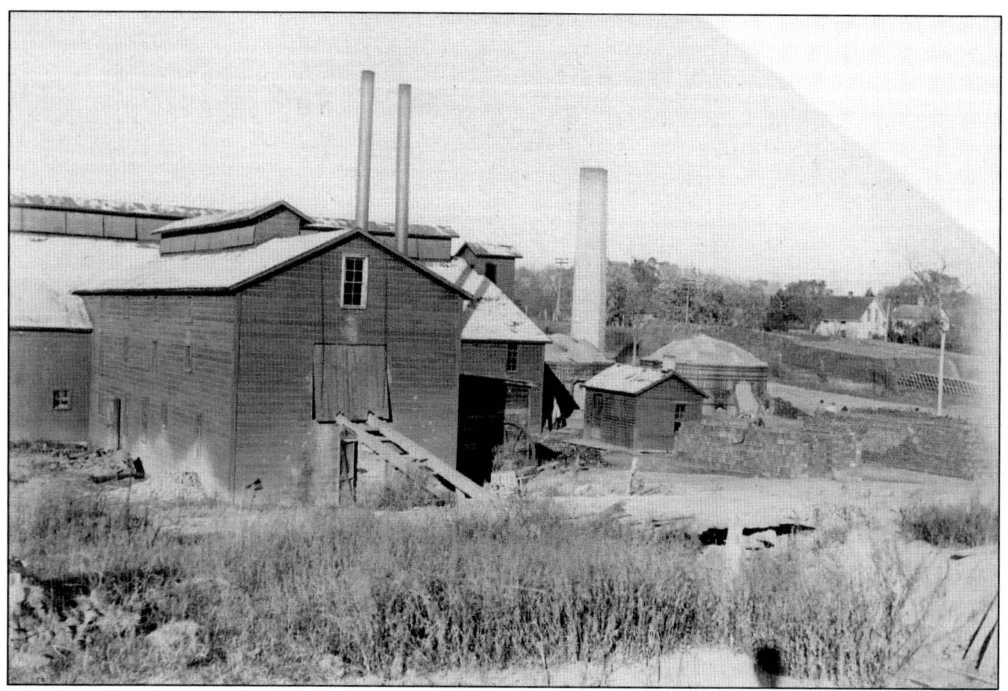

The Mount Pleasant Brick and Tile Manufacturing Company was an important local industry in the early 20th century. Bricks are critical to the development of a settled town, as they have the power to slow the spread of fire. Bricks can also transform a muddy lane into a fortified street, safe for travel. (MPPL.)

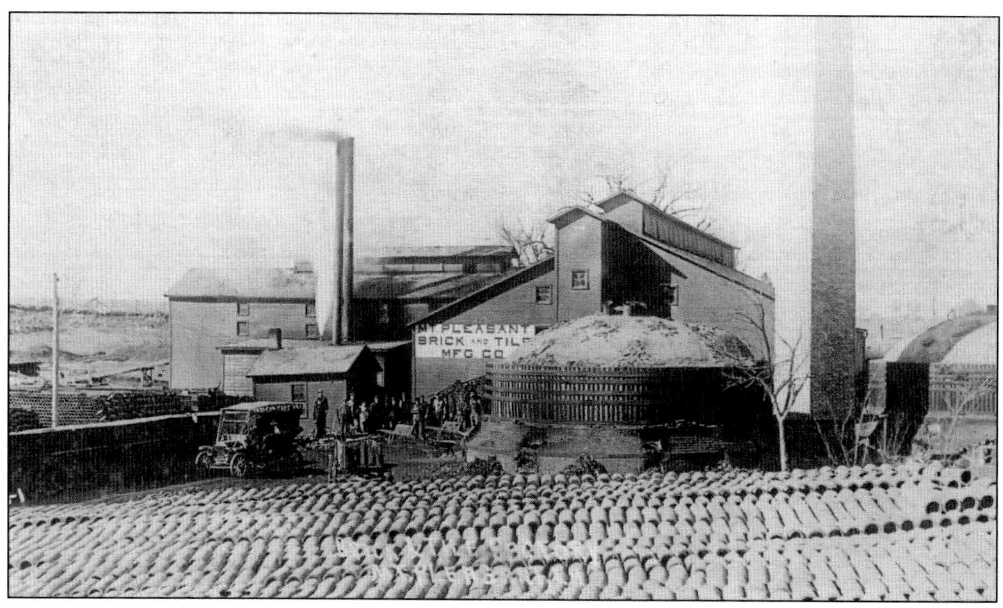

A massive domed kiln at the Mount Pleasant Brick and Tile Manufacturing Company rises in the center of this photograph. A second kiln is partially visible at far right. The adjacent collection of workers and the nearby truck give scale to the kiln's size. This industry was located on West Monroe Street until the 1930s. (Don Young Collection, HCHT.)

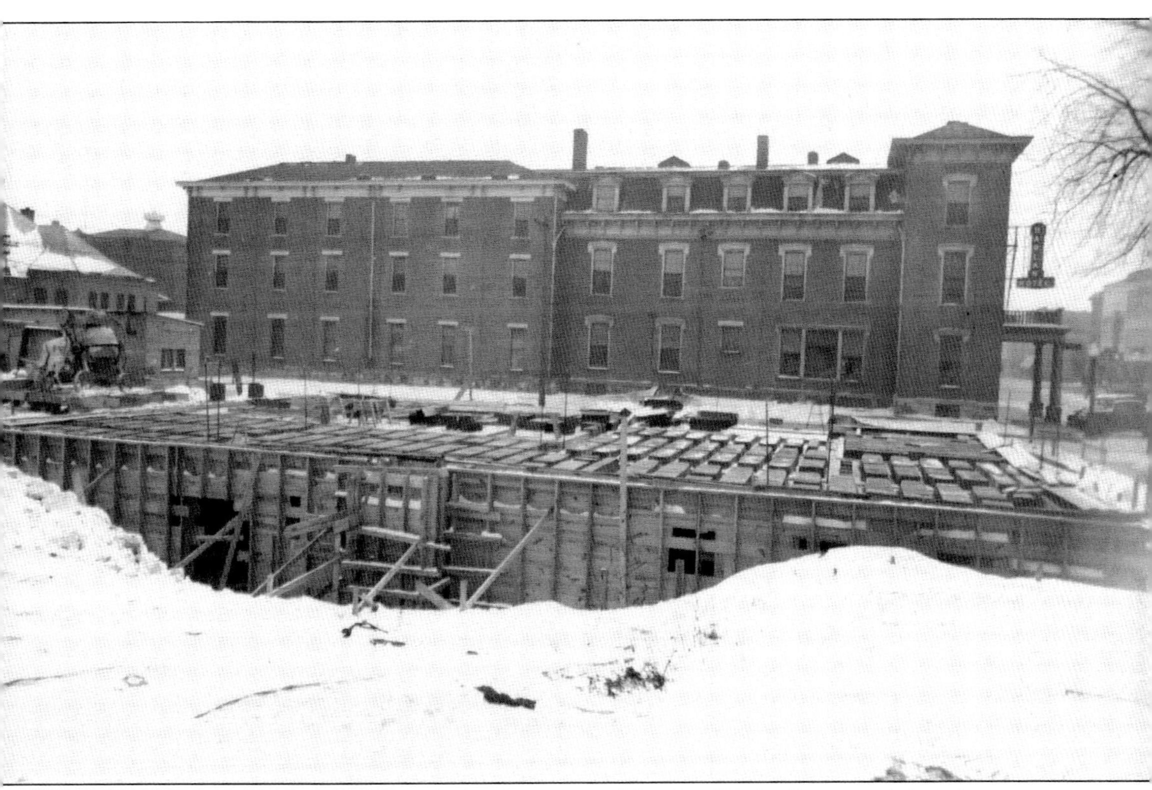

A new US post office was built with funds generated by the Works Progress Administration, part of Pres. Franklin D. Roosevelt's efforts to combat the Great Depression. The James I. Barnes construction company took this picture on February 1, 1936. In the background is the Harlan Hotel. Today, a cornerstone of the post office is dedicated to President Roosevelt's secretary of the treasury, Henry Morgenthau Jr., marking the completion of the facility. (MPPL.)

Mt Pleasant, Iowa, NOV 1 1909 19

Mr Gus Jericho, Sr.

To ELECTRIC LIGHT DEPARTMENT, CITY OF MT. PLEASANT IOWA, Dr.

Balance		
Minimum Monthly Charge, including Meter Rent, 50c.		
Meter Statement this date	1770	
Meter Statement September 1,	1720	
Watts Consumed	50	Minimum, $1.00
Amount Material		
Amount of Bill		$

Received Payment

J. W. McMillan Superintendent

This Mount Pleasant Electric Light Department statement for Gus Jericho was dated November 1, 1909. The people living in Mount Pleasant during this new electrical age were experiencing one of the most profound technological transformations in world history. In the late 19th and early 20th centuries, agencies like the Electric Light Department, and small businesses like the electrical supplies outlet on East Monroe Street, were part of this grand transformation. (MPPL.)

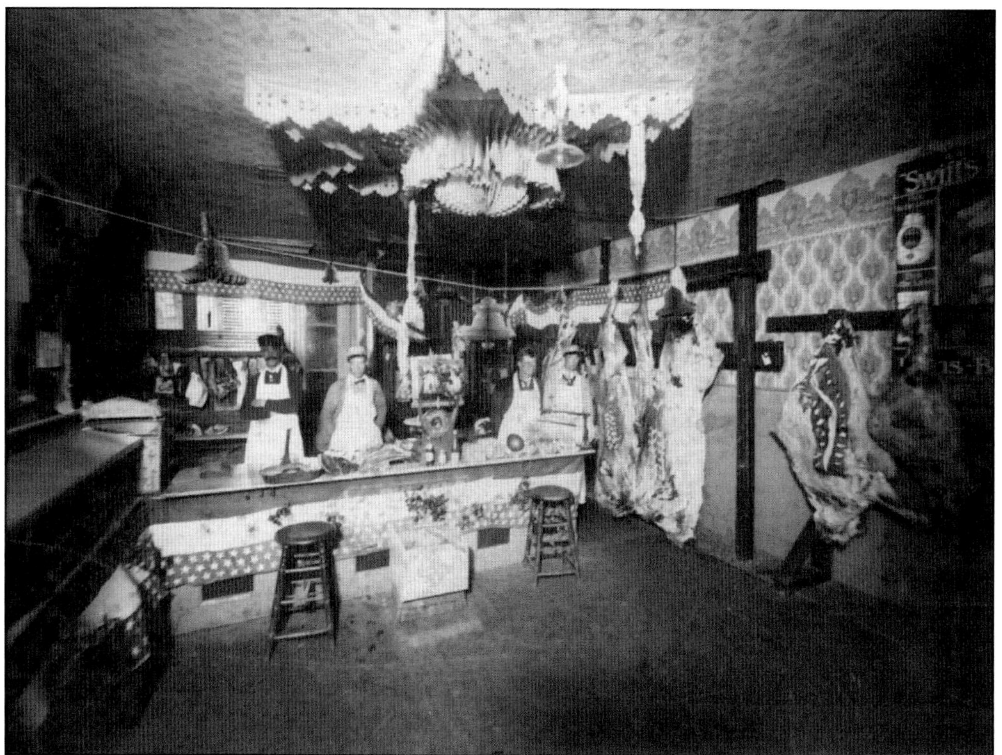

Meat hangs from the walls inside Brown's Meat Market on North Main Street. Iowa became America's breadbasket very early in its history. The widespread availability of meat was a unique feature of the American diet. By the late 19th century, the value of Iowa cattle and swine outperformed entire multi-state regions, making this state invaluable both for livestock and corn. (MPPL.)

RECEIPT FOR TRANSFER OF MONEY BY TELEGRAPH.

American Express Company.

Mt. Pleasant, Iowa, July 9 1889

Received *of* G Janicho

Fifteen —— 15 00/100 *Dollars,*

to be paid to Rich Janicho

No. 1217 East Main *Street,*

at Terre Haute, Ind

subject to the following terms and conditions:

It is understood and agreed that the AMERICAN EXPRESS COMPANY assumes no responsibility, and is not to be held liable for errors or delays of the Telegraph Co's, or otherwise, in the transmission of any messages connected with this transfer of money, but such risks are assumed by the sender.

Geo G. Will *Agent.*

Amount of Transfer, $	15 00
Telegraph Service, - $	50
Express Charges, - - $	50
Total, $	16 00

The telecommunications revolution was in full swing in Mount Pleasant during the late 19th century. Business clicked at a fast pace. This American Express Company receipt for money transfer by telegraph was issued on July 9, 1889. The $1 charge for telegraph and express services was considered well worth the cost. Time was money in Mount Pleasant in 1889. (MPPL.)

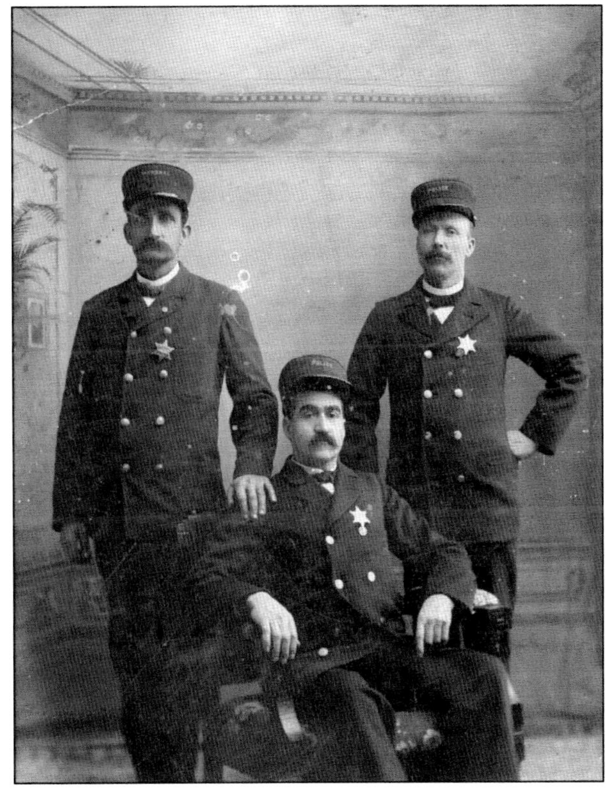

Mount Pleasant, as the county seat, has a long tradition of law. The 1879 *History of Henry County* recorded, "Henry [County] ranks first among all counties of the State in point of freedom from crime. The records show almost a total absence of noted cases of crime." The officers pictured here are, from left to right, John Cox, Ike Martin, and Tom Freeman. (MPPL.)

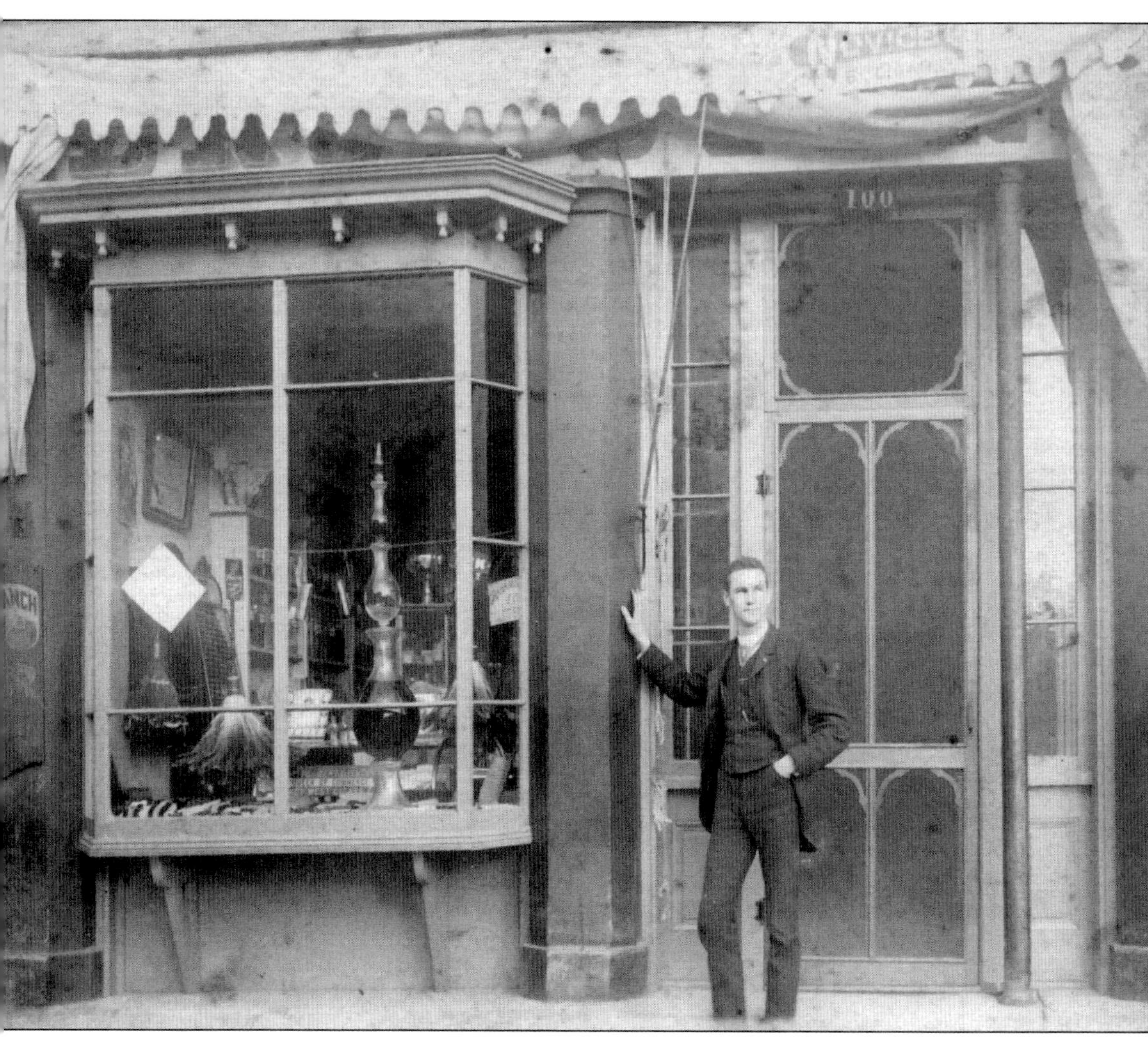

John Jericho, a druggist, stands in front of his store in 1895. The store was located at the intersection of Monroe and Main Streets, in the southwest corner of the Brazelton Hotel, the same venue currently occupied by RadioShack. Notice the goblets and feather dusters in the display window. (MPPL.)

Six

The Square

The heart of the town is the fine, sylvan park in the central square. The trees provide beautiful shade on a summer's day, and the fountain makes an inviting site. The square has acted like a spring from which the town has grown. Mount Pleasant found itself a center for early Iowa roads, connecting the infant community to Fort Madison, Burlington, and Iowa City. Travelers from the east followed Washington Street along the south end of the square. Horse teams could turn onto Jefferson Street and find a large trough up the way. The courthouse was originally in the center of the square, built at the astonishingly early date of 1839. Commerce blossomed around the square, the frame buildings soon giving way to sturdy, brick structures.

The year 1857 was a watershed year for the town. Railroad tracks had recently arrived, linking Mount Pleasant to Burlington and the wider east. Almost instantly, the nature of the city and the ambiance of the square transformed. By 1856, the city's population exploded from some 1,300 people to over 3,000. Shortly after the railroad's arrival, Old Central School was built just a few blocks east of the square, as was the beautiful Asbury Methodist Church. Old Main at Iowa Wesleyan was recently completed at that time as well. The Brazelton Hotel, which still dominates the northeast portion of the square, was built to accommodate the new traffic drawn from the railroad. Other brick buildings, including large banks with tall windows and chamfered entrances, appeared on the square. The Union Block was built in 1861. A stroll around the square in 1850 was very different than the same stroll in 1860.

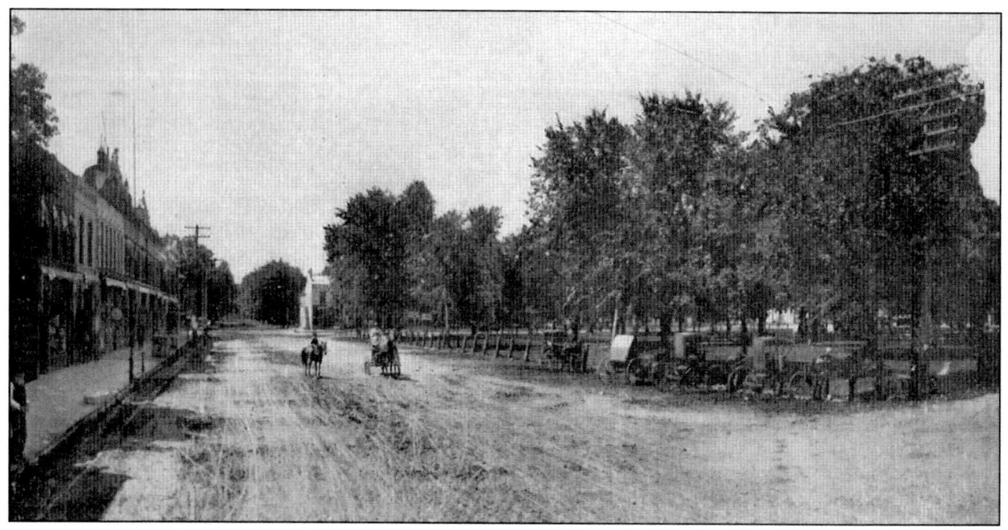

This pre-automobile view of the east side of the square shows the early conditions of the city streets. The 1893 *City Directory* records that the four sides of the plaza had been macadamized, that is, improved with broken stone, as had certain adjacent blocks on Jefferson and Main Streets. The directory mused, "The younger generation may see the streets of our beautifully shaded city all paved with hard brick or asphalt, and given the more modern and metropolitan name of boulevards." The bricked boulevards would come to the square in 1908. (Don Young Collection, HCHT.)

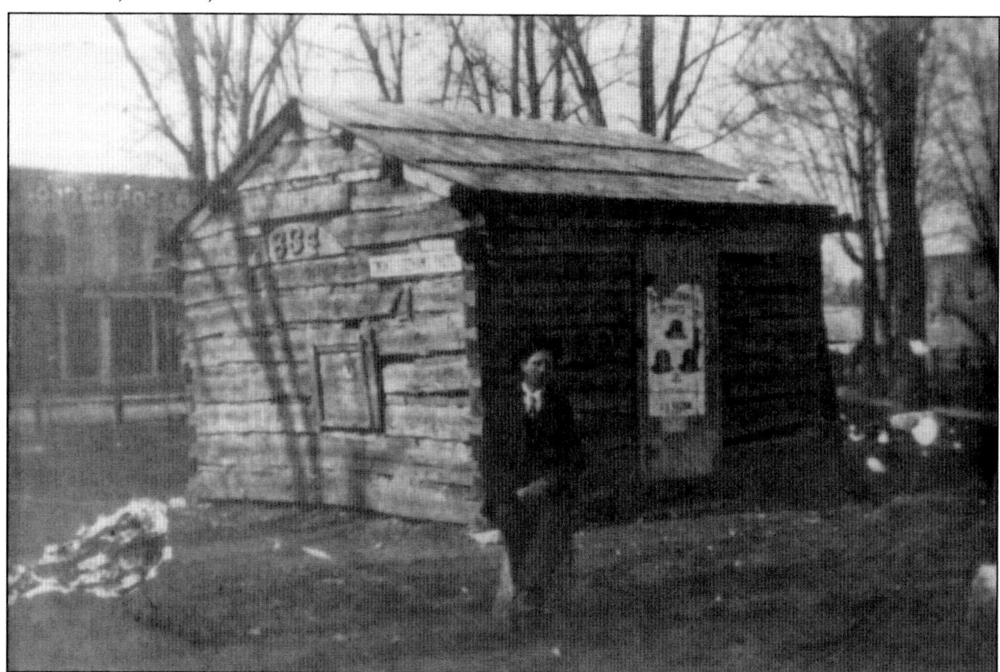

The James Dawson cabin, built in 1834 by the area's first settler, was moved from its original location west of town to the square in the 1880s, where it served as a historical keepsake for many years. Presley Saunders, the founder of Mount Pleasant, stayed with Dawson during his first expedition to the region during the summer and fall of 1834. This humble structure serves as a reminder of the hardships endured during a pioneer winter. (MPPL.)

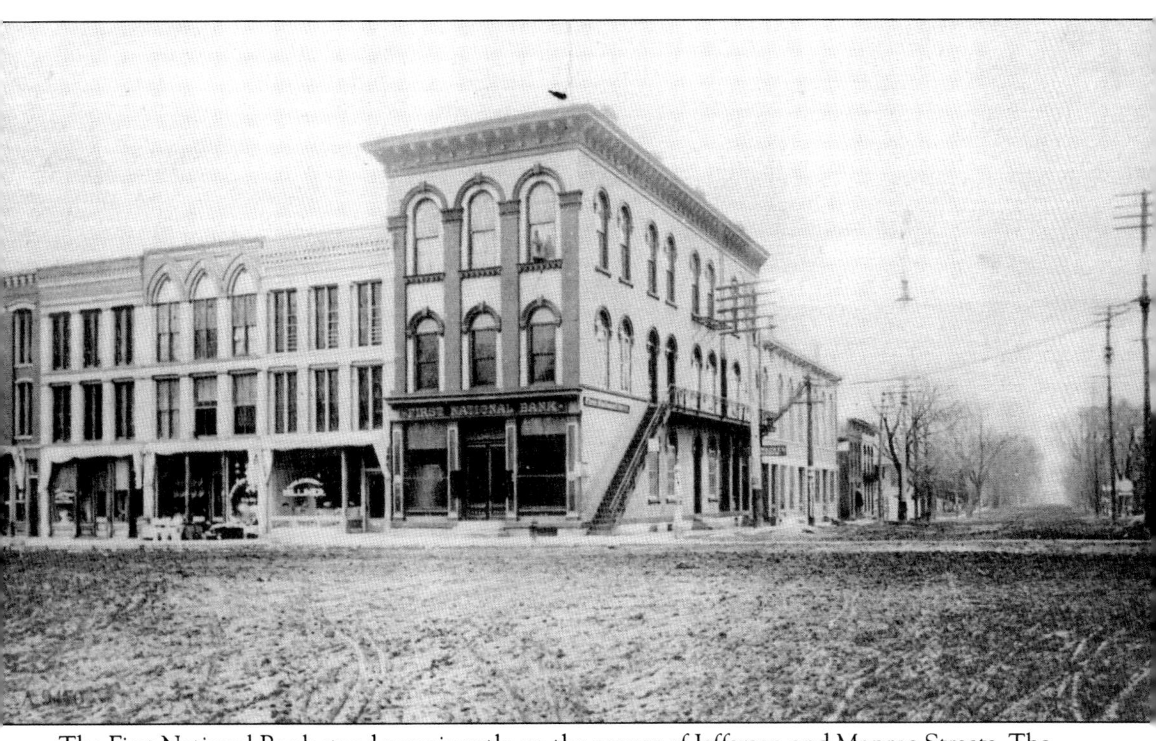

The First National Bank stood prominently on the corner of Jefferson and Monroe Streets. The bank was organized in 1864, and Mount Pleasant pioneer Presley Saunders served as its president. Though in good condition, the original building was replaced with the stone structure at the present location of Le Chic Boutique and Style Vault. (Don Young Collection, HCHT.)

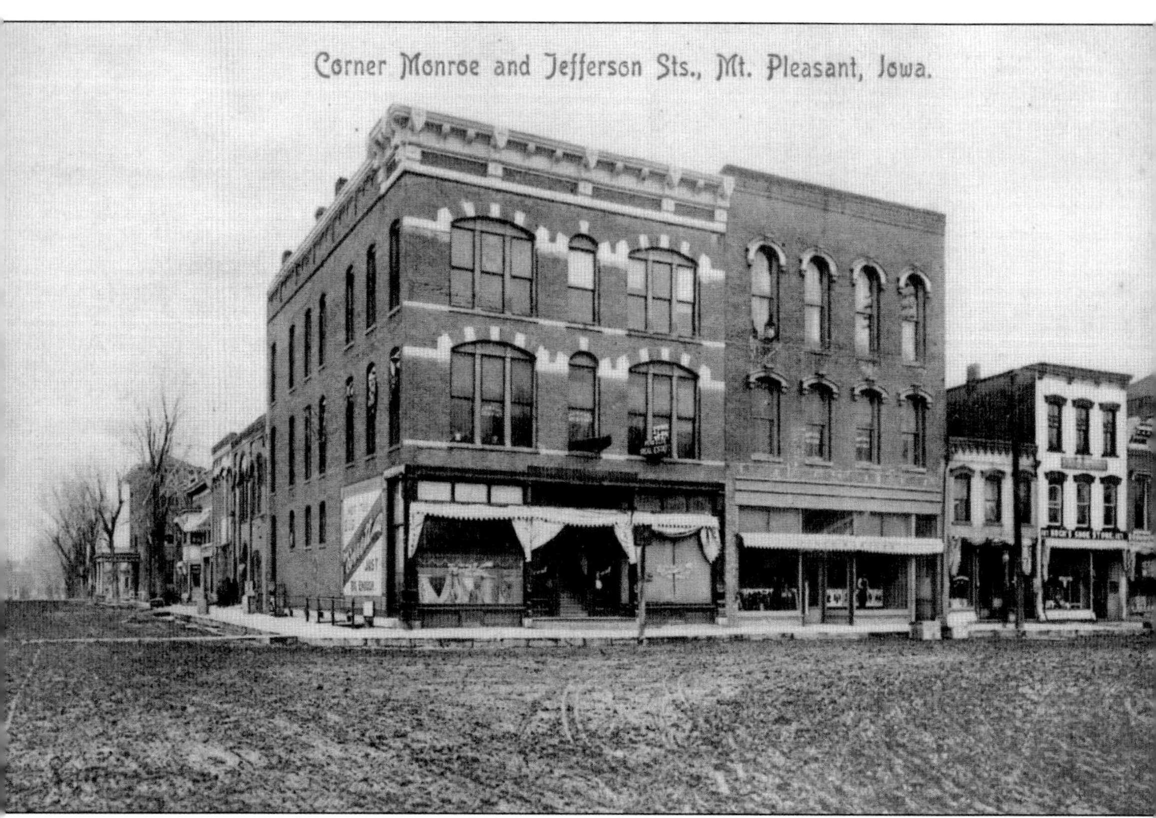

The Farmers and Merchants Savings Bank, identified by the checkered pattern of the arches, stood at the intersection of Monroe and Jefferson Streets in this late 19th century photograph. The bank is the current location of Subway. The street conditions are a prominent feature in this photograph. Before bricking or paving, the streets could easily turn wet and muddy after rainfall. (Don Young Collection, HCHT.)

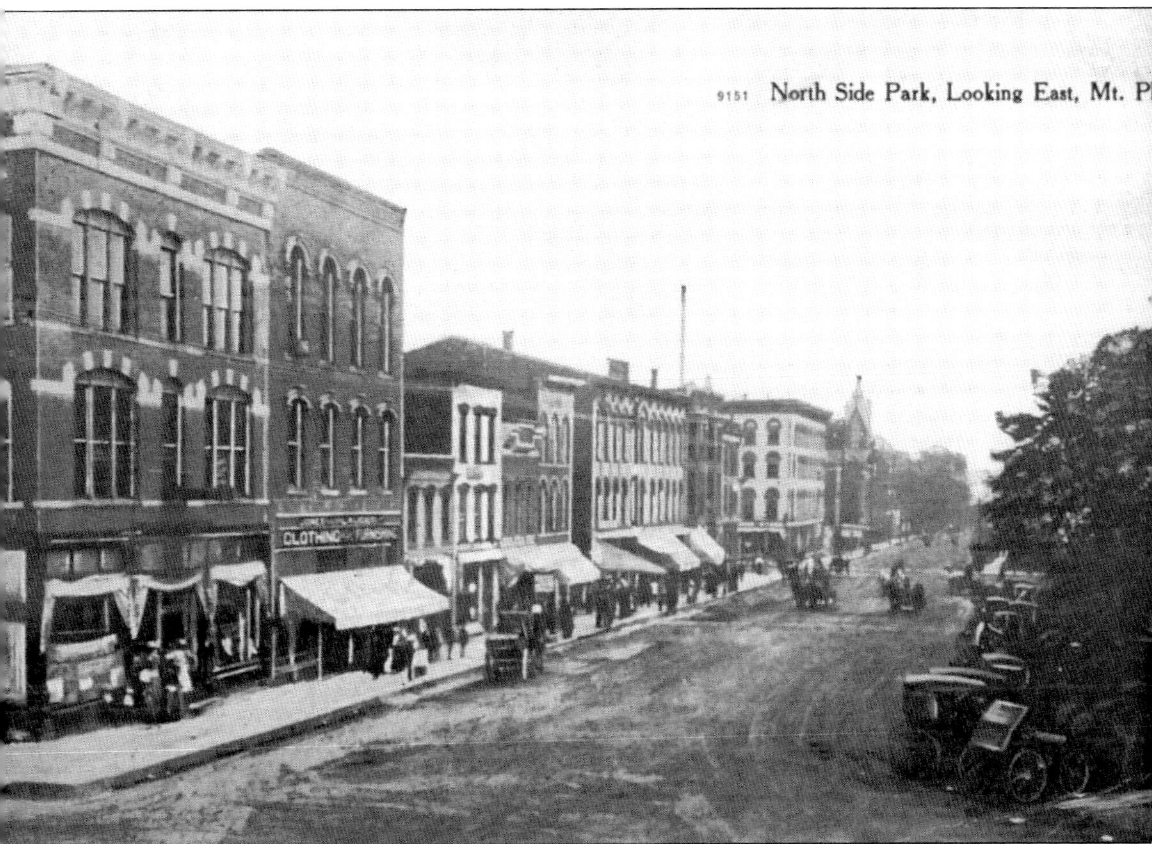

A heavy volume of shoppers passes beneath the storefront awnings in this late 19th century view of the north square. In an era before air conditioning, storefront awnings created shade, providing a comfortable space for potential customers to stop and peek inside. Carriages line the shaded north end of central park on Monroe Street. On the corner stands the Farmers and Merchants Savings Bank, adjacent to another three-story building, the Jones and Lauger Clothing and Furnishing store. The Brazelton Hotel is visible farther down Monroe Street. In the distance rises the Asbury Methodist steeple. (Don Young Collection, HCHT.)

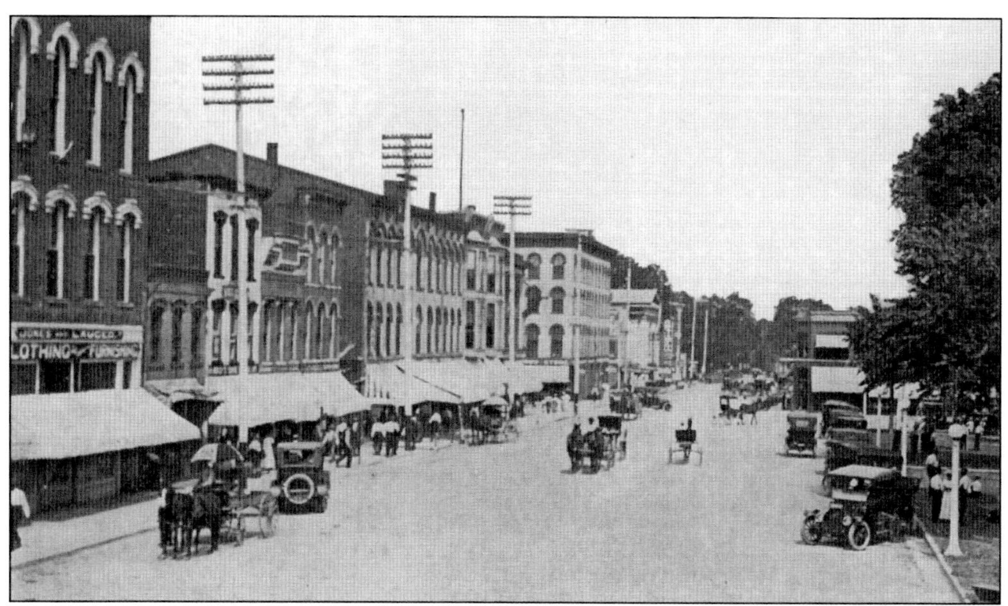

The Jones and Lauger Clothing store stood prominently on the northwest corner of the square in the early 20th century. This building is currently occupied by Becker's Jewelers. In the first few decades of the 20th century, the horse and buggy was forced to share the road with a newcomer: the automobile. (Don Young Collection, HCHT.)

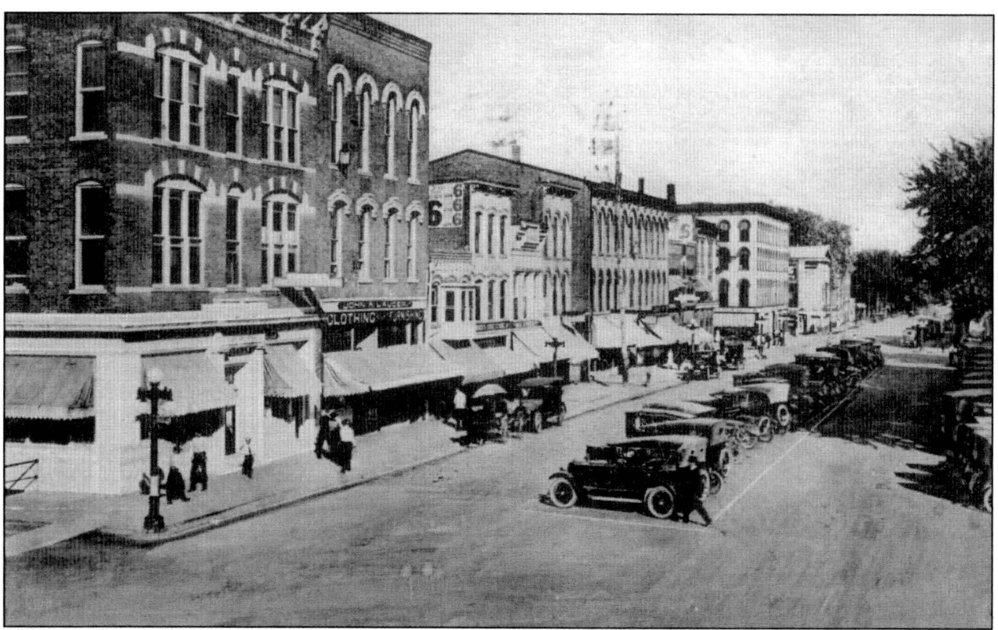

The era of the automobile was in full swing by the 1920s. Notice how the cars parked in the center of Monroe Street. Street lamps line the sidewalk, the specter of darkness washed away by industrial society. Less than a century after the first log cabin was built in Mount Pleasant, the whole structure of daily life had changed in fundamental ways. (Don Young Collection, HCHT.)

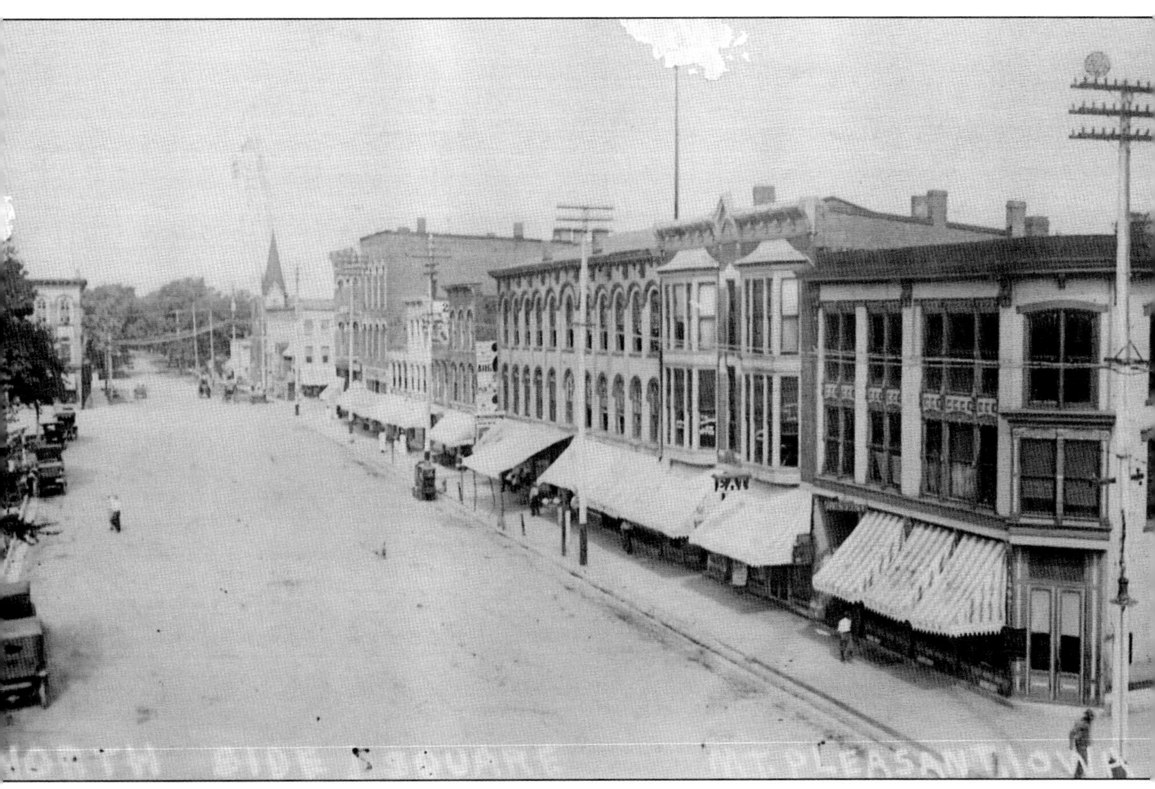

Monroe Street stretches west along the north side of the square. Awnings provide cool shade for pedestrians. In this image, dating from about 1910, the steeple of the Christian church is visible on the north side of Monroe Street, just beyond Jefferson Street. The Union Block, already a half-century old at the time of this photograph, stands in the center of the north square. (Don Young Collection, HCHT).

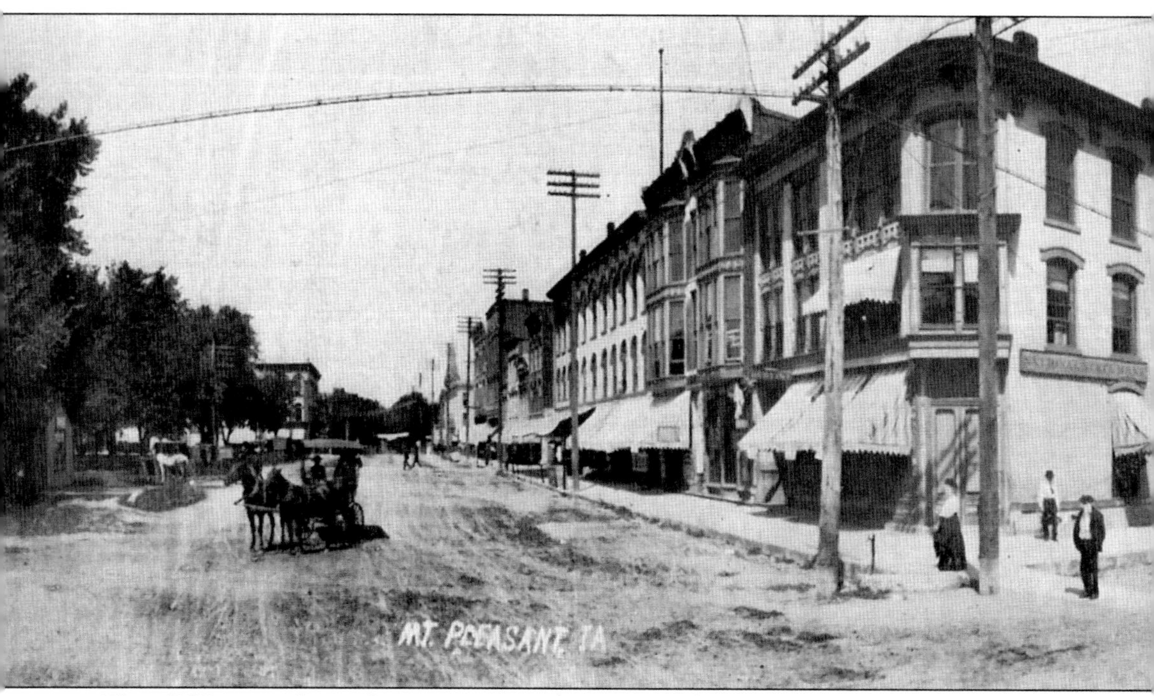

This 1907 image shows the intersection of Monroe and Main Streets, an area bustling with commerce. The 1911–1912 *Directory of Henry County* lists the many businesses located on the north side of the square and adjoining North Main Street, including seven physicians' offices,

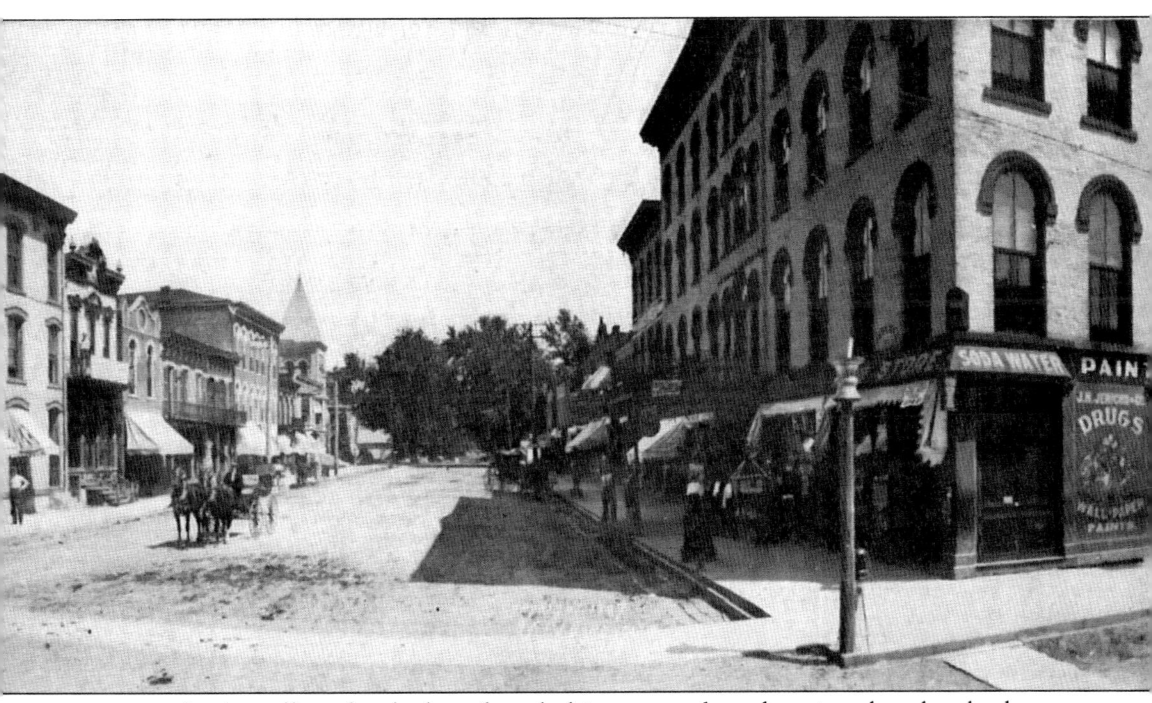

six grocers, five law offices, four barbers, four clothing stores, three druggists, three hotels, three jewelers, and a pool hall, among many others. (Don Young Collection, HCHT.)

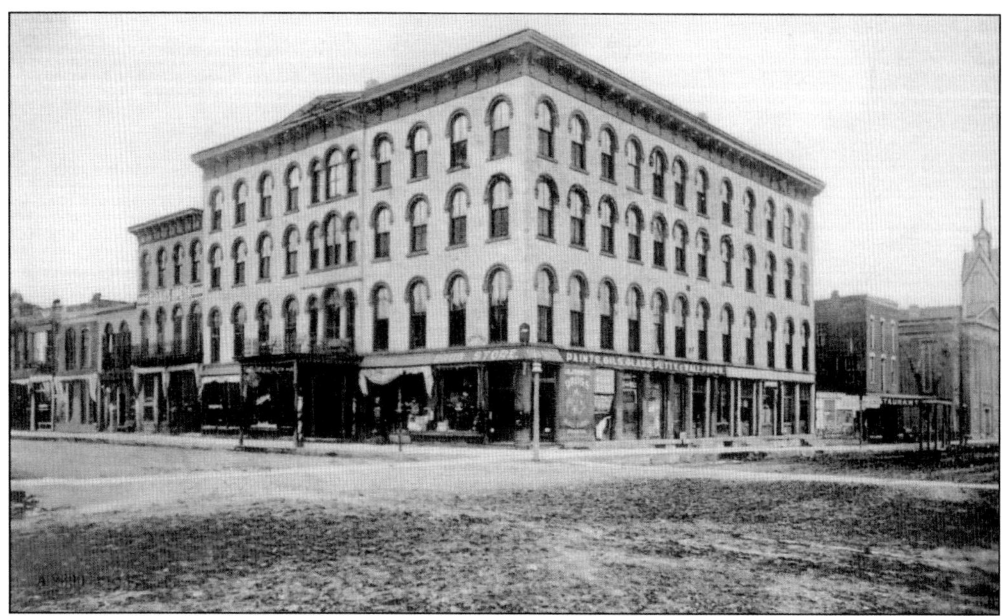

The construction of the Brazelton Hotel is directly related to the arrival of the Burlington and Missouri River Railroad. In July 1856, the railroad arrived in Mount Pleasant, and big city Chicago became a mere ticket purchase away. The Asbury Methodist Church, now Colonial Apartments, is at the extreme right. Notice the pedestrian crossing stones leading over both North Main and Monroe Streets. (Don Young Collection, HCHT.)

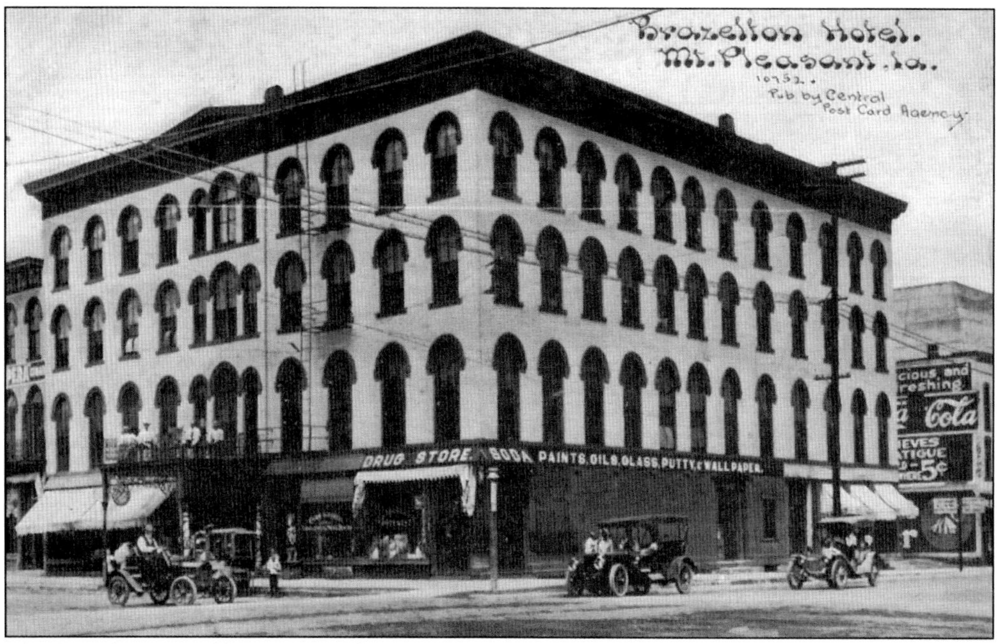

The Brazelton Hotel has remained an important local landmark for over a century and a half. The modern era was in full swing by 1910, as automobile engines cranked along the way and large Coca-Cola advertisements splashed across adjacent walls. The corner of the building, where RadioShack now stands, was a drugstore. Notice the people standing on the balcony overlooking North Main Street. (Don Young Collection, HCHT.)

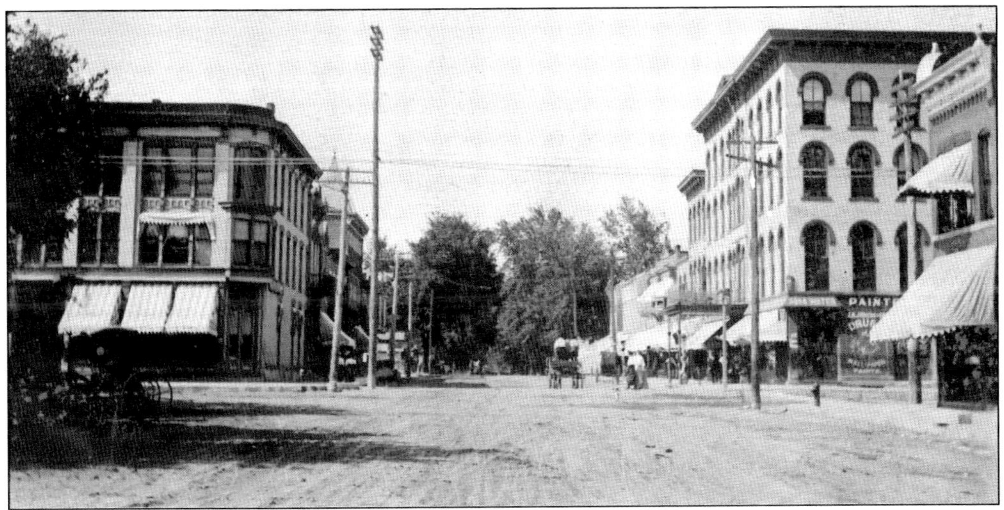

Horses and carriages dot the intersection of Monroe and Main Streets in this photograph from about 1900. The improvement of streets was an important concern for Mount Pleasant citizens at this time. Mount Pleasant's *Weekly News* reported in August 1893 that the Henry County Good Roads Convention met at Central Park and held a session in the old courthouse. The primary concern of the convention was improved road drainage. (Don Young Collection, HCHT.)

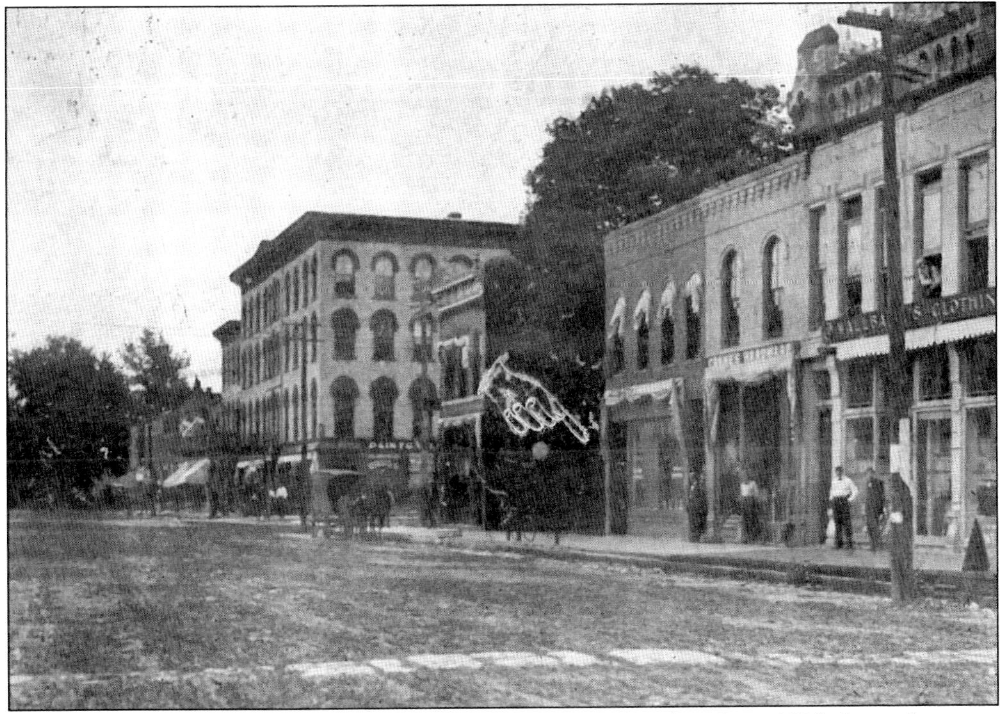

This photograph of the northeast corner of the square, captured in about 1905, shows the many businesses lining Main Street. An illustrated hand points to V.D. Morris' Jewelry, Book and Music Store. Crane and Company's Hardware stood adjacent to the jeweler. The building at far right, decked with an ornate pediment, was Wallbank and Sons Clothing and Shoes, currently Breadeaux Pizza and Anna's Pantry. Notice the crossing stones over Main Street. (Don Young Collection, HCHT).

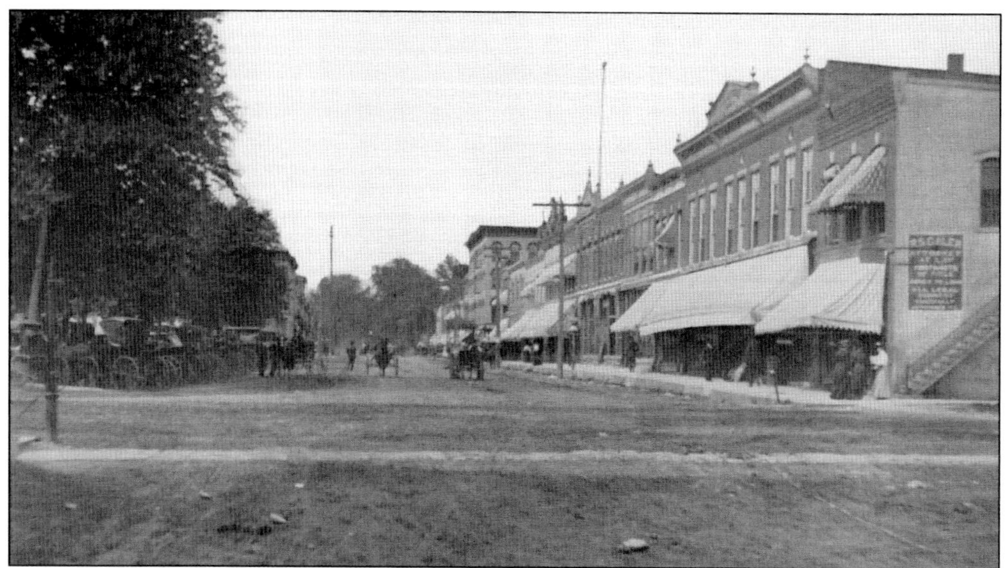

Carriages are parked along the east side of Central Park in this late 19th century photograph. Notice the depth of the sidewalk along the storefronts on Main Street. The 1893 *City Directory* discusses the issue of sidewalk improvement, noting that "the town needs to secure an improvement of walks to replace all walks when worn out with cement or asphalt, either of which is inexpensive and a decided improvement over plank, stone or brick." (Don Young Collection, HCHT.)

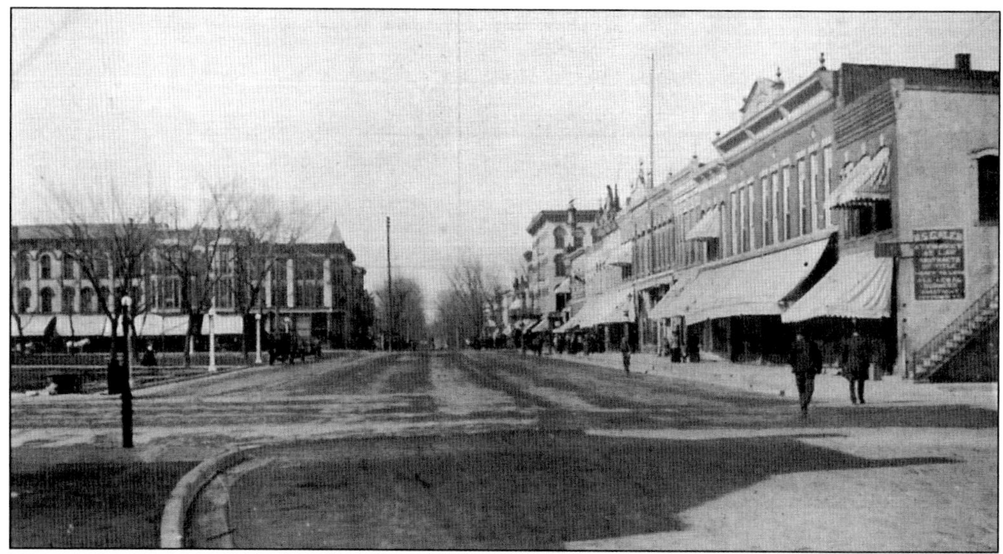

This photograph, taken in about 1910, looks up Main Street from the southeast corner of the square. The building situated at the corner of Main and Washington Streets advertises the law office of R.S. Galer; this is the current location of the Mount Pleasant Area Chamber Alliance. The Brazelton Hotel is visible down the block on the right. The triangular spire of the old Presbyterian church peeks above the other buildings farther down the way. (Don Young Collection, HCHT.)

Seven

CHURCHES

It is impossible to imagine the development of Mount Pleasant without its churches. The Methodist circuit rider John Ruble was the first Methodist preacher in southeast Iowa. He gave a sermon in Presley Saunders's cabin in 1835. Methodist circuit riders like Reverend Ruble were missionaries sent into the frontier wilderness as a voice of support and communion for the first pioneers in prairie country. The Rev. John Ruble traveled hundreds of miles over dangerous, unsettled lands to shepherd his flock, a voyager in a prairie sea.

The arriving settlers brought many denominations to Mount Pleasant. Methodists, Presbyterians, Catholics, Congregationalists, Universalists, Baptists, Episcopalians, and many others found a home here. In the early days, congregations would often meet in a home or in a public space, like the courthouse, before the congregation had the necessary resources or means to build a proper church. It is safe to say that all of these various denominations were present during the early years of the town's history, and they all played a critical role in Mount Pleasant's progression. In the 19th century, churches served as necessary networks for fellowship, charity, and learning. A humble cabin, once located in present-day Saunders Park, functioned as both a school and a multi-denominational house of worship during the pioneer days.

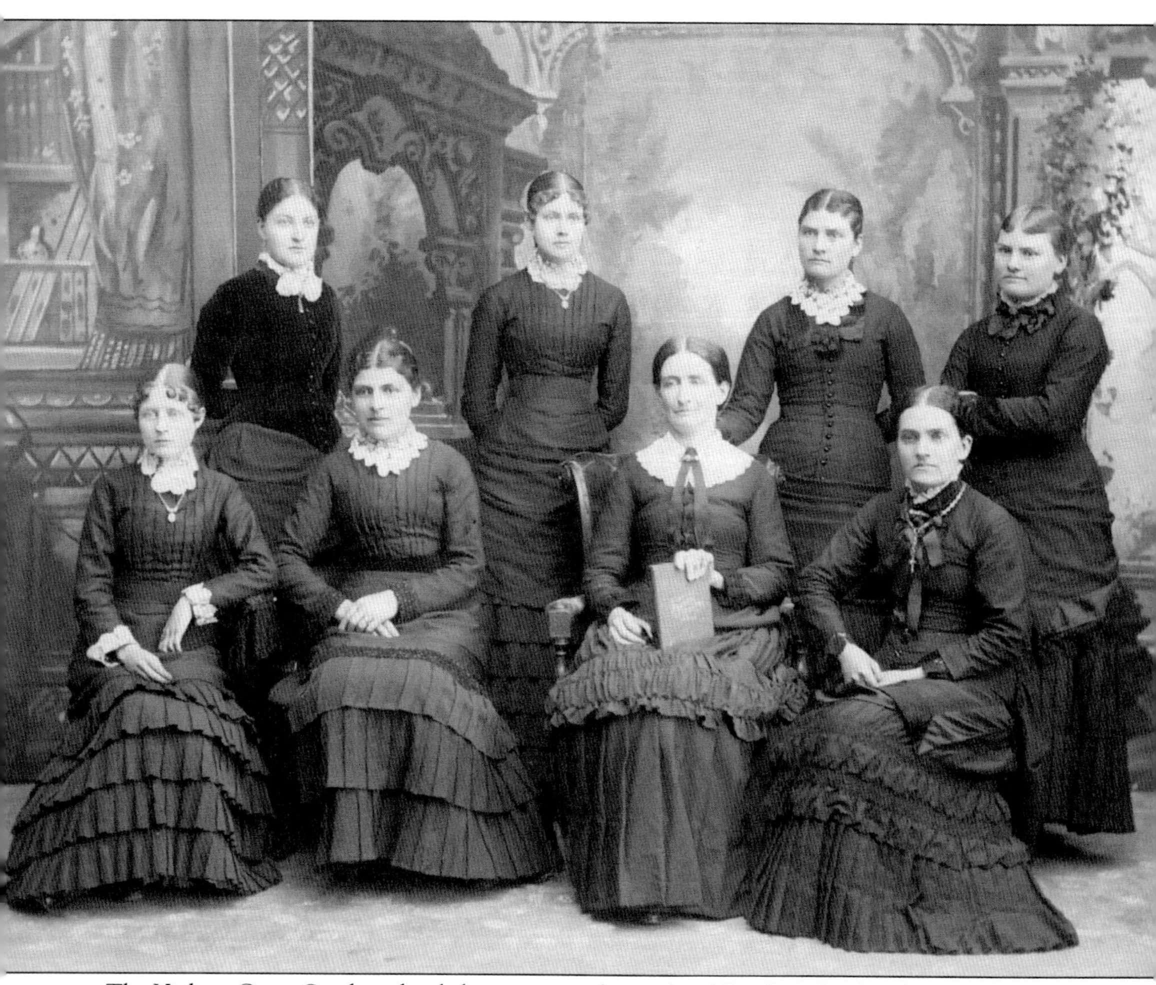

The Hickory Grove Sunday school class was one of many local Sunday schools. The 1867 convention of the Henry County Sabbath School Association reported that Henry County was home to 28 Sunday schools, consisting of 2,873 students and 311 teachers. The scholars shown here are, from left to right, (first row) Ann Lafferty, Lottie Kitch Smith, Elizabeth Jerrell, and Annabelle Cox; (second row) Allie Hall Leach, Mary Lafferty Traut, Mina Kitch, and Elnora Kitch. (MPPL.)

The original brick Congregational church stood on the east side of the square. The church, dedicated in 1852, originally had a large lawn with tall trees years before the adjacent lots filled with banks and businesses. The congregations of the Universalist church, seen in the background to the right, and the Congregational church developed a strong bond of friendship. (MPPL.)

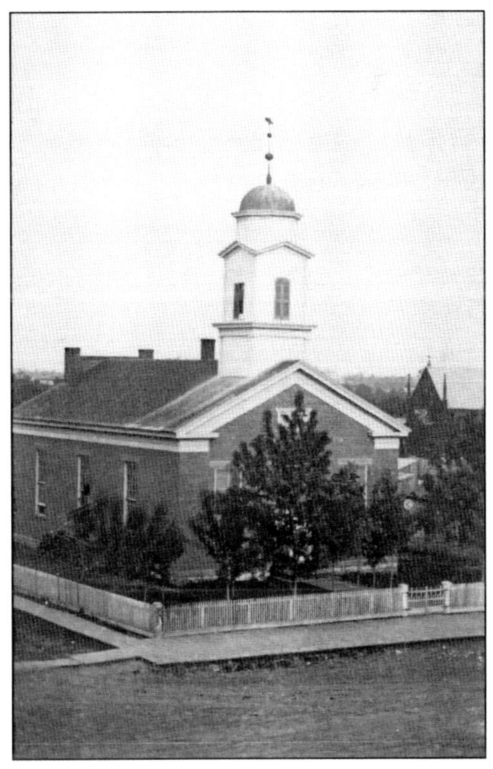

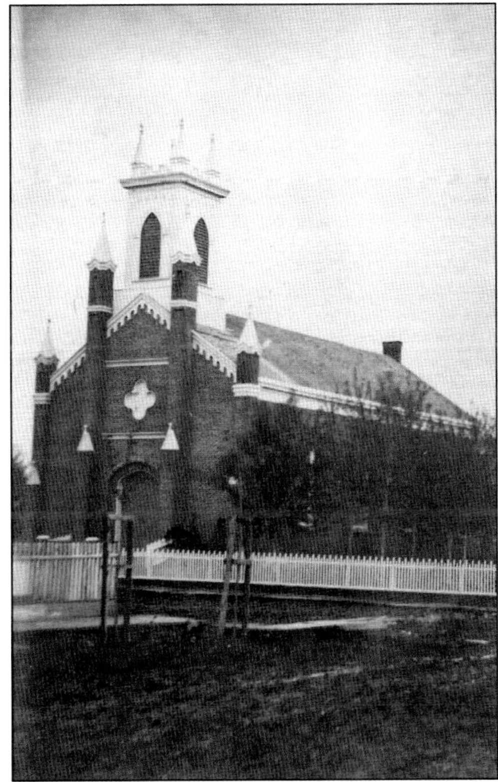

The distinctive steeple of the Universalist church rises skyward in this 1867 photograph. As the name implies, the Universalists held to a progressive doctrine, believing that most or all souls receive salvation. Though the steeple is no longer atop the building, the church structure still stands. Dr. Savage's office is located here today. (MPPL.)

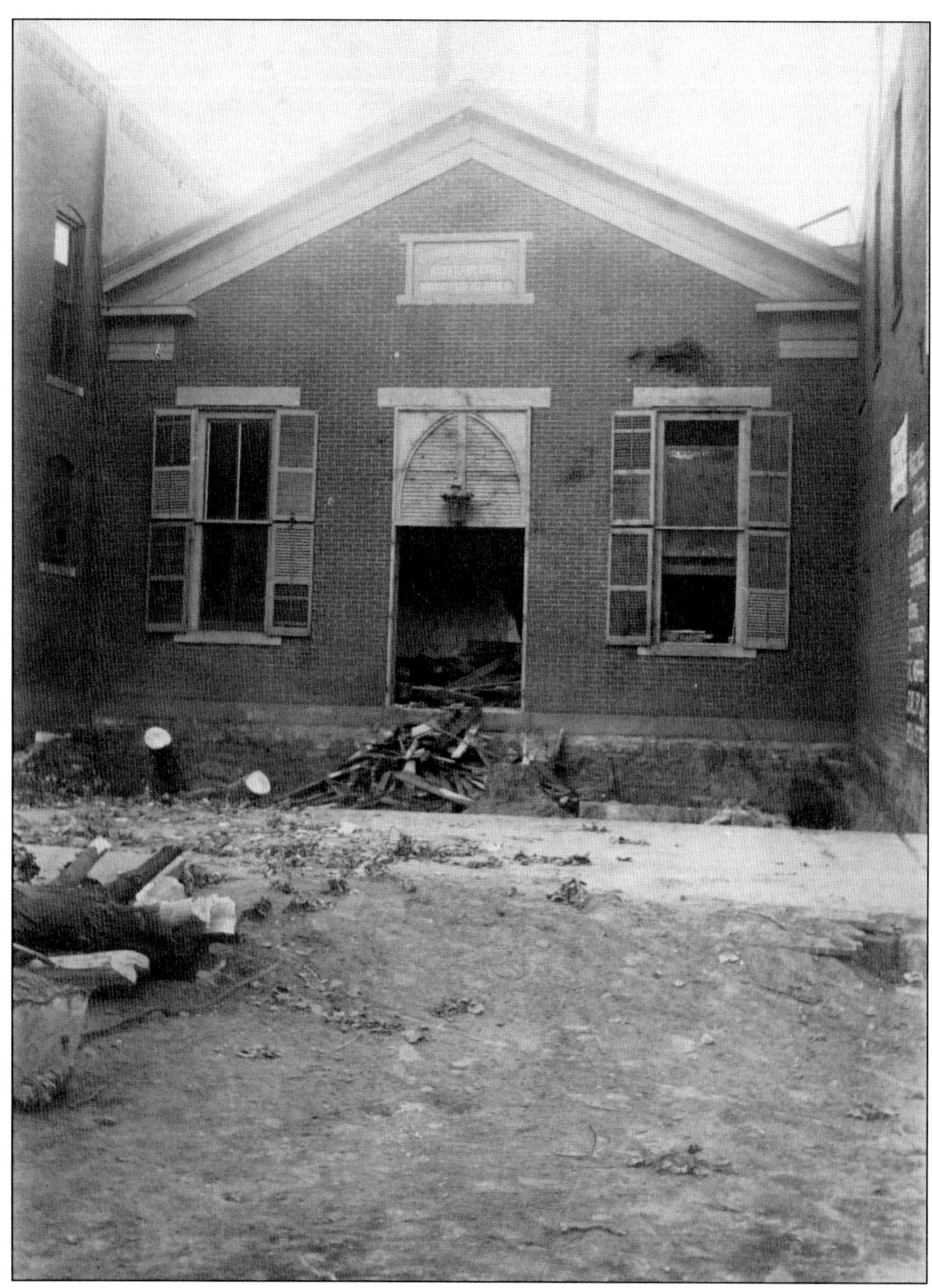

The city's rapid growth caught up with its earlier, pastoral landscape. By the early 20th century, the old Congregational church, once located on the east side of the square, had lost its lawns to development on Main Street. Here, the church is in the process of being gutted, with its trees cut down and its green lawns now occupied by other brick buildings. The signpost above the door reads, "Congregational Church Erected 1848." The Congregational church relocated to the stone building still used on East Washington Street. (MPPL.)

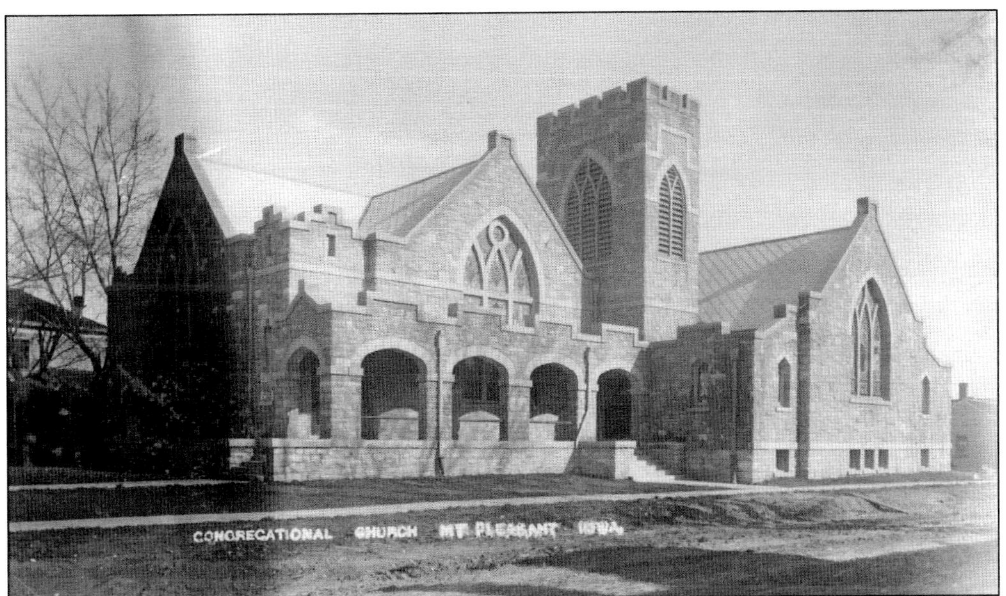

For over a century, the Congregational church has stood as a prominent feature on East Washington Street. This church, along with St. Michael's Episcopal Church, are among the oldest church buildings still functioning as worship spaces in the town today. (Don Young Collection, HCHT.)

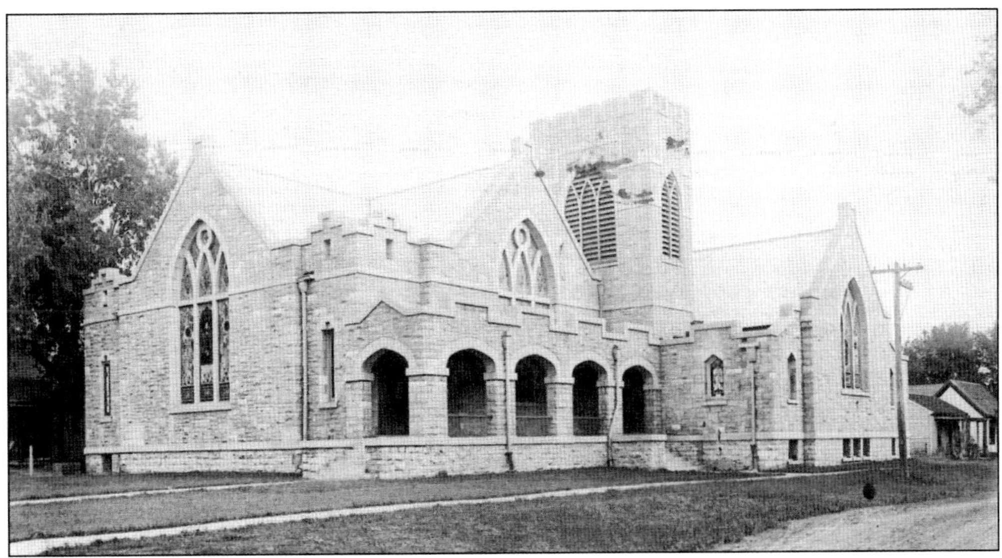

The Congregational-Universalist church on East Washington was a new building in 1908. The church combined two old Mount Pleasant communities: the Congregationalists, originally on the east side of the square, and the Universalists, originally at the intersection of Adams and Madison Streets. The two communities had a long partnership before their official union. On one occasion, in 1878, the Universalists provided space for the Congregationalists when the Congregational church was being mended. Over a century later, this stone church is still a dominant feature on Washington Street. (Don Young Collection, HCHT.)

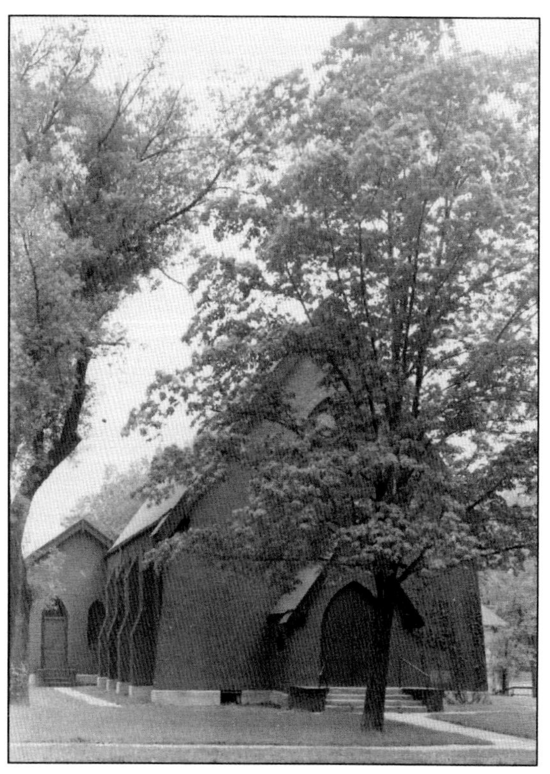

St. Michael's Episcopal Church on East Washington Street was built in 1865, making this church building among the oldest still standing in town. The buttresses and steep angles give the church a charming, Old World appearance, and the grounds have maintained a pleasant green lawn for all these years. The congregation has been active in Mount Pleasant since at least the early 1840s. (Don Young Collection, HCHT.)

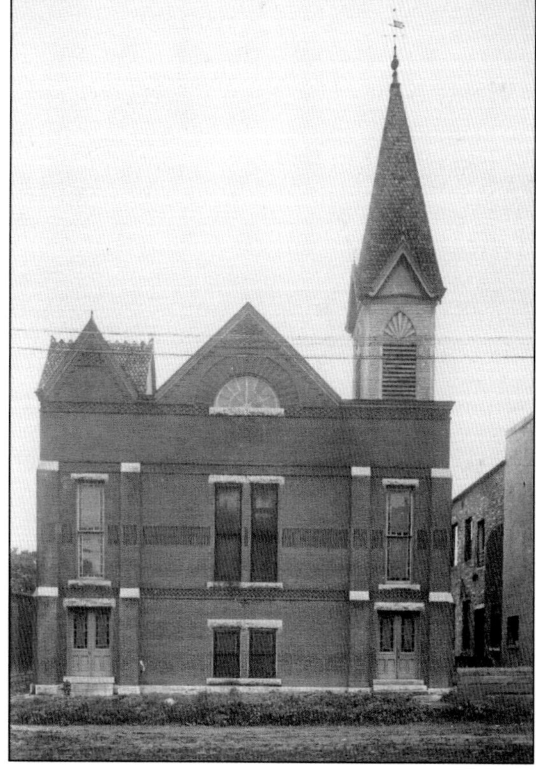

The Christian church, which once stood on West Monroe Street until 1914, was formed early in the town's history. The congregation began in 1845. The church building was constructed around 1855. The membership in 1879 was recorded at 150. Like many congregations, the Christian church would operate with or without an official presiding pastor. (Don Young Collection, HCHT.)

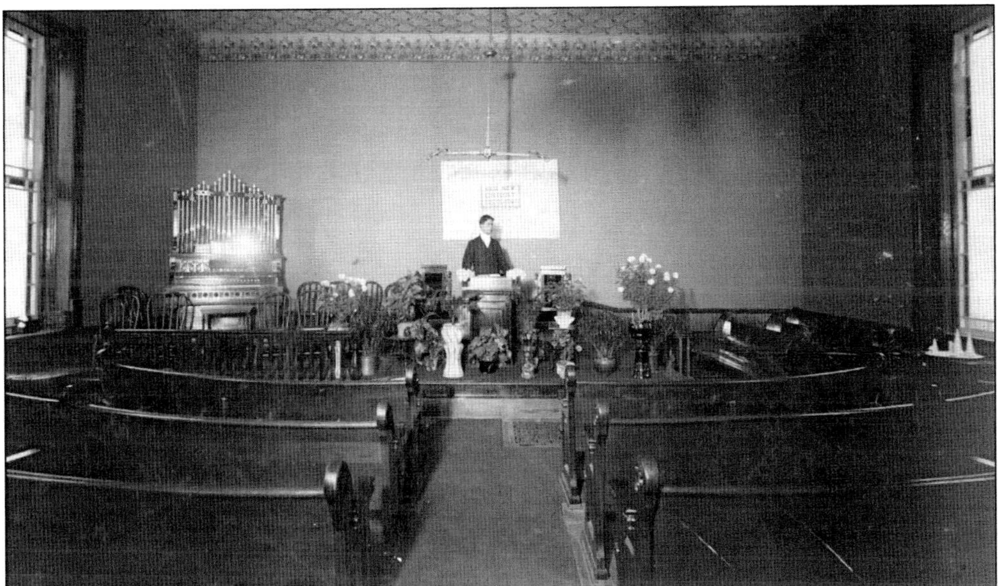

Flowers deck the altar of the Christian church on West Monroe Street. Notice the fine woodworking on the pews and the ceiling decor. The Christian church was consumed by fire on June 17, 1914, along with many other buildings between Jackson and Jefferson Streets. (MPPL.)

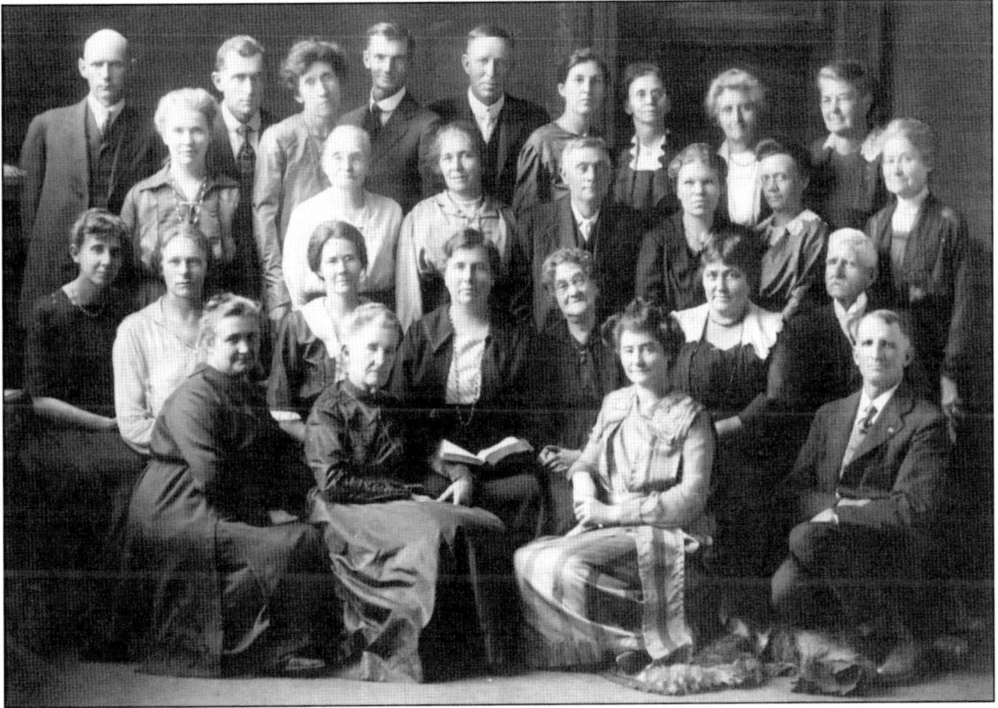

Mrs. Feidler held a coeducational class at the Christian church. Sabbath schools such as these provided thousands of Henry County residents with access to intellectual resources and environments that would have otherwise been inaccessible. In 1867, Henry County Sabbath schools had a combined collection of 6,222 books in their church libraries. Some Mount Pleasant churches appointed official librarians to manage their collections. (MPPL.)

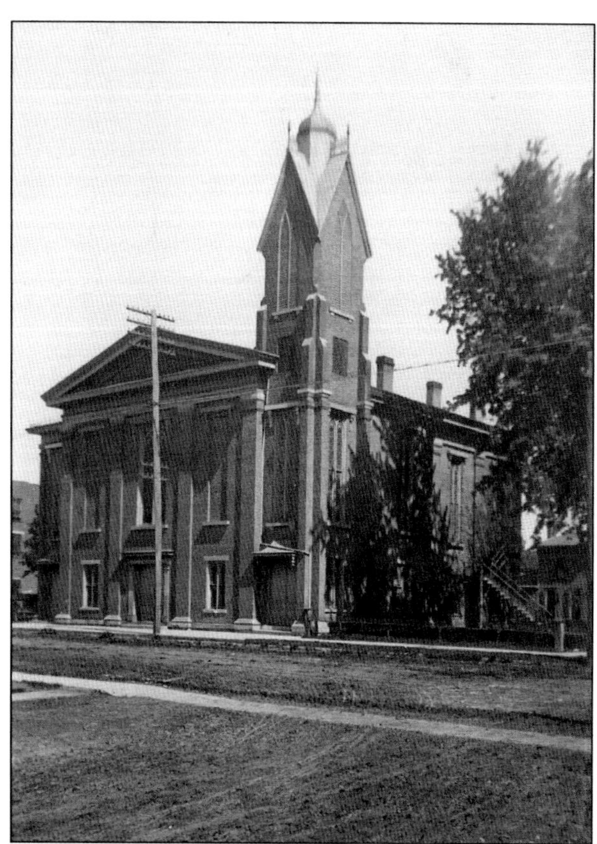

The beautiful Asbury Methodist Church stood proudly at the intersection of East Monroe and North Adams Streets hardly two decades after the first log cabin appeared in Mount Pleasant. At the time of its dedication in 1857, the church was considered among the finest in Iowa. The spire is no longer attached to the present building. This church was one of a number of Methodist churches to serve the community before the Bedford stone church was dedicated in 1912. This building is now Colonial Apartments. (Don Young Collection, HCHT.)

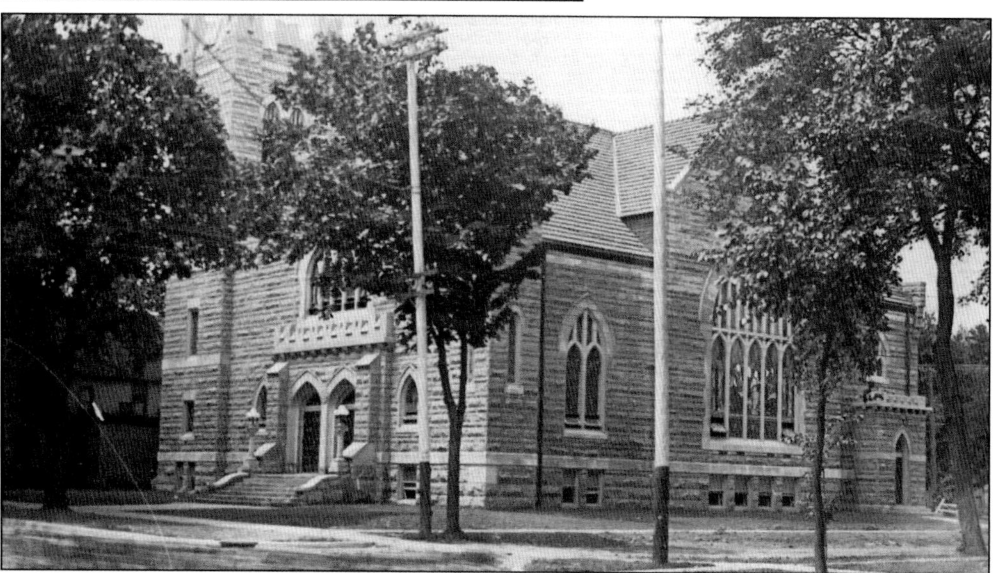

The Bedford stone Methodist church stood prominently on North Main Street. This photograph was taken in the church's first year, 1912. Important to the life of the Bedford stone church was Mr. Cromer's orchestra. This orchestra came to include some 25 instruments, the largest orchestra in the area. The orchestra inspired young people to attend and participate in Sunday school. (Don Young Collection, HCHT.)

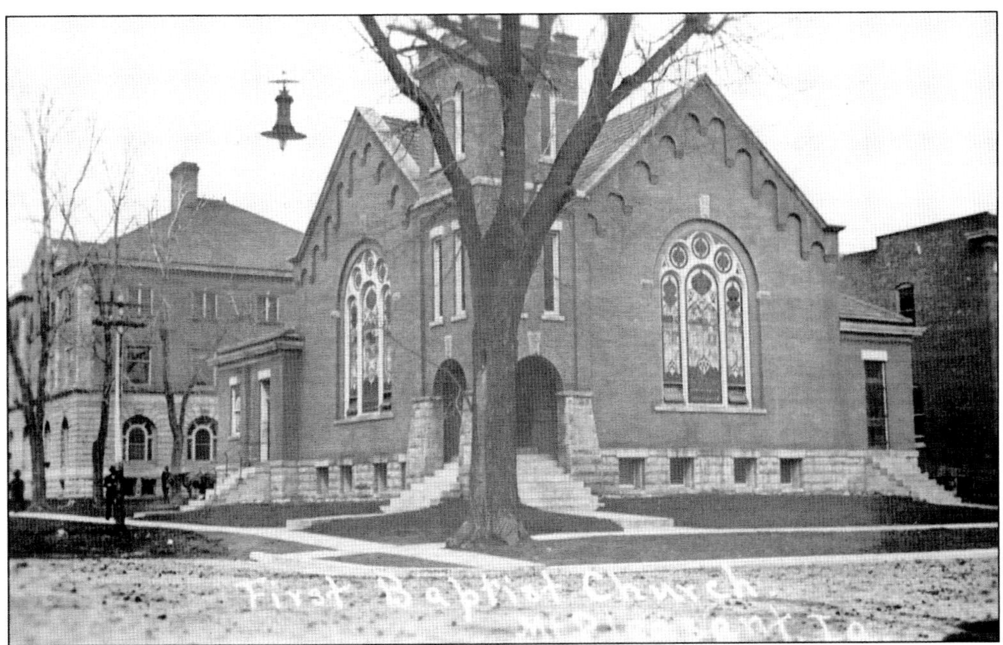

Magnificent stained-glass windows decked the old Baptist church at the intersection of Main and Madison Streets. This congregation had a dramatic history, enduring both the 1882 cyclone and a disastrous fire in 1905. Yet the Baptists picked up and rebuilt each time, facing every trial with determination. The YMCA building stands in the background to the left, at the current location of the post office. (Don Young Collection, HCHT.)

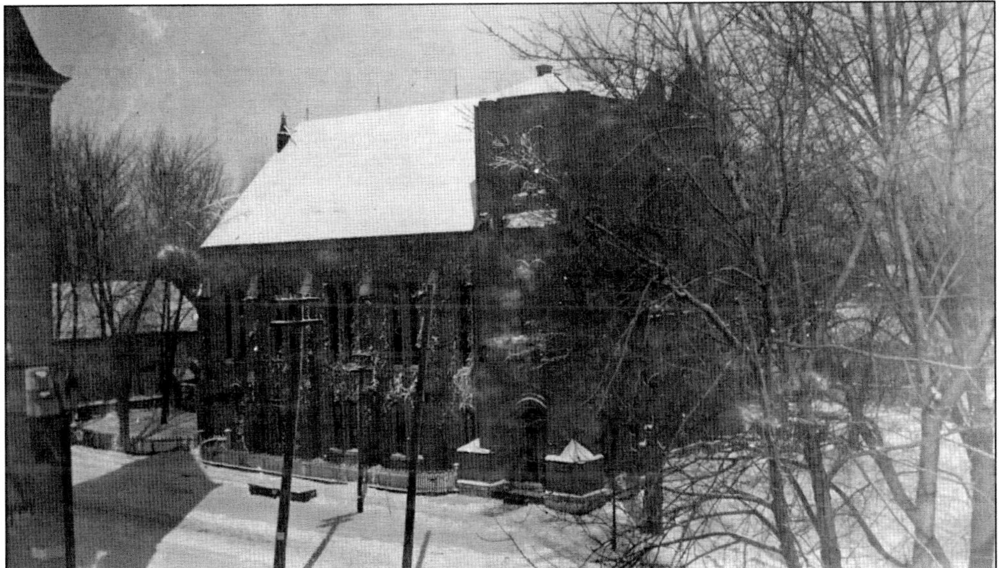

Snow covers the roof of the old Baptist church that once stood at the intersection of North Main and Madison Streets. The edge of the old Presbyterian church is at far left. The Baptist church formed early in Mount Pleasant's history, with the congregation organizing in 1843. This church at the intersection of Madison and Monroe Streets was built piecemeal. The foundation was set in 1867, and walls were built in 1868. In 1875, beautiful stained-glass windows replaced plank boards. The building was dedicated in 1878. (MPPL.)

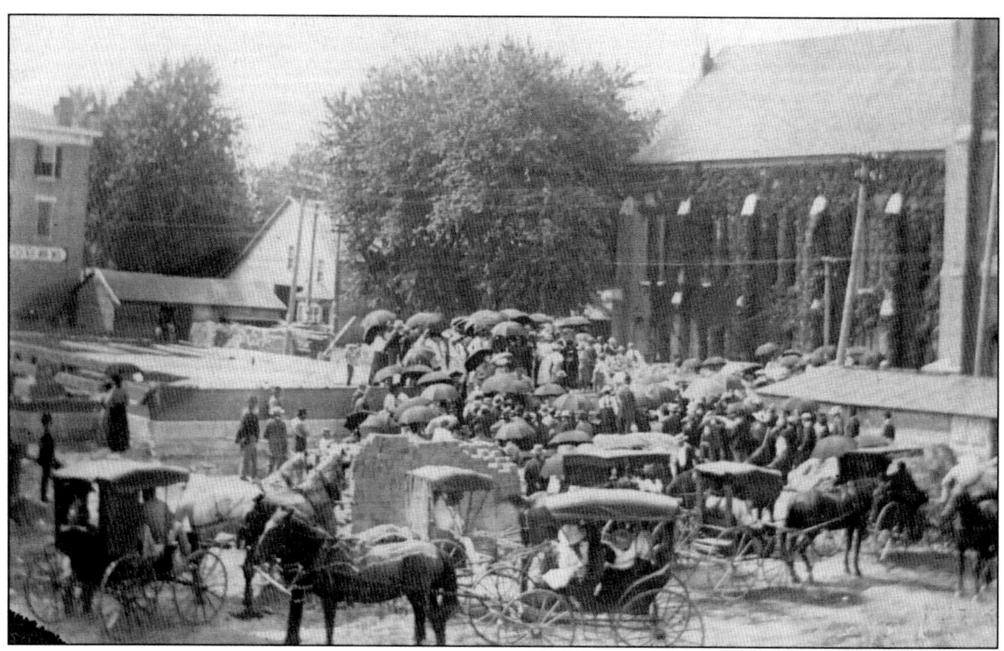

On July 15, 1897, people amassed to view the cornerstone laying for the Presbyterian church that once stood at the intersection of North Main and Madison Streets. The church at right was the old Baptist church. The Harlan House is at far left. Rev. Cedric Peterson, who preached at the Baptist church in the 1930s, served as Pres. Calvin Coolidge's pastor at Coolidge's Wisconsin retreat. (MPPL.)

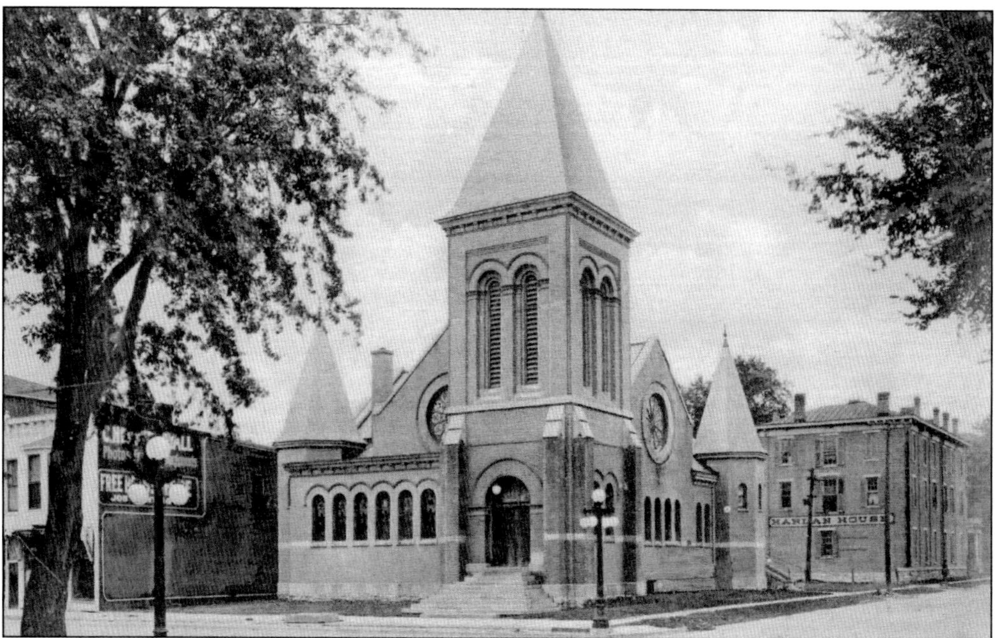

The old Presbyterian church, dedicated in 1898, stood at the intersection of North Main and Monroe Streets. The Harlan House is behind the church. During the Great Depression, Rev. E.L. Jeamby of Red Oak, Iowa, provided the congregation with a powerful voice and boundless energy. During his 12-year tenure, 200 new members joined the flock. (Don Young Collection, HCHT.)

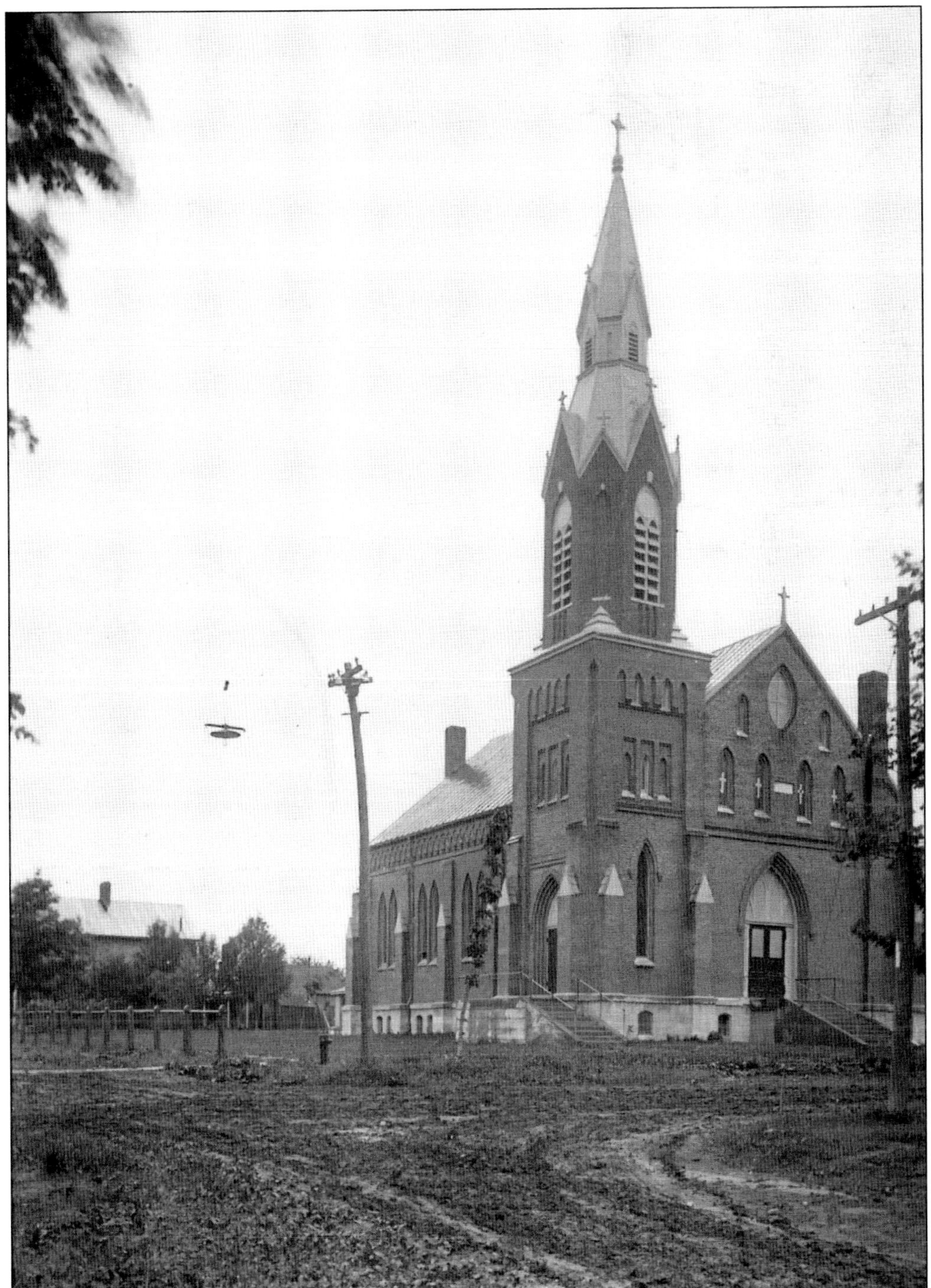

St. Alphonsus Church was over a half century old when this photograph was taken around 1905. Fr. J.J. Bassler was nearing the end of his fruitful 24-year tenure at this time. Under Father Bassler, St. Alphonsus began a church school and installed stained-glass windows. The Irish Catholic community adored their German priest. Notice the pre-automobile "parking lot" to the left of the church, with posts for hitching horses. (Don Young Collection, HCHT.)

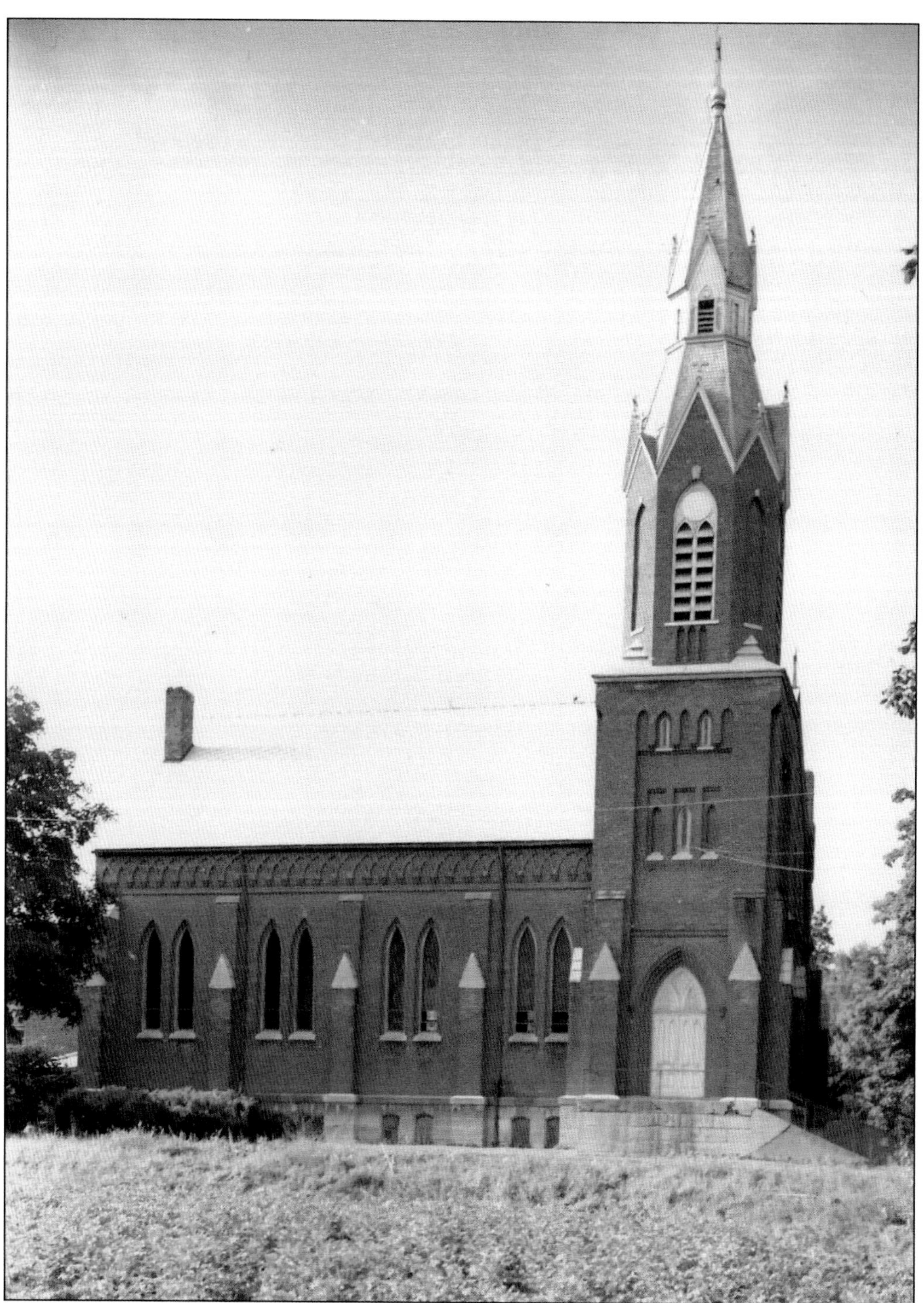

Fr. Myles Turner Gaffney served Saint Alphonsus Church for over two decades beginning in 1920. Father Gaffney, a friendly and compassionate priest, carried the parish through the difficult years of national economic depression, a struggle that began on the farm in the early 1920s. He also took up the responsibility of ministering to the asylum patients, often responding to calls in the late-night hours. (Don Young Collection, HCHT.)

Eight

Asylum

Mount Pleasant had developed into a significant community in Iowa by the time of the Civil War. Following Governor Grimes's impassioned plea for the care of Iowa's mentally ill persons, the state chose Mount Pleasant as the location for the mental health asylum. The asylum opened in 1861. In the 19th century, the act of assisting the mentally ill was perceived by many as a critical social mission, a civilized and responsible treatment for those suffering from mental illness. By the 1860s, Iowa's mentally ill were no longer limited to lives shut indoors or wandering homeless. The Mount Pleasant asylum provided a public facility to take in such persons.

The asylum held its staff to the highest principles, forbidding foul language, demeaning comments, and even tobacco use. The asylum doctors, nurses, attendants, and visiting clergy did what they could to help the mentally ill with the materials and techniques available at the time. Thousands of patients were received into the facility, and many were improved.

The *Portrait and Biographical Album of Henry County* from 1888 gave voice to the quality of service at the asylum, noting that Dr. Gilman's care had improved 131 patients in two years. The *Album* recorded:

> These results are gratifying to Dr. Gilman, and to all humanitarians, who have at heart the amelioration of the condition of those unfortunate human beings suffering from that worst of all disorders—brain disease and mental aberration. To the relief and cure of this class of diseases Dr. Gilman has dedicated his life, and his success in his chosen vocation is the legitimate result of his untiring zeal, constant study of the best modes of treatment, and personal care in insuring that the measures devised for the relief of those under his charge shall be carried out as directed.

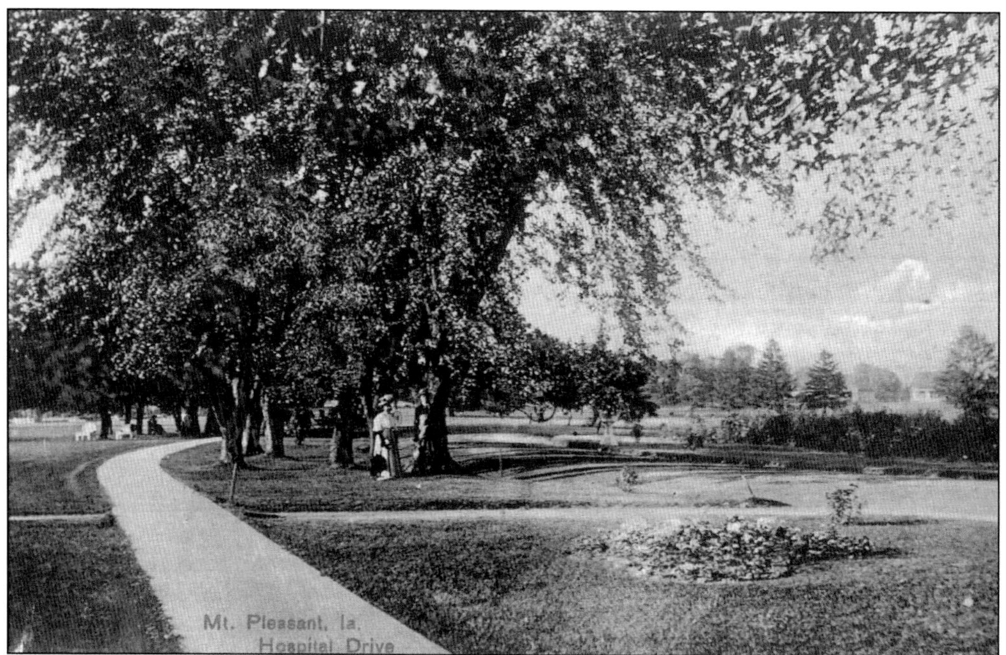

In the 19th century, a primary treatment method at the asylum hinged on the creation of a pleasing atmosphere. In 1901, Dr. A.W. McClure recalled that in 1875, "Mrs. Elliot, a member of the Board of Trustees, a very intelligent and practical woman, together with other philanthropic ladies of the community interested in the comfort of the many feeble and distressed inmates of the wards for women, suggested and urged the importance of having some other outside enclosure provided with shade and seats where this class could be out doors much of the time in pleasant weather and thus be relieved of the monotony of indoor life." (Don Young Collection, HCHT).

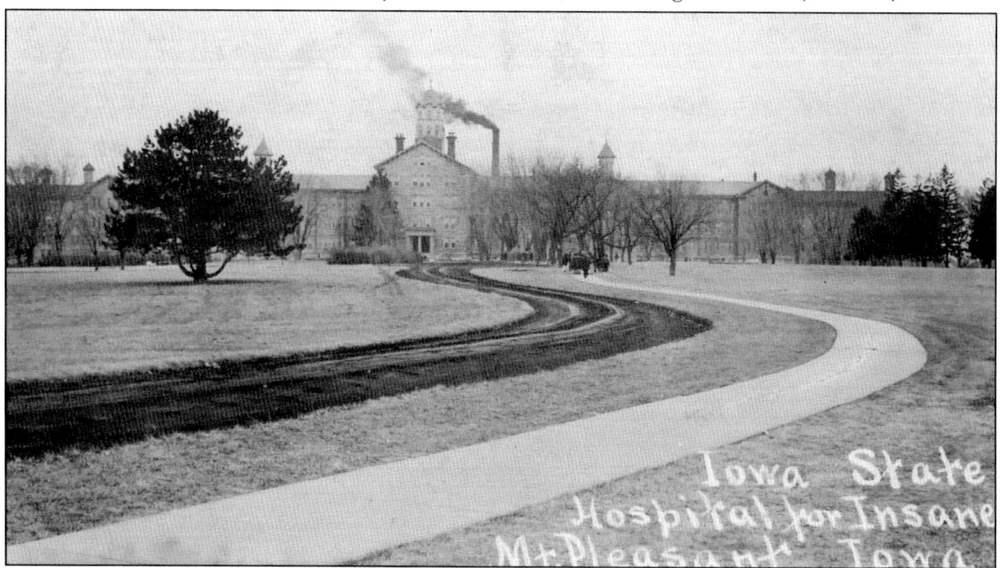

All efforts were made to create a healthy, positive environment for asylum patients. The facility's 1860 bylaws required that staff treat patients "with respect and civility," and necessitated that staff communicate with patients "in a mild and gentle tone of voice avoiding all violence and rudeness or undue familiarity, nicknames, or disrespectful terms." (Don Young Collection, HCHT.)

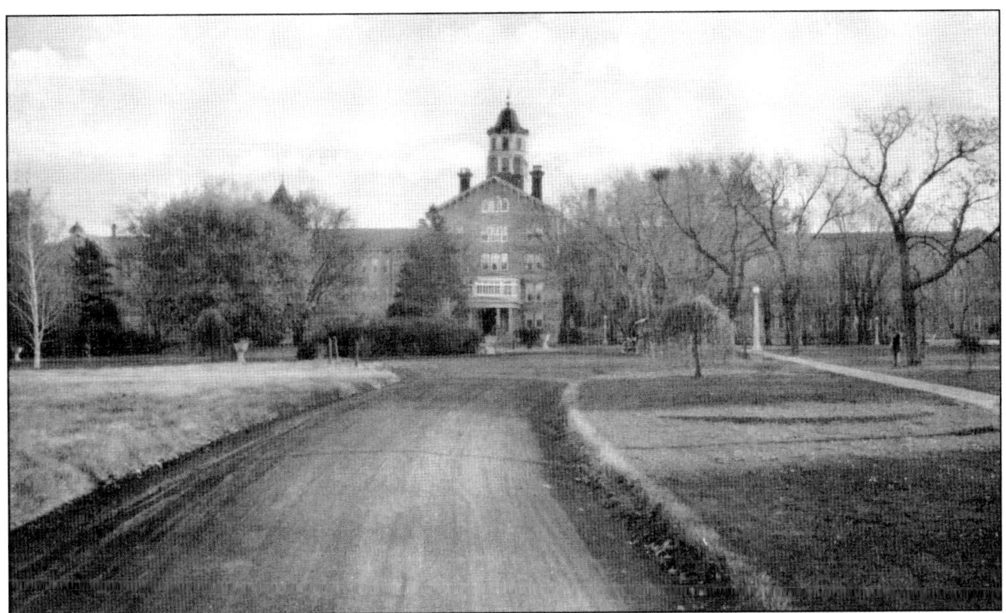

The 1879 *History of Henry County* provided detailed statistics for the asylum at a time when the facility had been less than 20 years in service. By 1879, a total of 3,584 patients had been admitted. Of these, 1,141 were recovered, 505 had improved, 589 had shown no improvement, and 740 had died. One patient was deemed "not insane." (Don Young Collection, HCHT.)

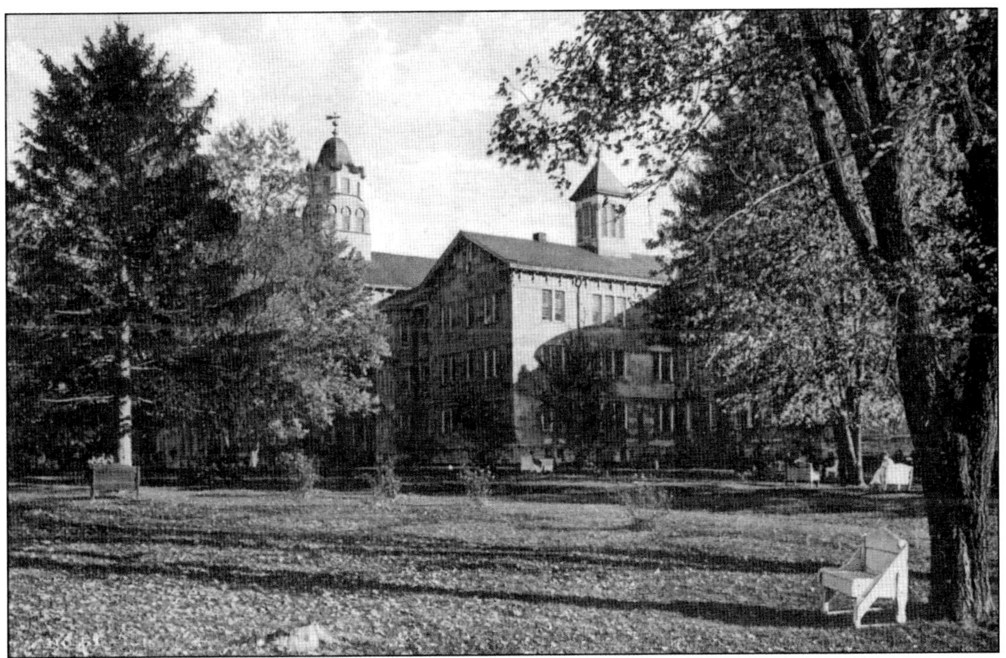

Facilities were composed of a cut-stone main building with adjoining wings in the highly geometric Elizabethan style. Cupolas were seated upon the roofs. Notice the benches in the yard, an important feature of treatment, as the grounds provided a healthy, outdoor environment to heal ailing minds. (Don Young Collection, HCHT.)

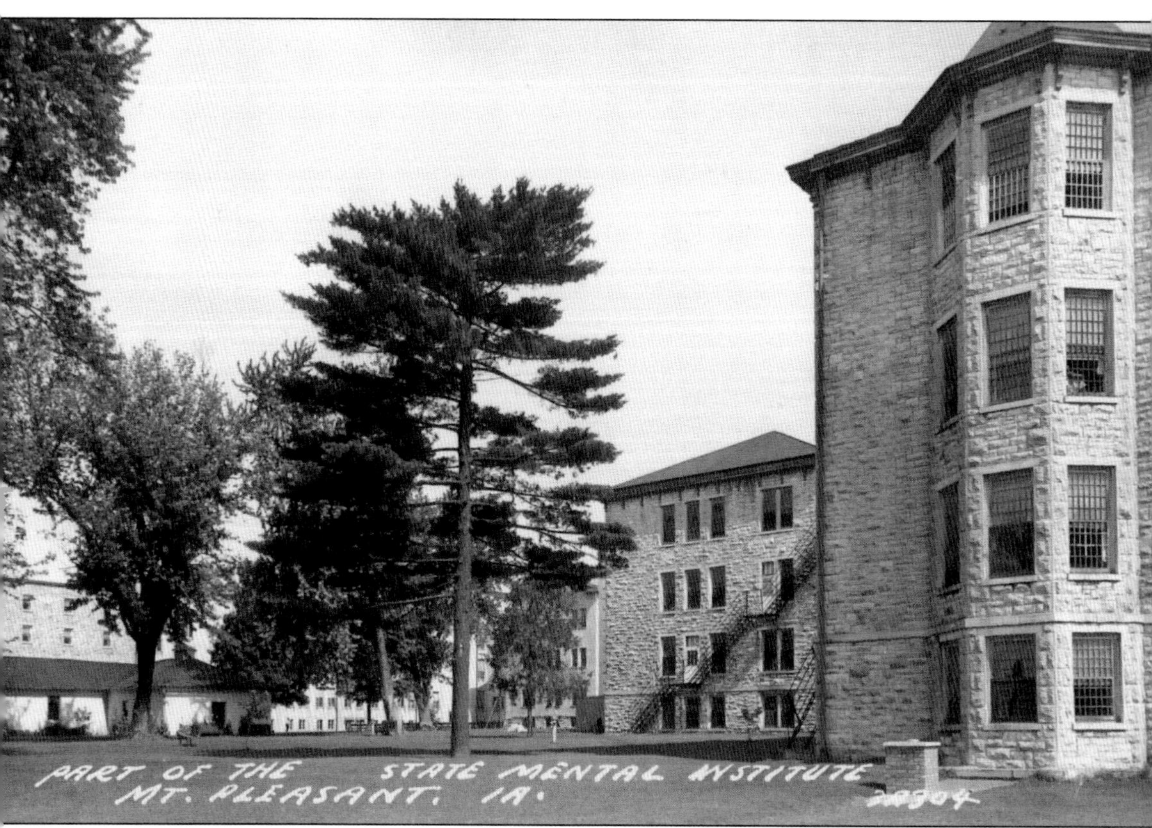

The asylum's administration continually appealed to the state for additional funding in order to accommodate the needs of periodic overcrowding. In 1882, a total of 98 patients died from ailments rooted in overcrowding. In that year, over 100 men and women slept on the floors in simple straw beds as the facility struggled to handle the high demand for more patients; however, new wings and wards were added to absorb the rising asylum population. (Don Young Collection, HCHT.)

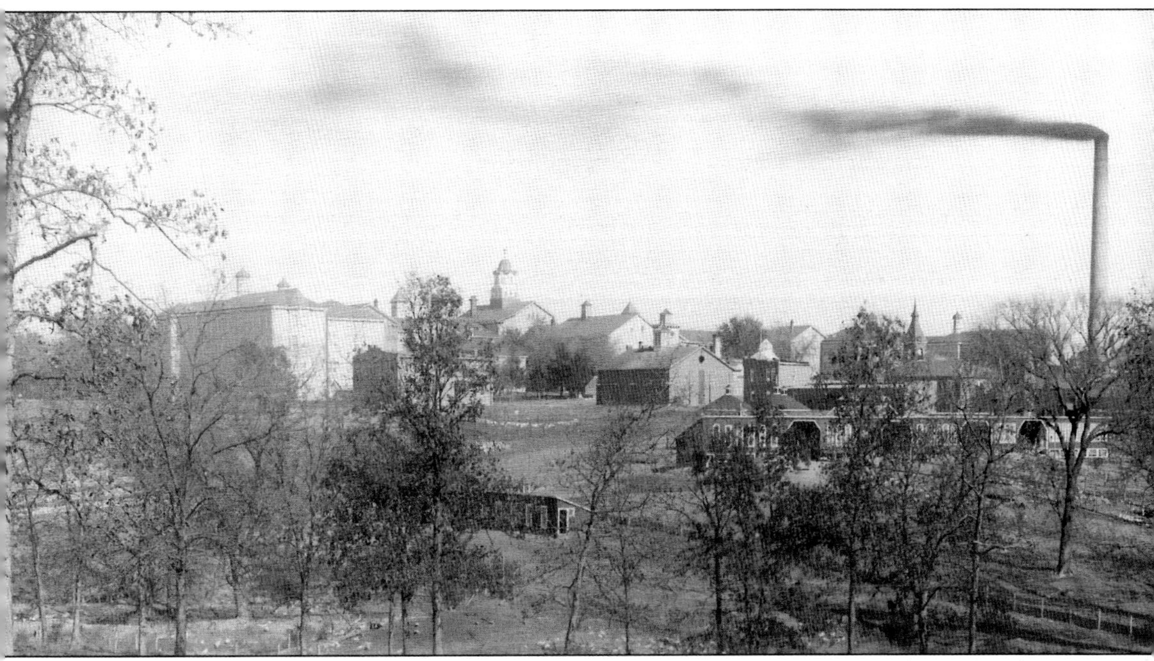

After opening in early 1861, the asylum received hundreds of patients previously confined to jails and poorhouses. The facility was filled to capacity within a few years. Through the 19th century, additional wings were added to the original structure in order to accommodate the rising population. In 1888, the asylum housed 700 patients. (Don Young Collection, HCHT.)

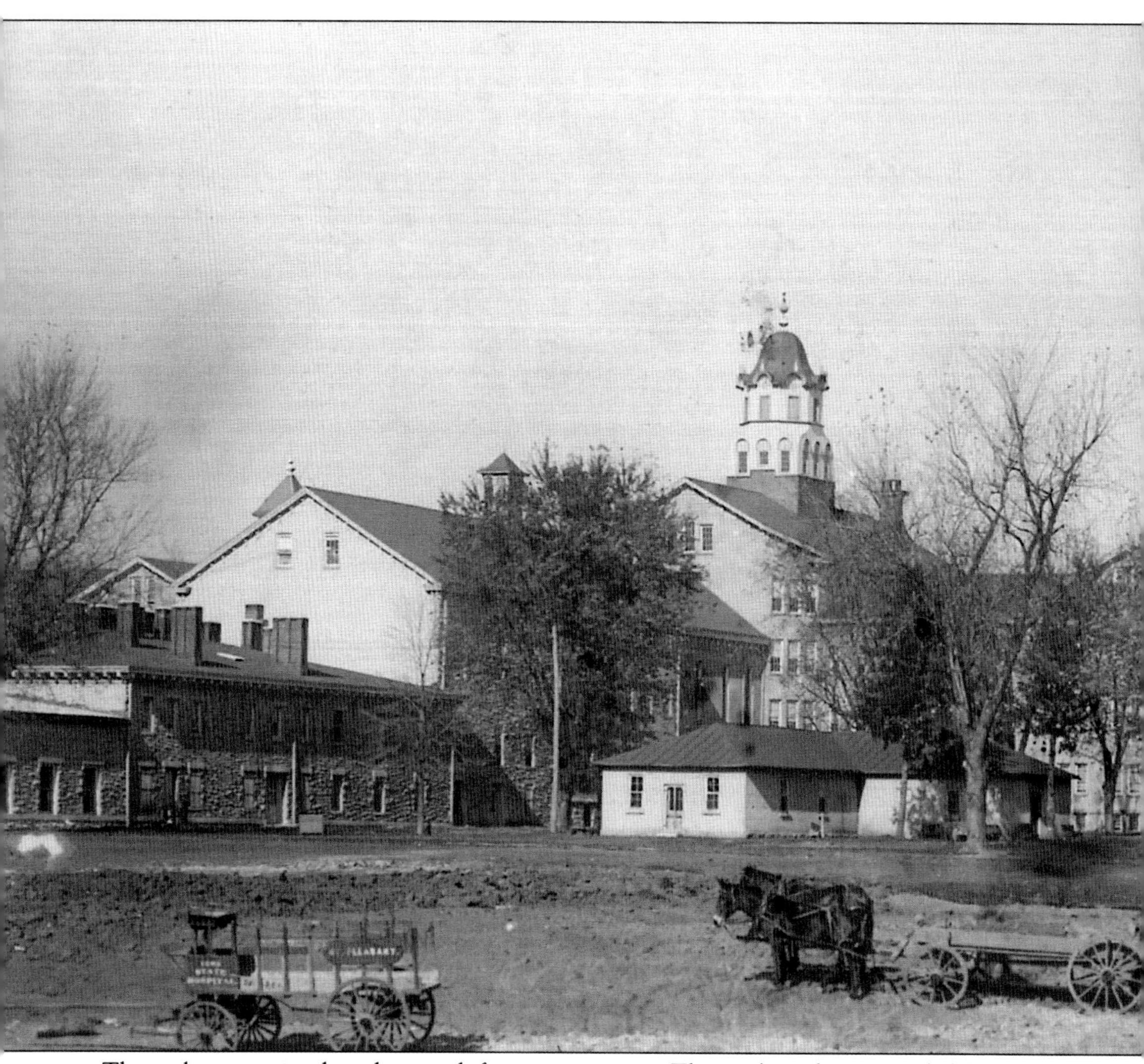

The asylum permitted outdoor work for many patients. The working farm provided food for the facility. In 1901, Dr. A.W. McClure recalled that the asylum land was "sufficiently diversified to make it attractive, and being partly rich prairie land and partly broken woodland, it affords

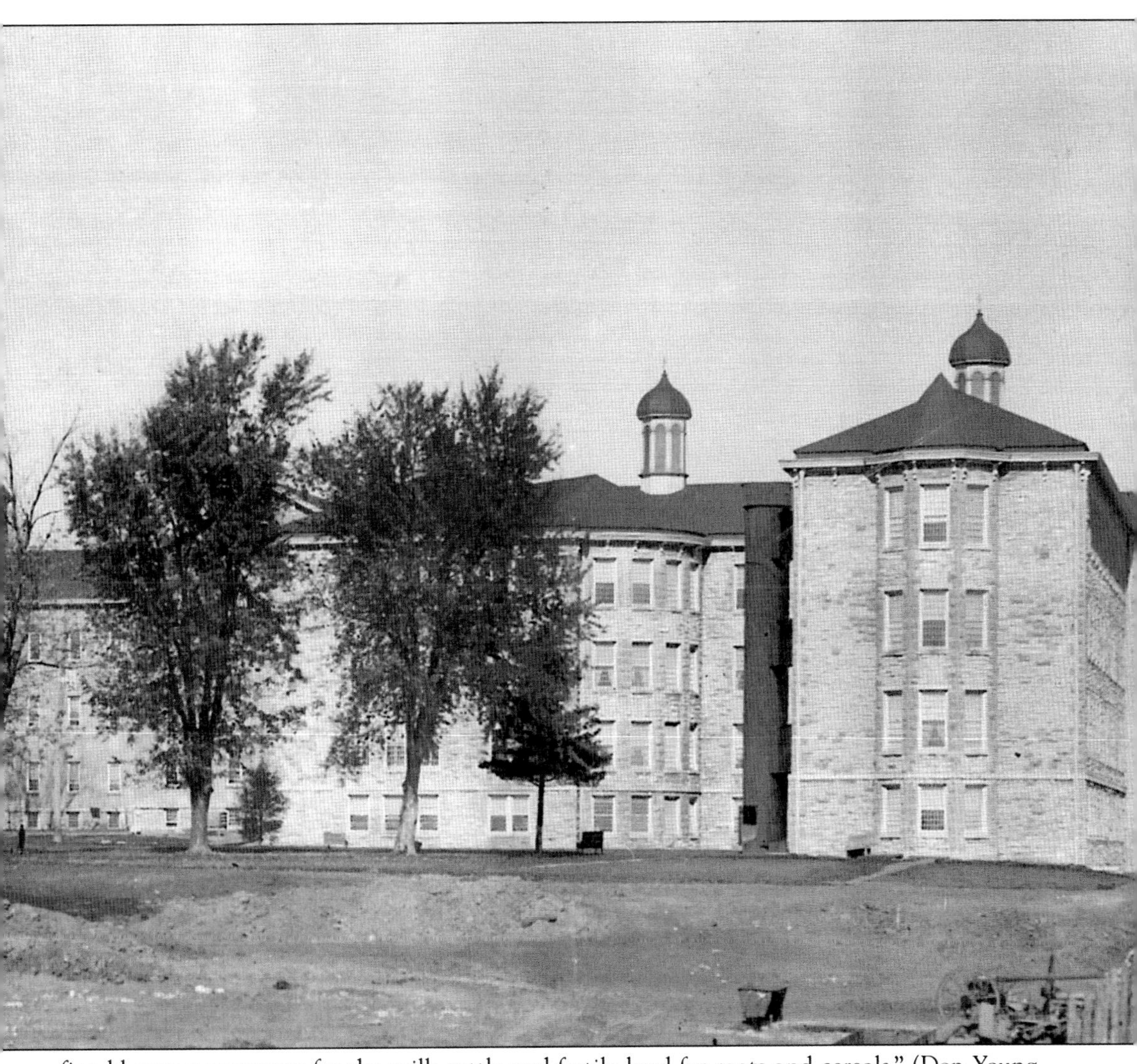

fine bluegrass pasturage for the milk cattle and fertile land for roots and cereals." (Don Young Collection, HCHT.)

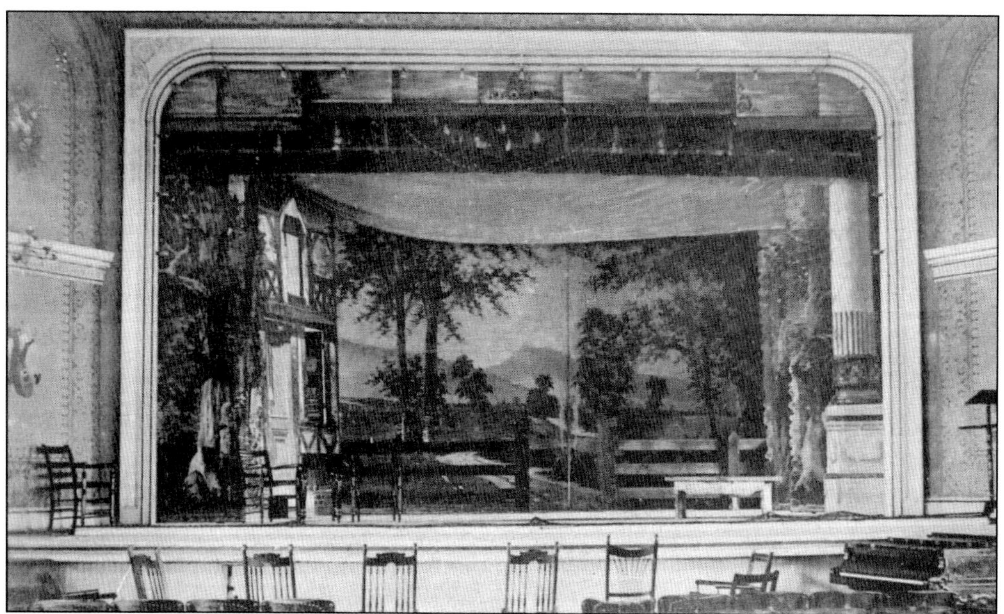

Amusement Hall was built in 1891. This colorful room improved the quality of life for patients. Classical frescoes lined the walls. The hall accommodated plays, dances, and musical concerts. Notice the movable background settings on stage, as well as the piano at lower right. (Don Young Collection, HCHT.)

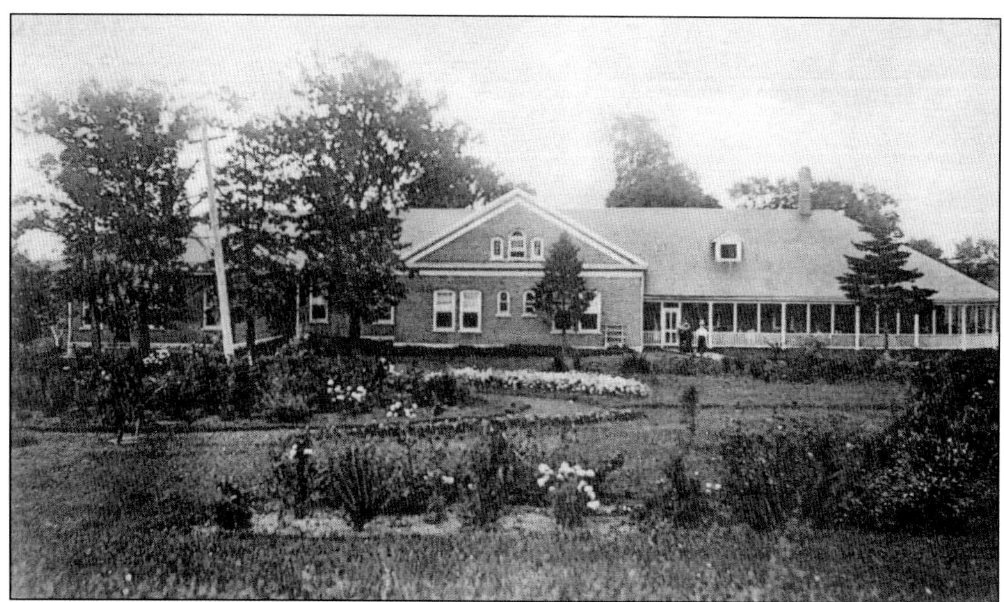

The asylum provided separate infirmaries for men (pictured) and women. The institution's 1860 bylaws had many health regulations that were far ahead of the general population. For instance, chewing tobacco and smoking were strictly forbidden, even for state officers and workers. The 1860 code noted that "the use of tobacco, from its universally injurious effects upon the physical and mental faculties" was strictly prohibited for patients. It would therefore be "inconsistent and unjust that the officers or attendants should use it." (Don Young Collection, HCHT.)

Nine

Trials

Mount Pleasant has endured a number of challenges, ranging from harrowing storms to large fires. The most dramatic trial in its history was likely the Civil War. The conflict began just three decades after the first cabins appeared in Mount Pleasant, yet the community was thrust into the struggle, its sons serving in its bloody battles. The town was also a location of a military camp during the war. The largest natural calamity to strike Mount Pleasant was possibly the twister of June 1882, which tore off roofs and steeples all over town and left broken trees in the streets. The most common threat has been fire. In the days before electricity, there was the often incendiary combination of firelight and wooden buildings. Whole sections of town could become inflamed. Fire, not age, is the reason why few church buildings remain from the 19th century. Even as late as the summer of 1914, Mount Pleasant suffered two large fires that scorched numerous buildings, decimating whole blocks. Yet the community pulled together and progressed forward.

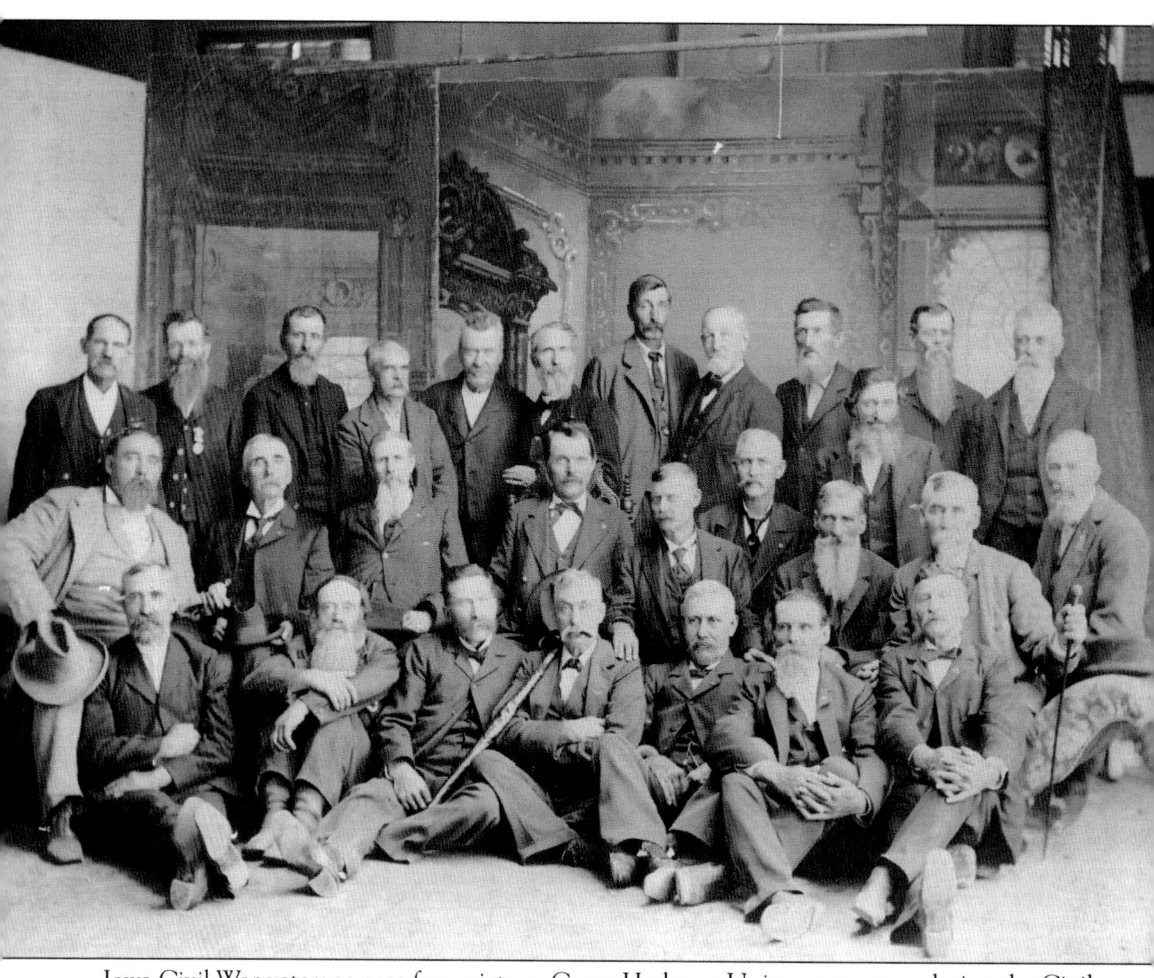

Iowa Civil War veterans pose for a picture. Camp Harlan, a Union army camp during the Civil War, once stood near the present Mount Pleasant Golf and Country Club. At Camp Harlan, the 4th Iowa Cavalry mustered under Col. Asbury B. Porter, an expert horseman and Mount Pleasant resident. The 4th Iowa Cavalry consisted largely of men from Mount Pleasant and Henry County. (MPPL.)

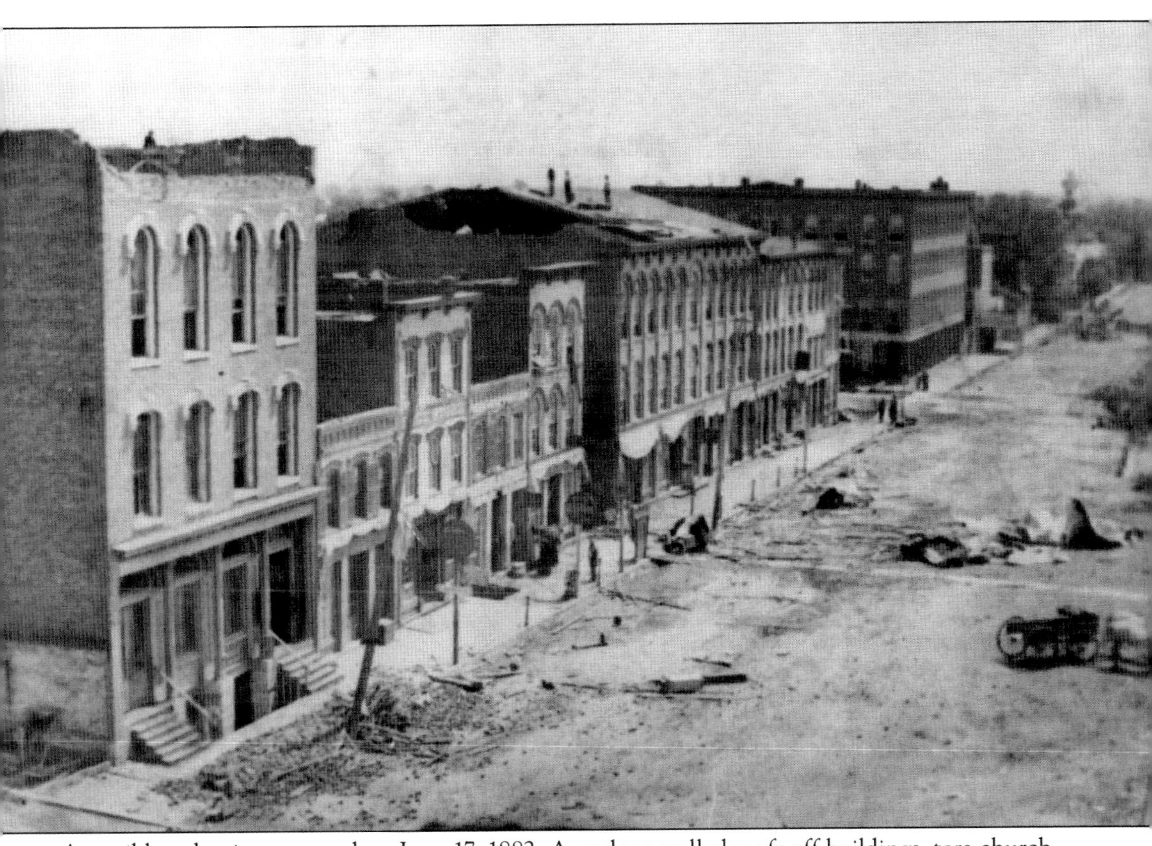

A terrible calamity occurred on June 17, 1882. A cyclone pulled roofs off buildings, tore church spires to the ground, and tossed trees like kindling. This view shows the damage on Monroe Street on the north square. The June 22, 1882, *Free Press* detailed the aftermath of the "Terrible Tornado," reporting, "Never before in the history of Mt. Pleasant has there been such a general need of repairing and every body that can use the trowel, saw, or hammer or do anything to assist in replacing roofs or chimneys or skylights is busy from early dawn till dark." (MPPL.)

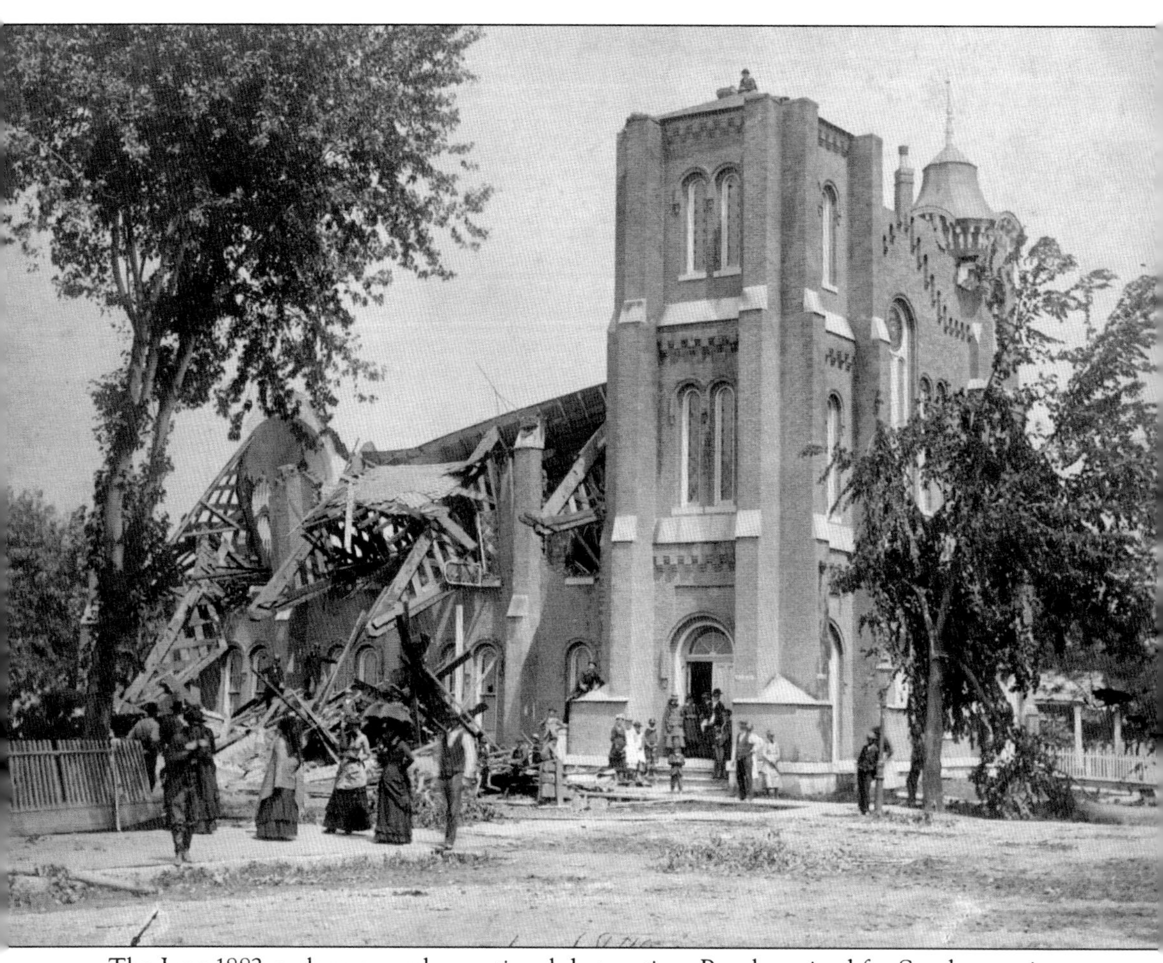

The June 1882 cyclone caused sensational destruction. People arrived for Sunday services to discover their churches badly damaged. Like other churches in town, the Baptist church, once located at the intersection of Main and Madison Streets, was severely damaged. (MPPL.)

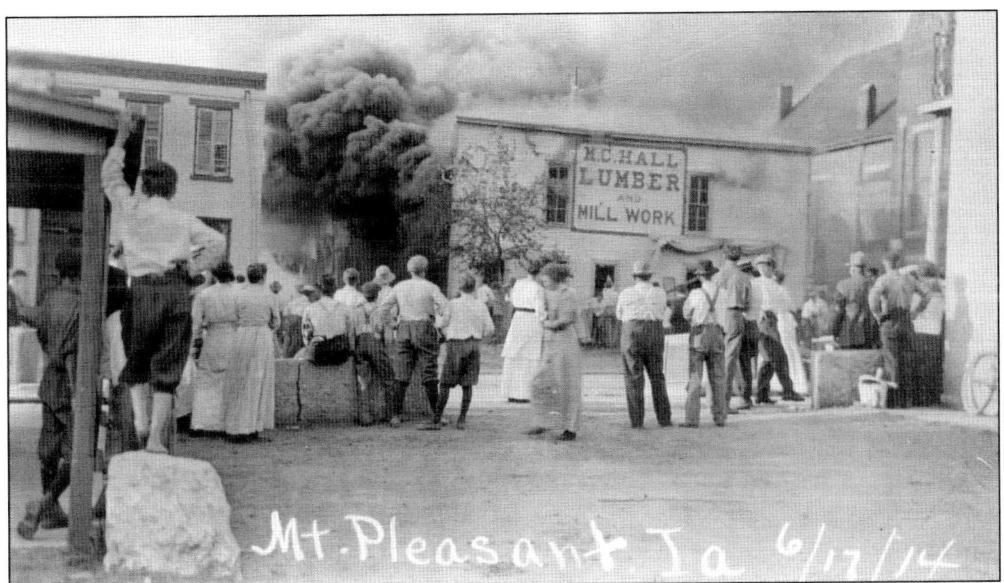

Mount Pleasant's calamitous summer of 1914 began with the June 17 blaze, the fire raging on the north side of West Monroe Street near the present location of the *Mount Pleasant News* office. M.C. Hall Lumber burned (above), and the Christian church (right) also caught fire. The *Mount Pleasant Daily News* estimated that fire damages accumulated to $120,000. (Both, MPPL.)

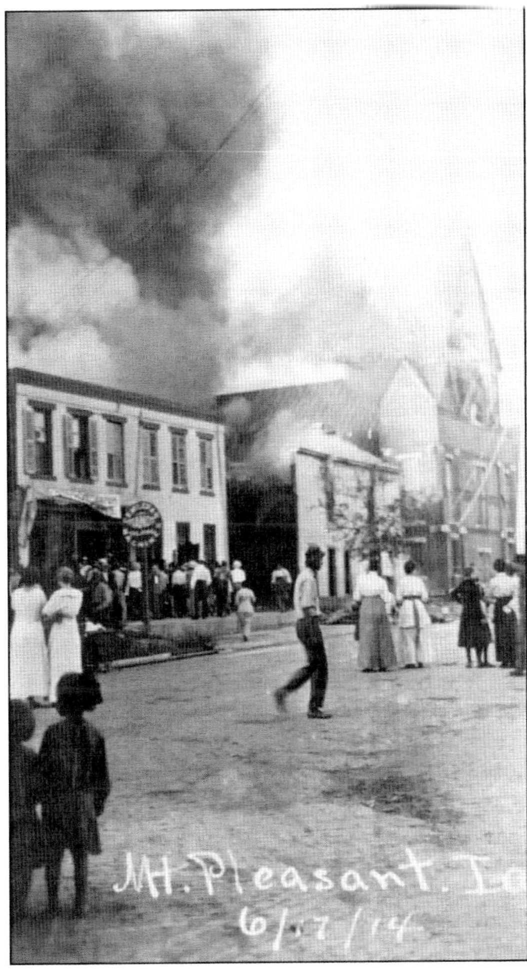

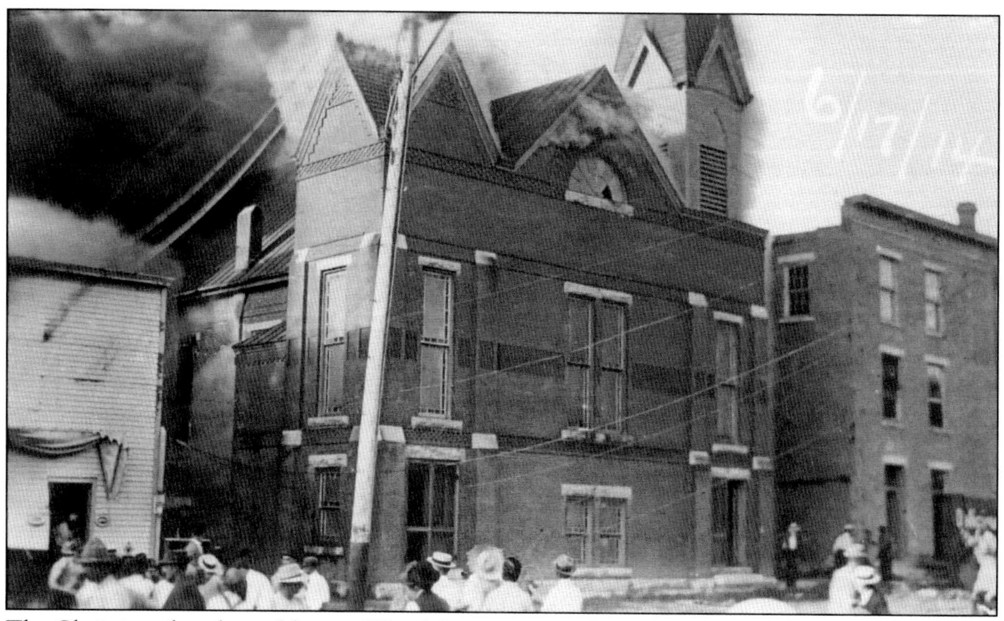

The Christian church smolders on West Monroe Street during the June 1914 fire, a tragic end to a congregation with a long past in Mount Pleasant. The church was formed in Mount Pleasant in 1845, and this building was constructed around 1855. Hundreds of persons over multiple generations had worshipped in this building. (MPPL.)

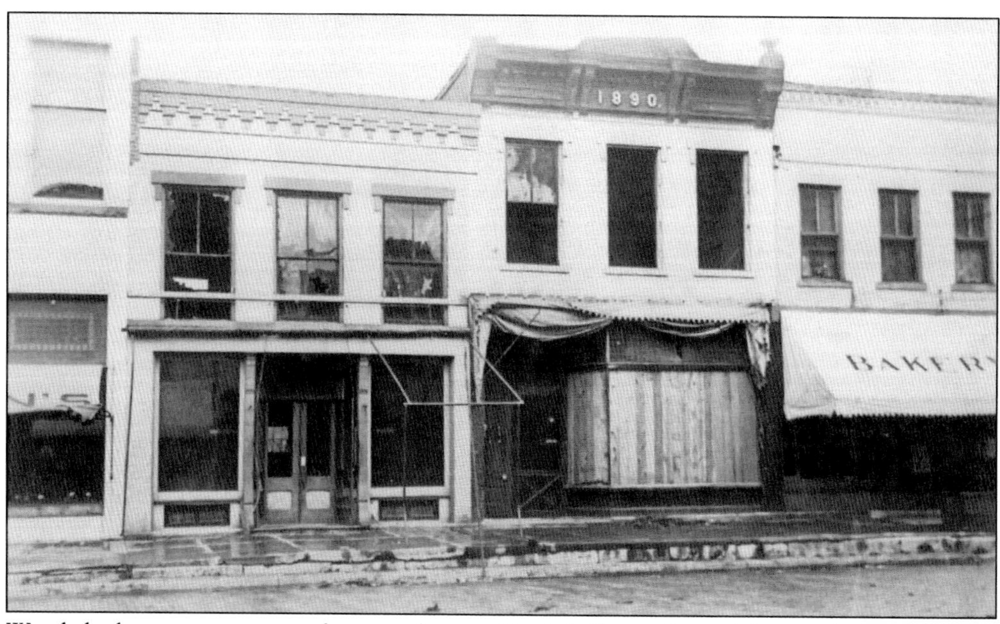

Wood planks were set into storefront windows on North Jefferson Street following the June 17, 1914, fire. The inferno had spread along West Monroe Street, burning many lots between North Jefferson and Jackson Streets. The June 18, 1914, *Mount Pleasant Daily News* reported, "No one seriously injured, water supply ample, pressure good and firemen magnificent in action." (MPPL.)

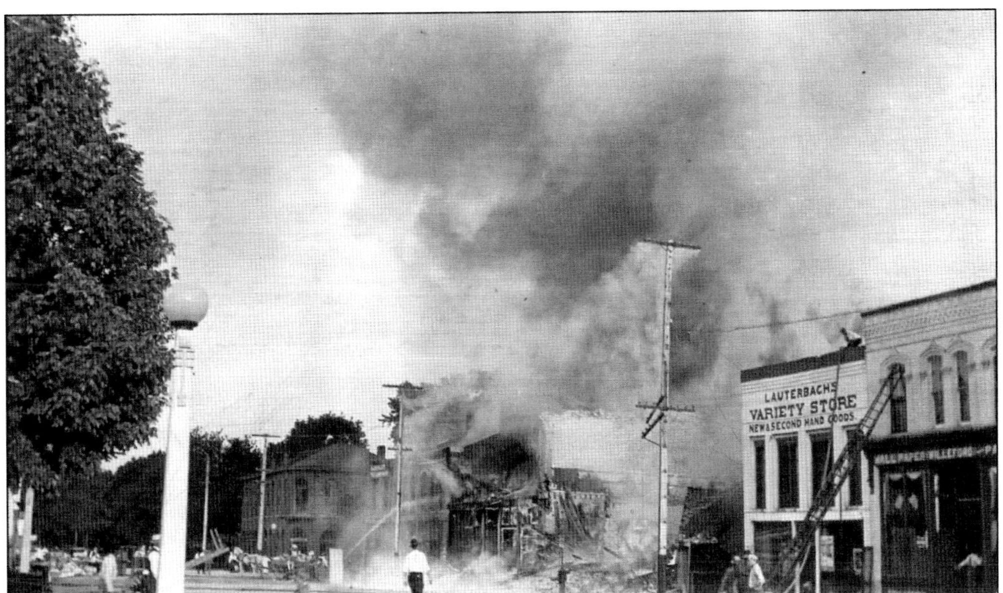

Mount Pleasant suffered another major fire in the summer of 1914, this one occurring on the south side of the square on August 14. The *Mount Pleasant Daily News* reported, "It was just about five o'clock last evening when a terrific explosion occurred in the rear of Smith's Dress Club on the South Side of the square." The *Daily News* office itself was a casualty of the blaze, the paper reporting that the "fine machinery and printing equipment, paper stock and work in process of manufacture was all destroyed." (Don Young Collection, HCHT.)

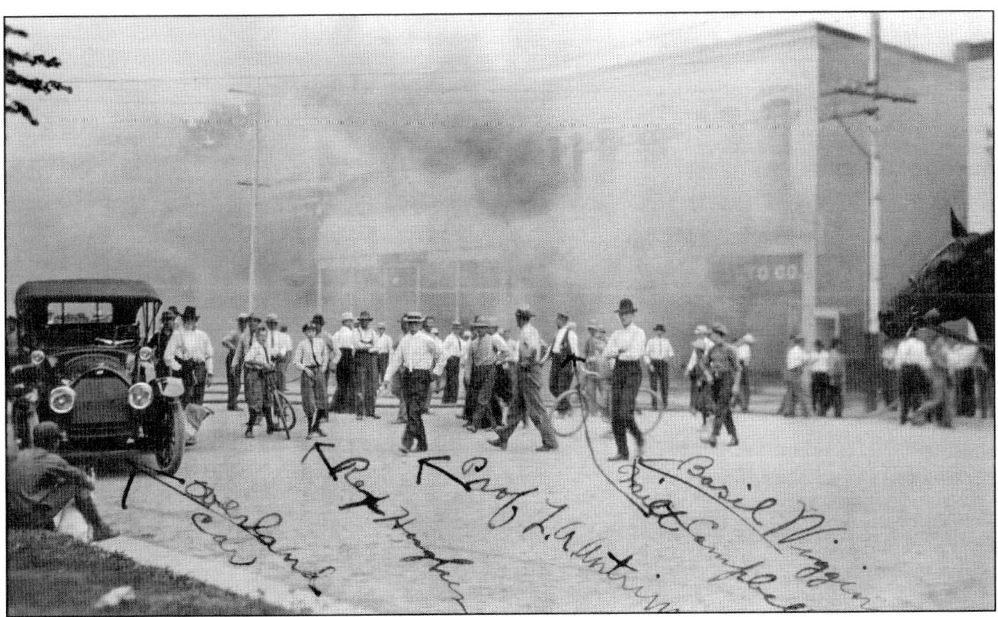

The south side fire consumed the Wind Brothers Garage and Smith's Dress Club. Citizens amassed at the scene. Professor Antrim of the Mount Pleasant Academy is visible at center. The *Mount Pleasant Daily News* recorded that a "grown of anguish went up from the crowd" as the fire raged. Fortunately, the people inside the buildings safely escaped. (MPPL.)

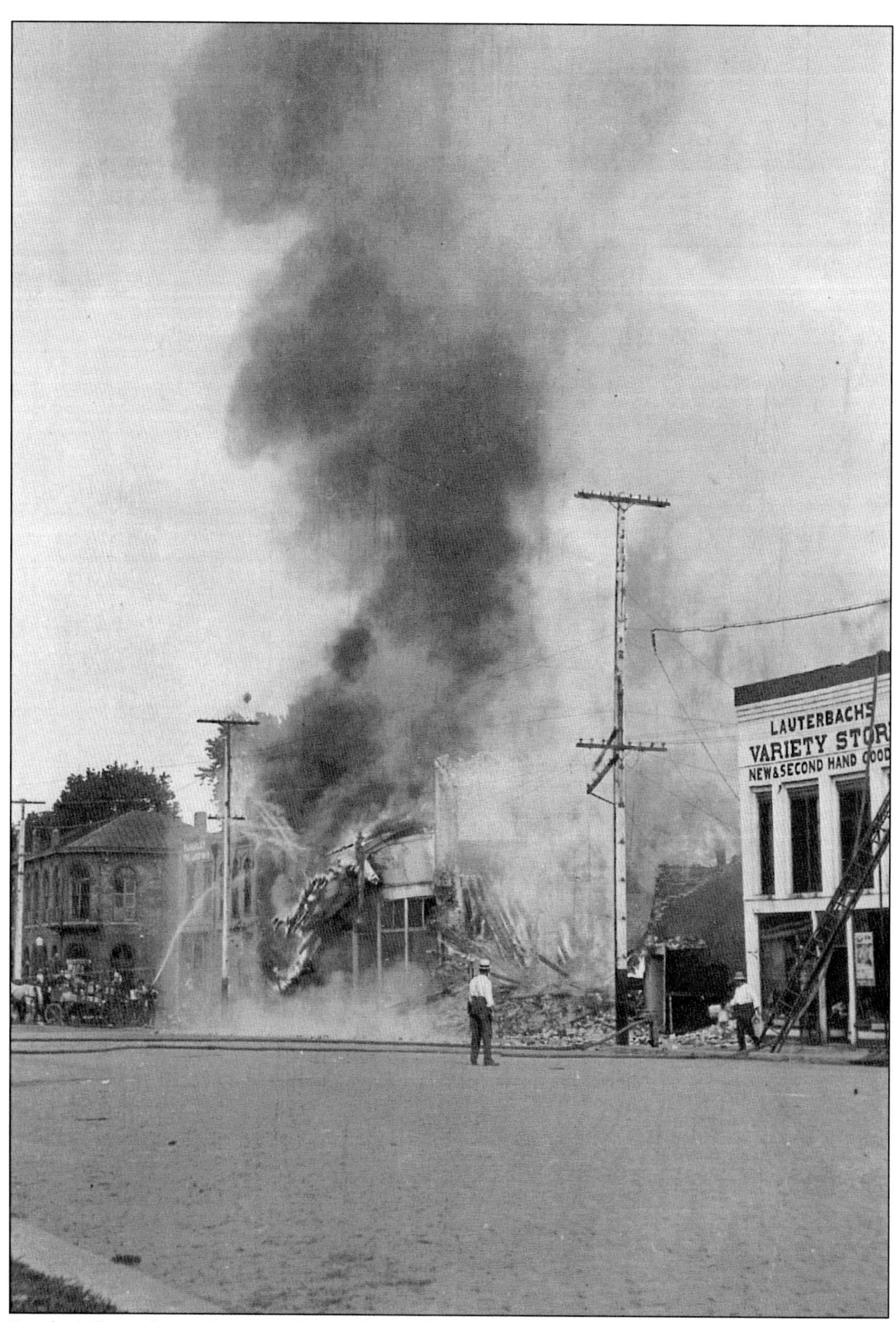

Smoke billows skyward during the south side fire. Fire crews battle the blaze at left with a stream of water from a horse-drawn fire engine. The old courthouse is at far left. (Don Young Collection, HCHT.)

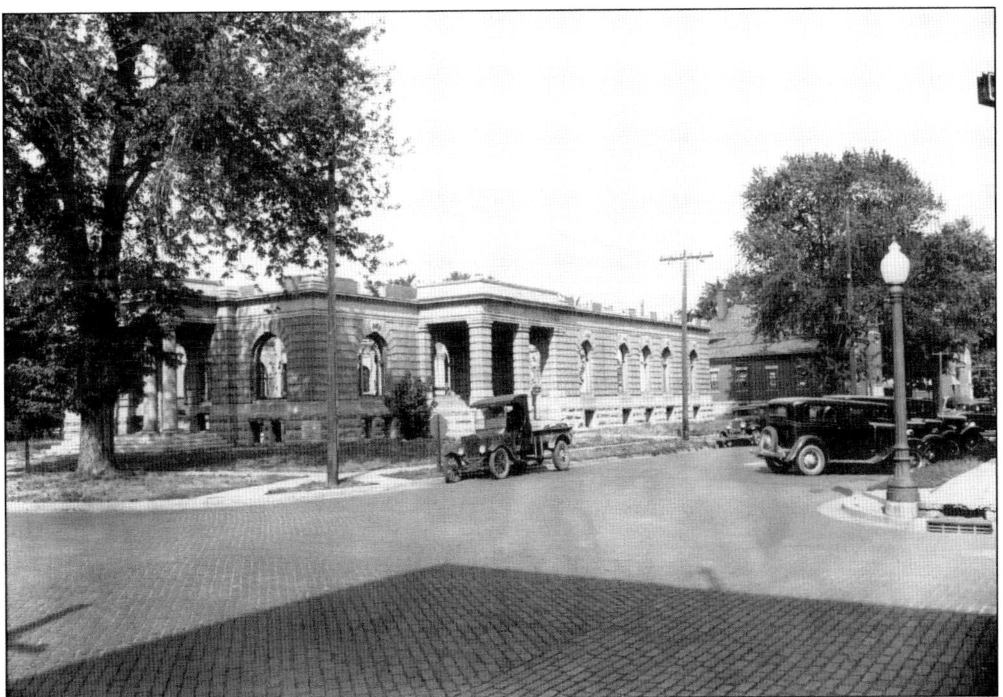

The ground floor of the YMCA building is all that remained after the 1932 fire. The story goes that an airplane "buzzed" the town in the early morning to alert citizens to the fire. The building was destroyed before firemen could mobilize. Stone from this ruin, however, was salvaged and used in the construction of the city hall building in 1936. Notice the bricked streets of the 1930s above. The photograph below was taken at the corner of Monroe and Jefferson Streets facing northeast. (Both, MPPL.)

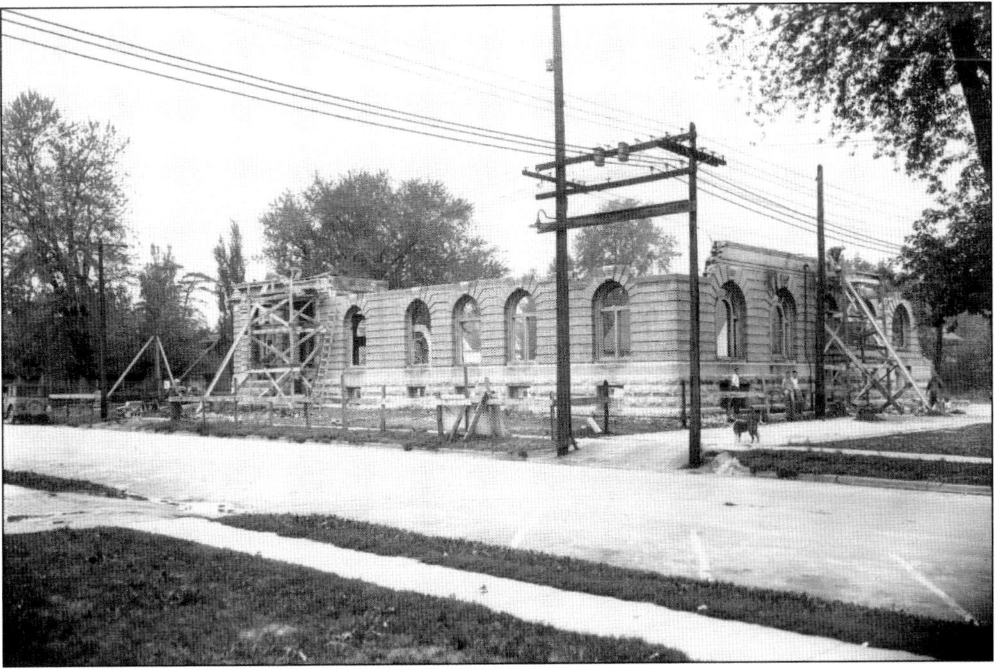

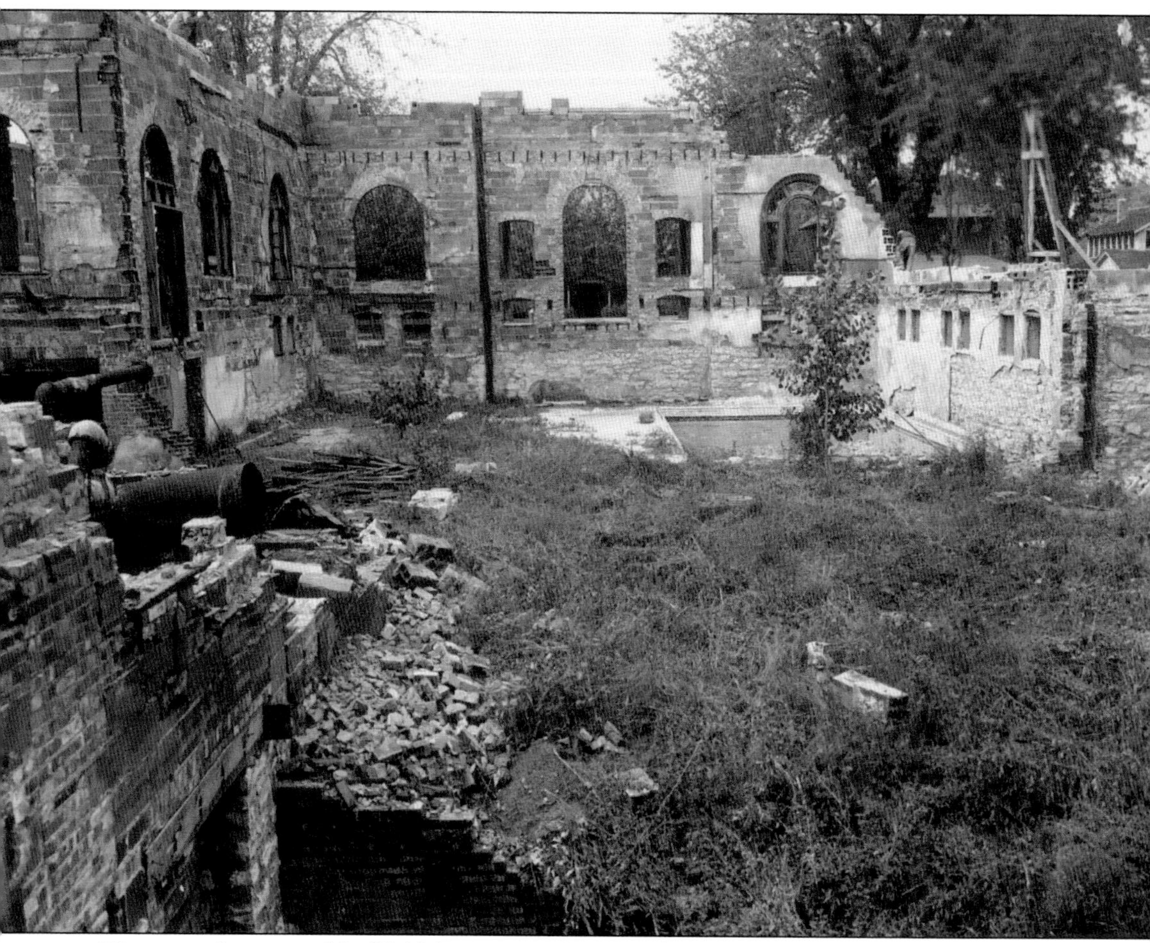

This is another view of the YMCA ruins in 1934. Grass has already sprung up within the building's shell. The surviving Roman arches are shadows of this once magnificent building. It is easy to understand why building materials from such ruins would be salvaged and reused. These stones were given new life in the construction of city hall. (MPPL.)

Fire spread quickly through multiple wings of the mental health institute on August 10, 1936. The next day's *Mount Pleasant News* reported that the "roaring inferno swept the interior of the main building of the state hospital Monday night from 10:30 on until the early hours of the morning." (Pat White.)

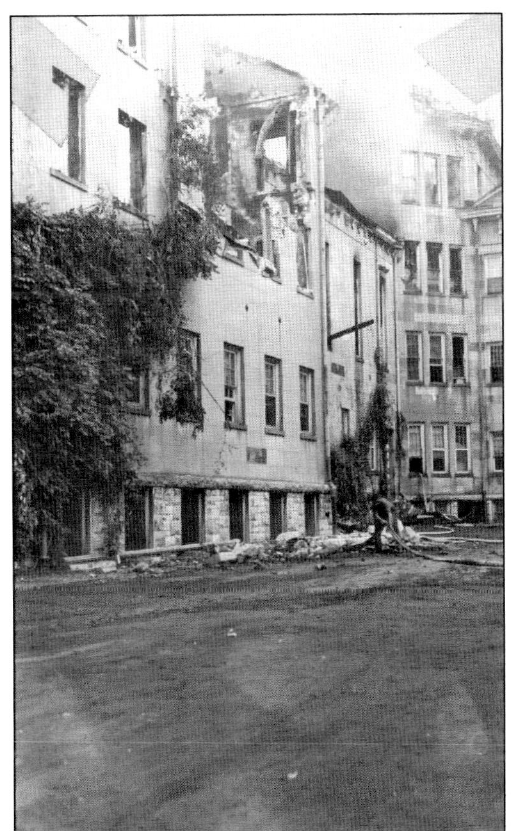

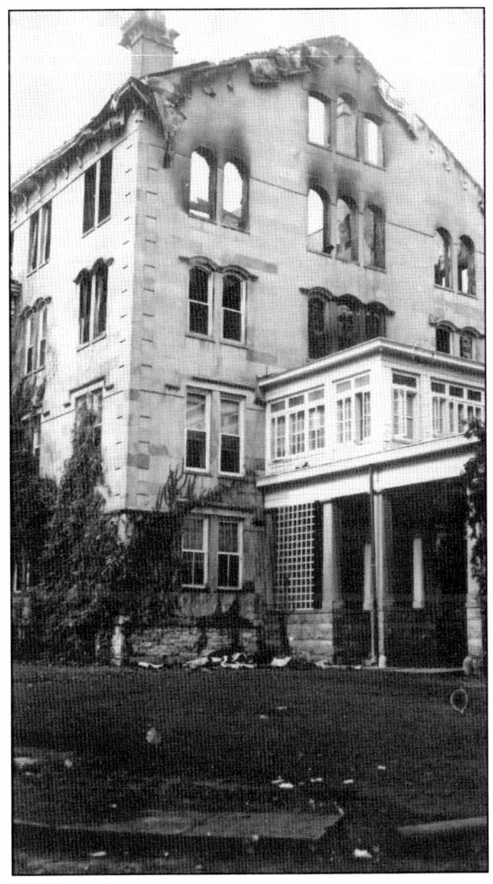

Flames swept through the asylum's main building. The August 11, 1936, *Mount Pleasant News* recorded, "It is almost impossible to believe that a fire of such proportions and under such circumstances could occur without loss of life. The actions of the entire staff from Supt. Ristine down to the newest attendant functioned like clockwork. Cool heads saved many a life during the night." (Don Young Collection, HCHT.)

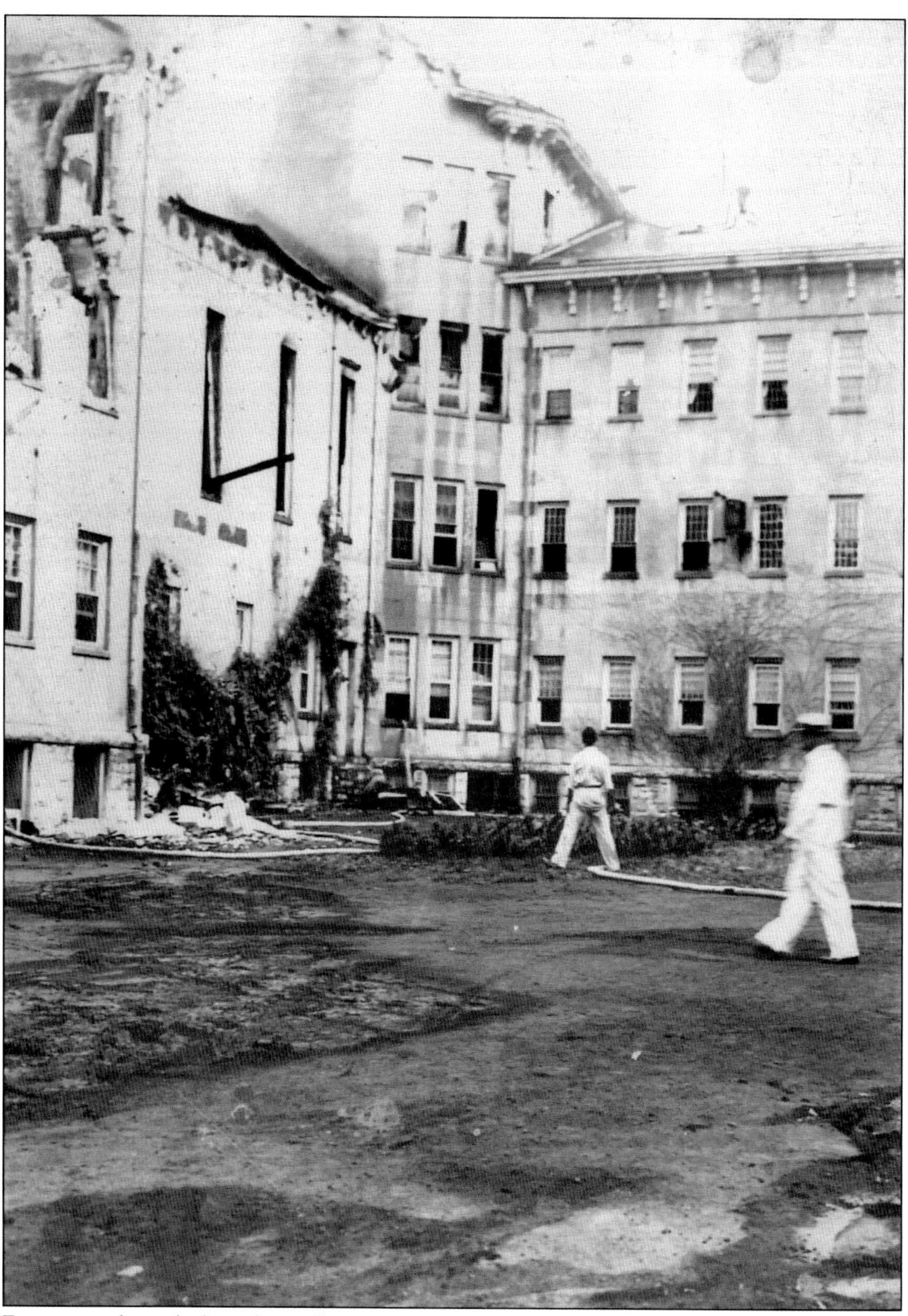

Firemen performed a herculean effort to save the asylum from total destruction. The August 11, 1936, *Mount Pleasant News* reported that four fire departments battled the blaze, including two fire trucks from Mount Pleasant, two trucks from Burlington, one truck from New London, and another truck from the hospital itself. (Don Young Collection, HCHT.)

Ten

LEISURE

Mount Pleasant is blessed with a beautiful landscape, scenery that has for many generations given its citizens relief from stress. The 1870 *City Directory* recorded:

> By strangers visiting the place its situation and surroundings are considered peculiarly beautiful. At a distance of four miles the Skunk river, one of the principal streams of the State, takes its south-easterly course to the Mississippi: while Big creek, a small clear stream, surrounds us in the shape of a horse-shoe, one and a half miles distant north, west and south. In these directions, thickly studding the loamy bottom lands, are seen heavy forests of oak, hickory, walnut and maple, which on the little tributary Saunders' run, approach on the west to the very limits of the corporation; and feathering here into a luxuriant growth of sapling among the large trees, invite many a merry picnic group to find enjoyment in their shade.

Since the 1830s, the trees have tempted the afternoon crowds, and the country streams have lured fisherman.

For many people today, Mount Pleasant is synonymous with festival, as thousands come each year to the Old Threshers Reunion. The fairgrounds have a long history, originally made festive by the Henry County Agricultural Society in 1865. Since the 19th century, the fairgrounds have been a place of autumn festivals, an occasion for people to watch horse races or mingle in large crowds. Mount Pleasant has always drawn crowds.

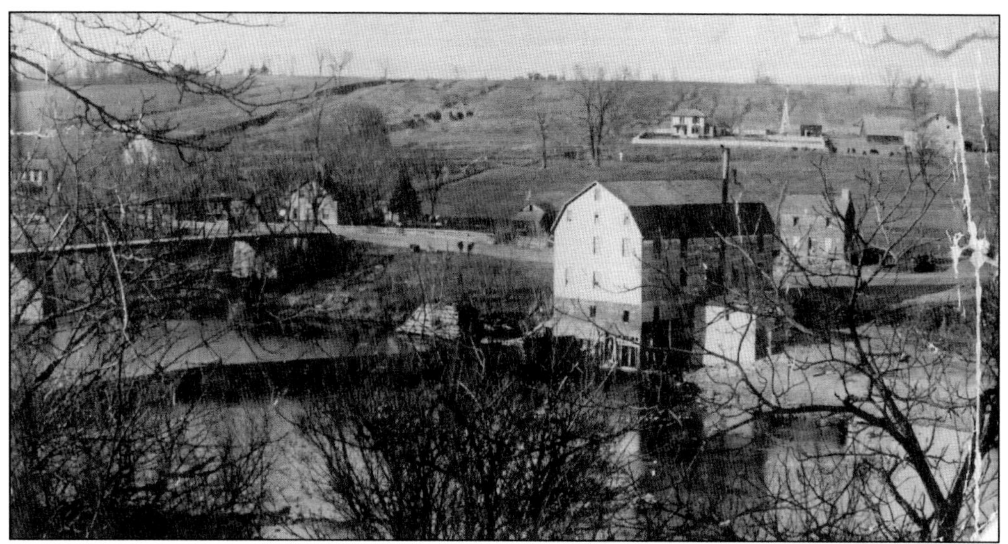

Oakland Mills has long provided a beautiful retreat for Mount Pleasant residences. The 1879 *History of Henry County* described the natural beauty of the "region through which runs the river Skunk, and the banks of which are embroidered the chains of picturesque hills." (MPPL.)

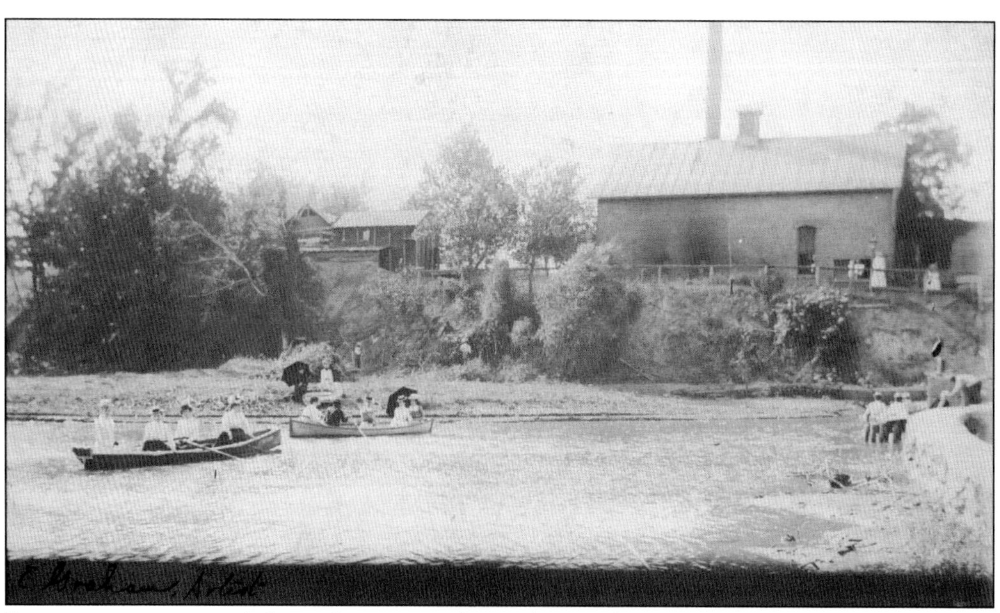

Boaters enjoy a summer's day at the waterworks southwest of town. Youngsters play atop the stone wall at right. Water, tree shade, and sun were as enjoyable and relaxing in the 19th century as they are today. (MPPL.)

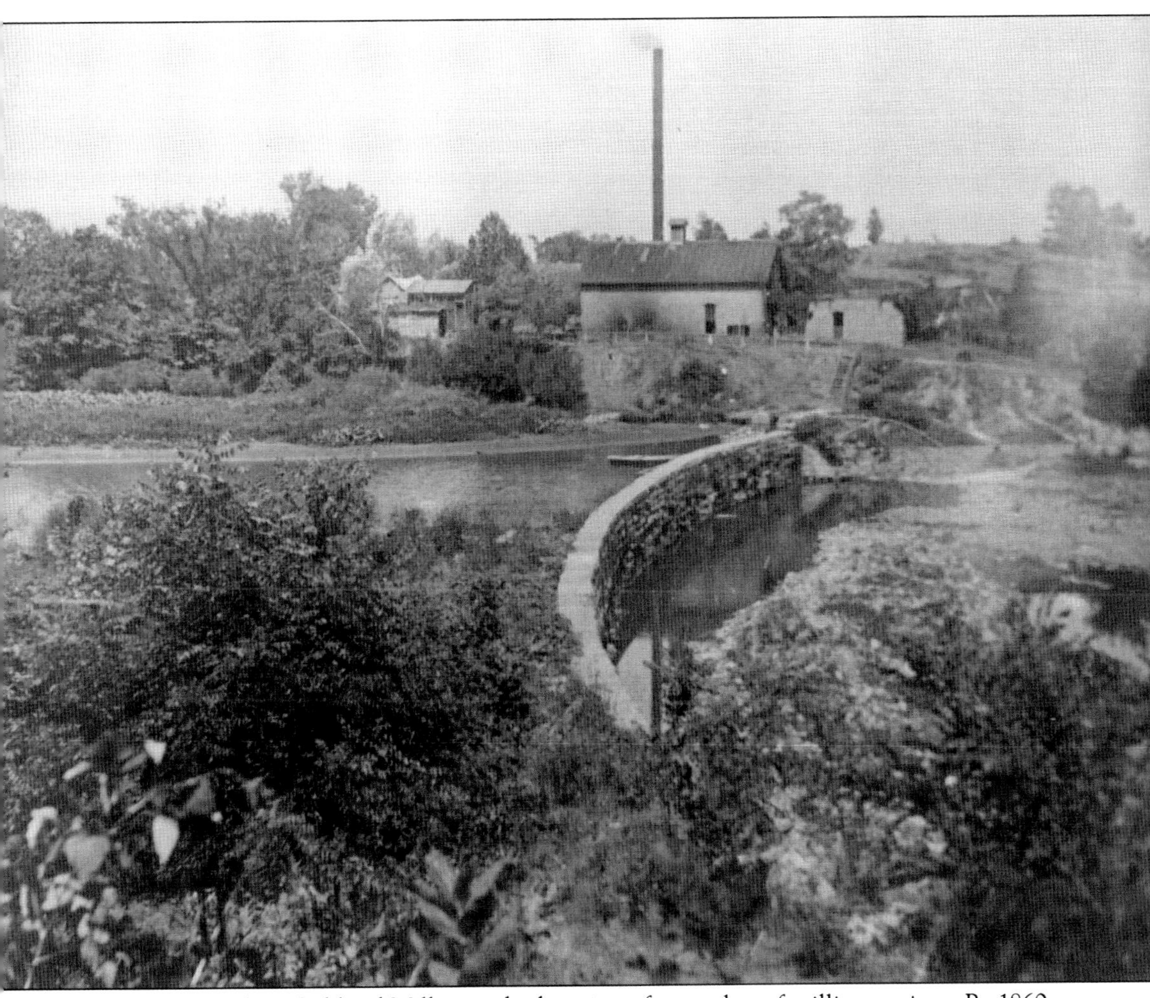

As the name implies, Oakland Mills was the location of a number of milling stations. By 1860, Oakland was home to a sawmill, a gristmill, and a woolen mill. The stone dam contains the water behind the wall, which is very different than the rush of water seen today. Visitors to Oakland Mills today will find Butch's River Rock Café here. (MPPL.)

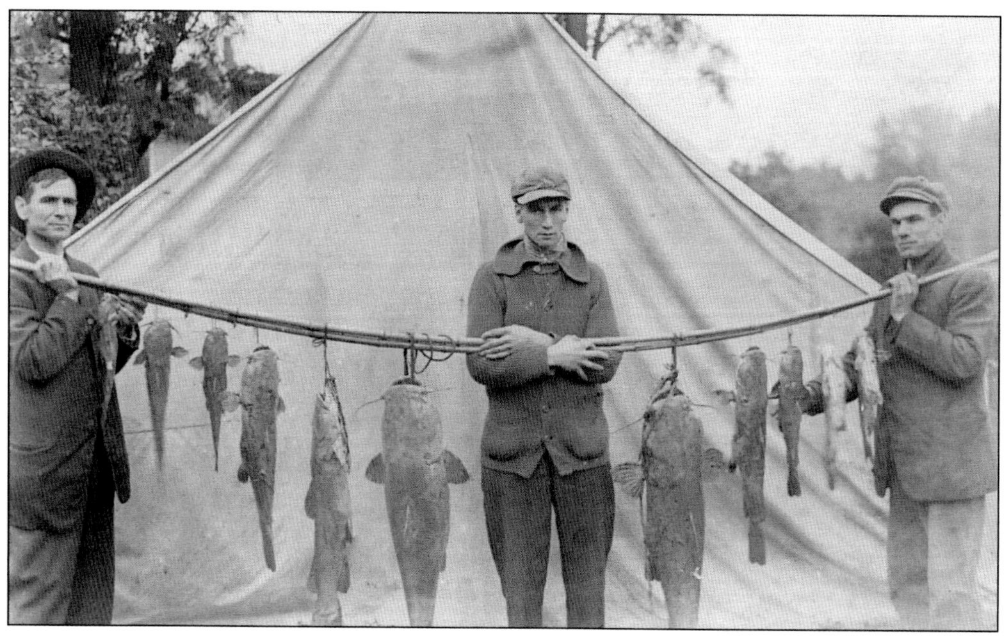

These 19th-century photographs of the Jericho boys and their friends reveal an age-old pastime: fishing. These young men were among many Mount Pleasant folks who have enjoyed fishing on the Skunk River at Oakland Mills. Notice the large size of the catfish. The 1893 *City Directory* stated, "The water works are another favorite resort for fishermen and a nice string may be caught there most any spring day. Catfish, buffalo, and suckers are the principal varieties found." (Both, MPPL.)

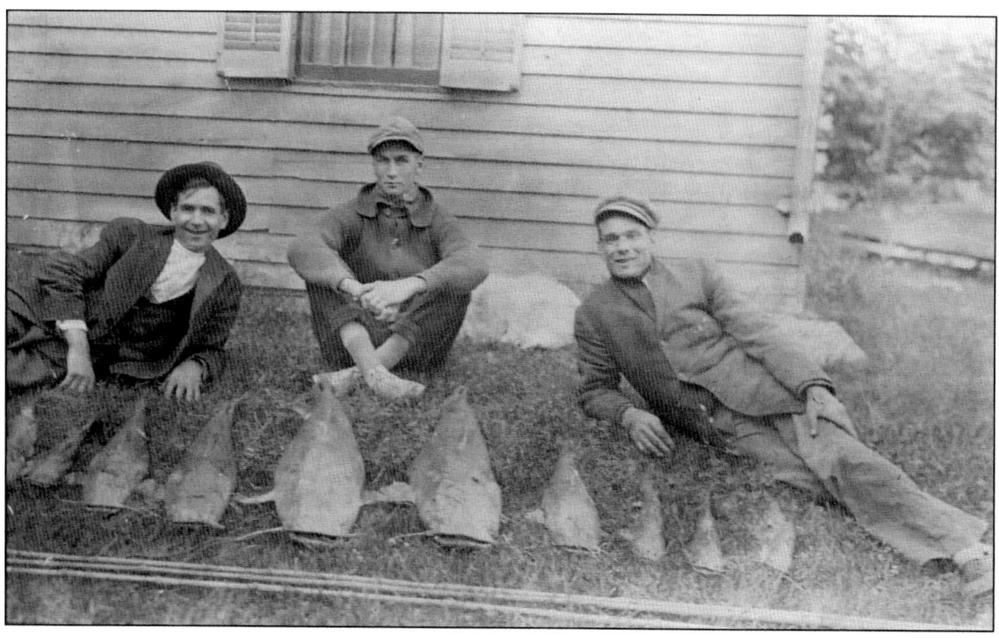

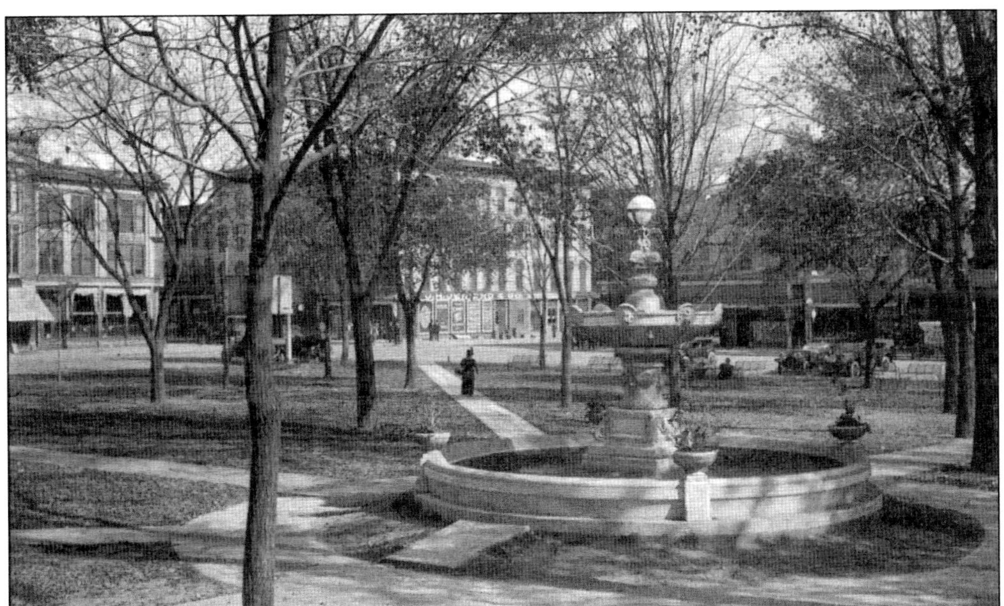

The P.E.O. Fountain stands in the center of the plaza, a work long in the making. Some two decades before this photograph, the 1893 *City Directory* imagined the day "when a better water supply is obtained for the city mains, fountains should be built." Originally built in 1911, and modified thereafter, the fountain still spouts water during the warm parts of the year. During the Christmas season, the fountain is decked in sparkling light. (Bth, Don Young Collection, HCHT.)

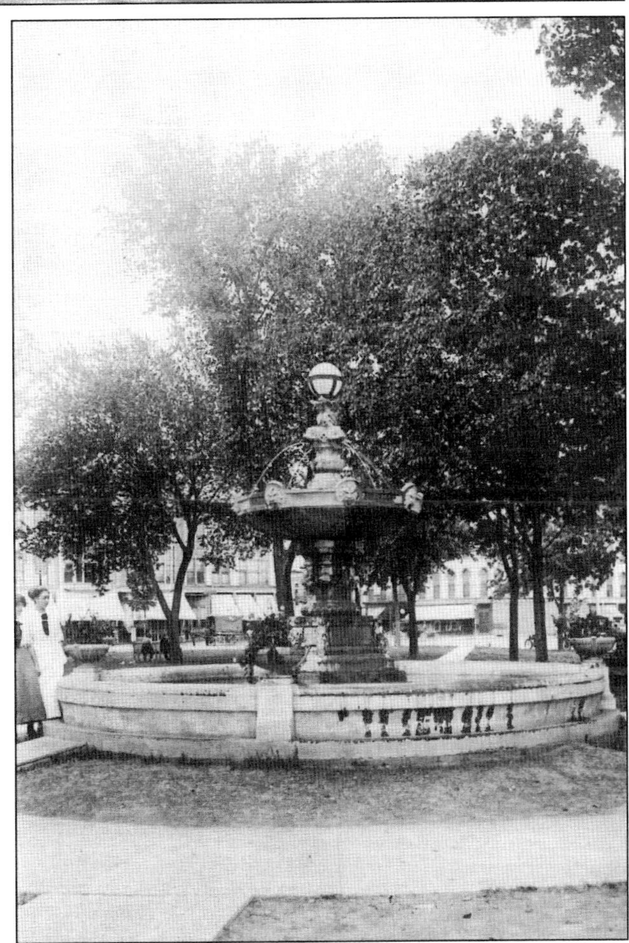

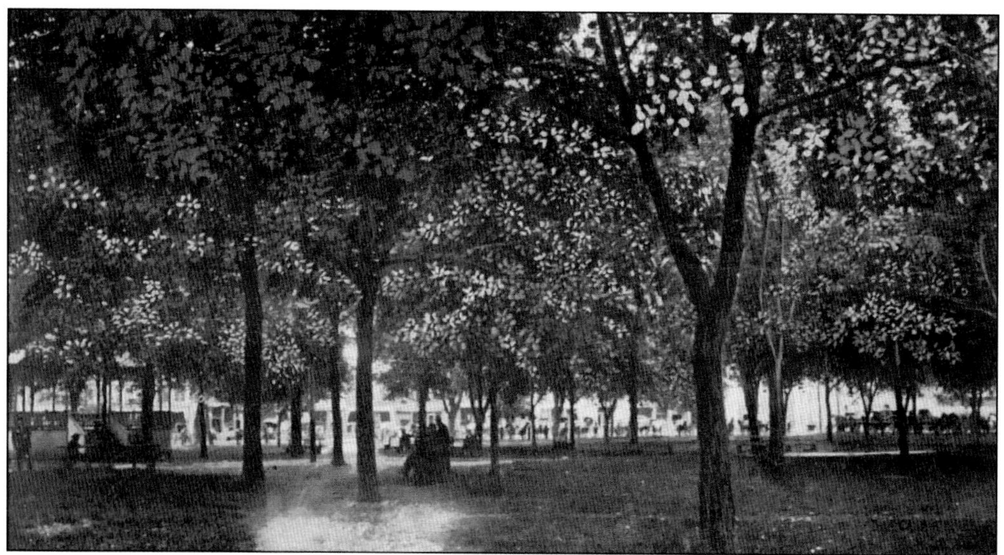

The square was always the central hub of town, purposely established in the center of the business district. In this early 20th century photograph, the trees are thick, creating an almost forest-like atmosphere. The 1893 *City Directory* noted, "A luxuriant shade is cast by its elm and maple forest, and a well kept greensward makes it a favorite retreat for all during the heated days of summer." (Don Young Collection, HCHT.)

In Mt. Pleasant, Iowa, in 1863, Wm.
M'Clure was city marshall.
He had made a collection of liquors from
all the saloons and drug stores, and stored
them in his room in the Brazzleton Hotel on
Main Street.
One morning he rolled the barrels across
the ~~street~~ sidewalk, ~~into the street~~, and broke
the barrels making quite a pool of mixed
liquors.
Along came a cow, smelled the mixture,
tasted it, — then taking a second swig,
gave a bellow, raised her tail straight
into the air, and started up Main Street.
Every body laughed ~~boisterously. to~~
much to the amusement of the Crowd—
H. Whiting.

Mr. H. Whiting recorded a funny moment in Mount Pleasant in 1863. The city marshal "had made a collection of liquors from all the saloons and drug stores, and stored them in his room in the Brazelton Hotel on Main Street. One morning he rolled the barrels across the street sidewalk, into the street, and broke the barrels making quite a pool of mixed liquors. Along came a cow, smelled the mixture, tasted it,—then take a second swig, gave a bellow, raised her tail straight into the air, and started up Main Street. Every body laughed boisterously, much to the amusement of the Crowd." (MPPL.)

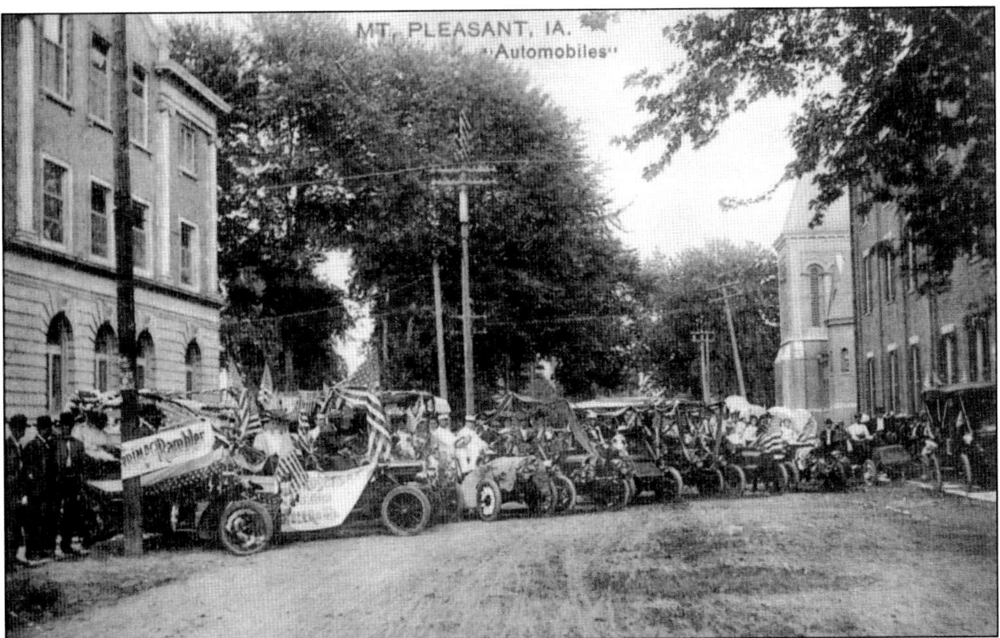

A patriotic assembly of automobiles gathered on Madison Street in the early 20th century. The YMCA building (left) stands on the north side of the street, opposite the Harlan House (right). The spire of the old Presbyterian church is visible behind the Harlan House. (Don Young Collection, HCHT.)

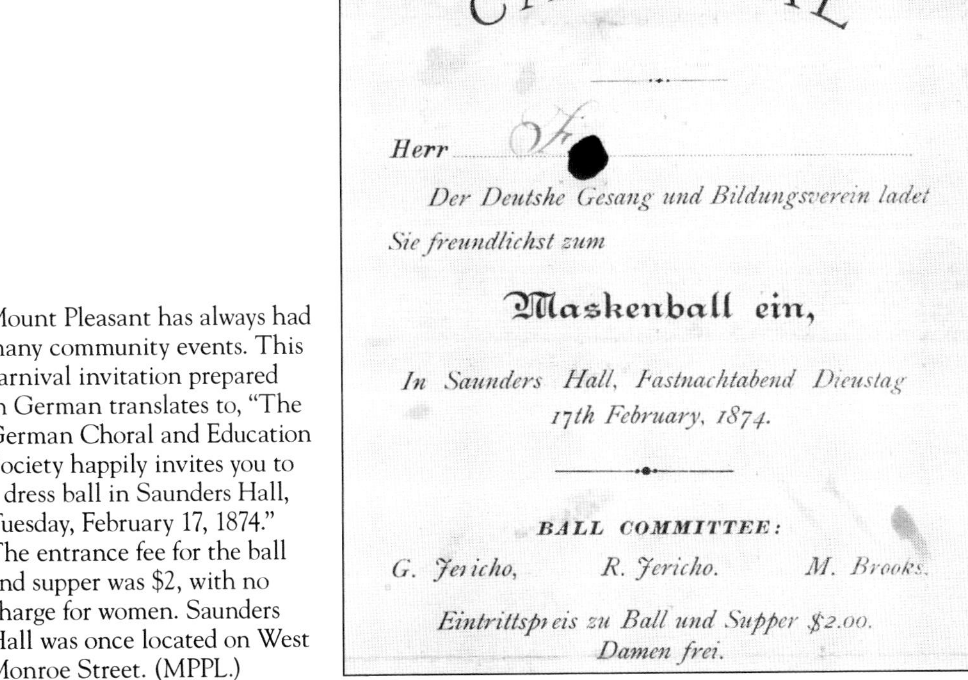

CARNIVAL

Herr ....

Der Deutshe Gesang und Bildungsverein ladet Sie freundlichst zum

Maskenball ein,

In Saunders Hall, Fastnachtabend Dienstag 17th February, 1874.

BALL COMMITTEE:

G. Jericho, *R. Jericho.* *M. Brooks.*

Eintrittspreis zu Ball und Supper $2.00.
Damen frei.

Mount Pleasant has always had many community events. This carnival invitation prepared in German translates to, "The German Choral and Education Society happily invites you to a dress ball in Saunders Hall, Tuesday, February 17, 1874." The entrance fee for the ball and supper was $2, with no charge for women. Saunders Hall was once located on West Monroe Street. (MPPL.)

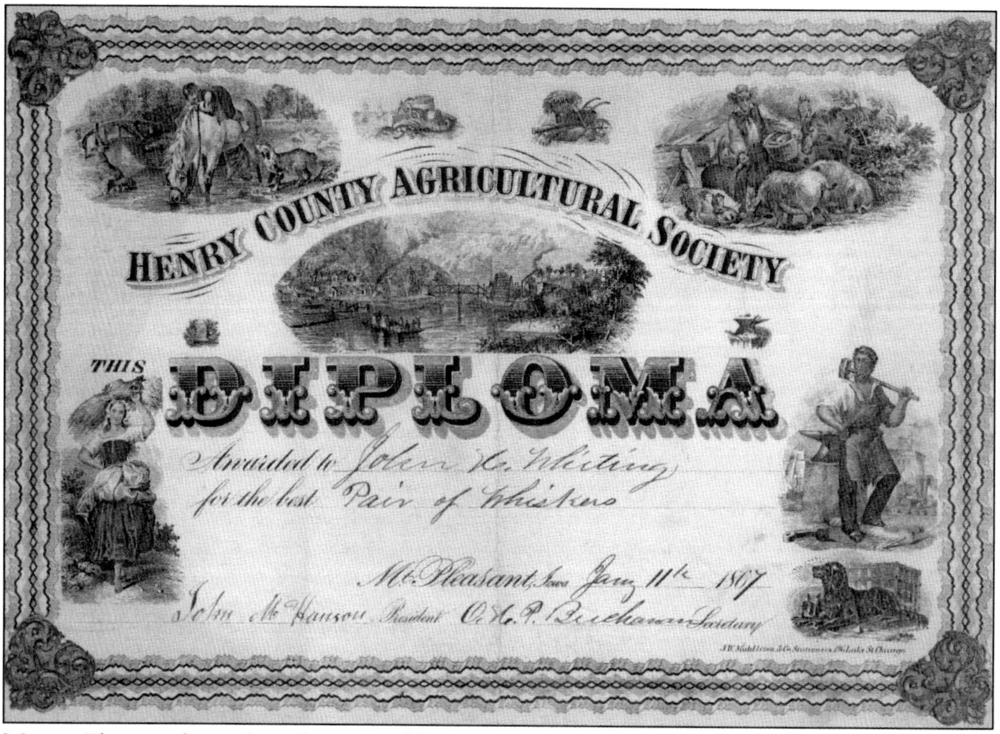

Mount Pleasant has a long history of fair-going, beginning with the creation of the Henry County Agricultural Society in 1865. The 1879 *History of Henry County* reported that the "Society owns a good fair-ground, to which an addition has recently been made of twenty acres, by purchase." Those old fairgrounds remain fairgrounds today, contained within present-day McMillan Park. (MPPL.)

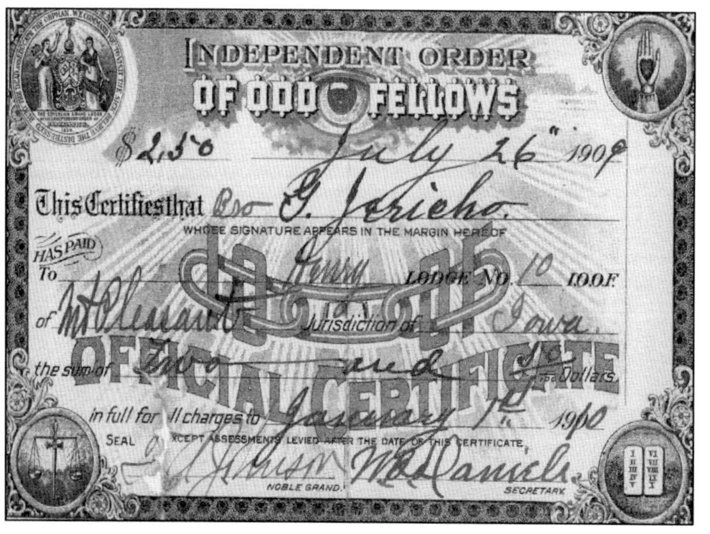

INDEPENDENT ORDER OF ODD FELLOWS

$2.50 July 26th 1909

This Certifies that Geo G. Jericho

WHOSE SIGNATURE APPEARS IN THE MARGIN HEREOF

HAS PAID To Henry LODGE No. 10 IOOF

of Mt Pleasant Jurisdiction of Iowa

the sum of Two and 50/100 Dollars

OFFICIAL CERTIFICATE

in full for all charges to January 1st 1910

SEAL EXCEPT ASSESSMENTS LEVIED AFTER THE DATE OF THIS CERTIFICATE,

NOBLE GRAND. SECRETARY

A number of secret societies once operated in Mount Pleasant, including the Independent Order of Odd Fellows. "Secret society" is a bit of a misnomer, as these organizations posted meeting dates and the names of officers in local directories. The Odd Fellows, like other secret societies, functioned as benevolent charitable organizations. This 1909 Odd Fellows membership certificate belonged to G. Jericho. (MPPL.)

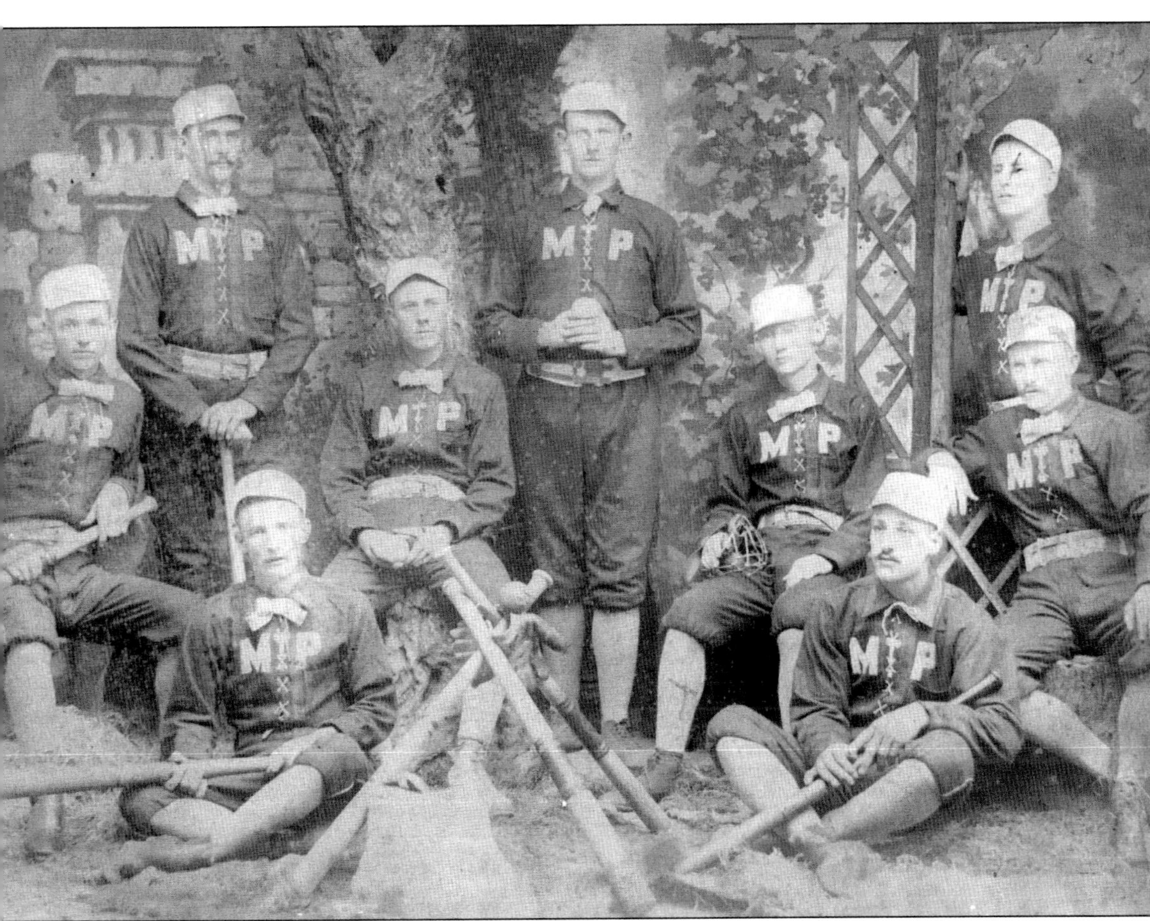

Baseball has long been a Mount Pleasant tradition, as illustrated by this 19th-century team picture. The 1906 Iowa Wesleyan *Croaker* noted, "Baseball early won favor as a popular sport at Wesleyan. In the early '70s [the 1870s] a team was organized which played games with the city team and teams from neighboring towns." Iowa Wesleyan had a properly organized team by the early 1880s. (MPPL.)

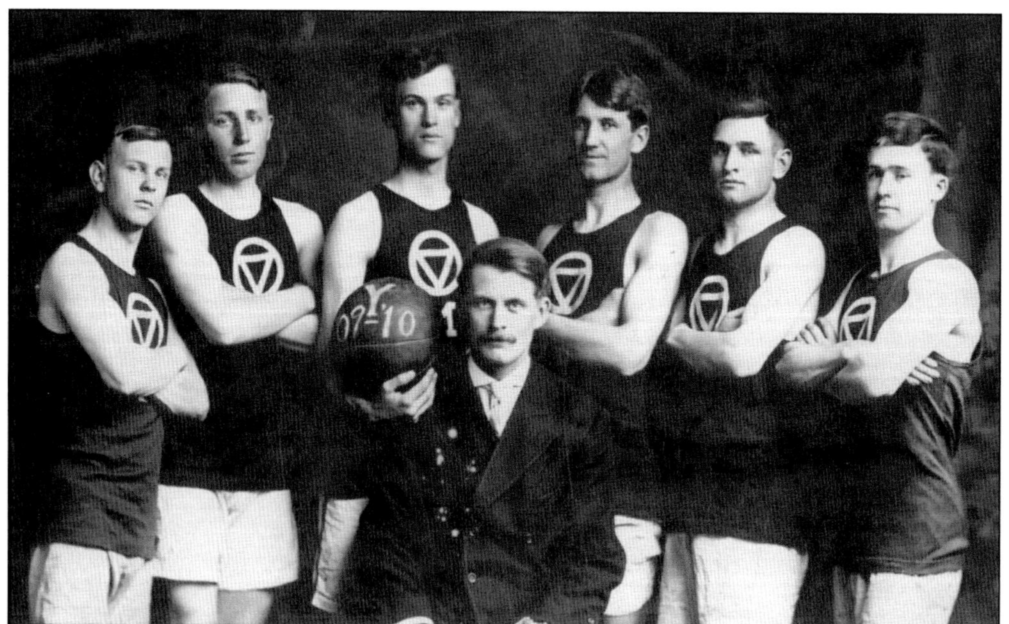

This 1909–1910 basketball team played in the old YMCA gymnasium. A number of Iowa Wesleyan athletic squads utilized the YMCA's facilities. Notice the "Y" for YMCA on the basketball, as well as the YMCA triangle logo on the jerseys, the three equal sides representing body, mind, and spirit. (Don Young Collection, HCHT.)

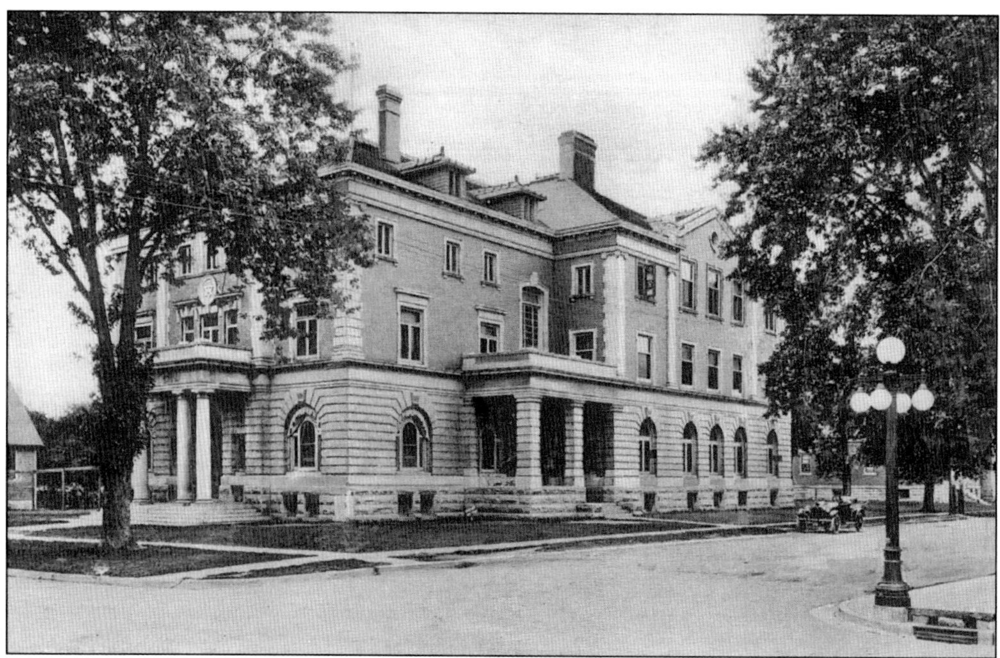

The YMCA building, an important center for local athletics, once stood at the corner of Jefferson and Madison Streets, at the present location of the post office. The Roman arches, pediments, and columned porches exemplify the classical design. The Baptist church, also no longer standing, is visible beyond the YMCA building at right. (MPPL.)

This advertisement for the August 1915 Henry County Fair shows a female jockey jumping a fence. The girl rides sidesaddle, both legs thrown over the same side of the horse. Notice the jockey's hat and formal attire. Horse shows were big draws for the fairgrounds. (Don Young Collection, HCHT.)

THE BIG
HENRY COUNTY FAIR
AUGUST 17, 18, 19, 20
1915

© 1914 "OVER THE FENCE"

The more things change, the more they stay the same. In this early 20th century photograph, older boys drive up Jefferson Street while younger boys follow behind on their bikes. Perhaps the big ball in the car is coming from the fairgrounds. Men on a horse-drawn carriage to the right watch the antics. The Harlan House is at left. (Don Young Collection, HCHT.)

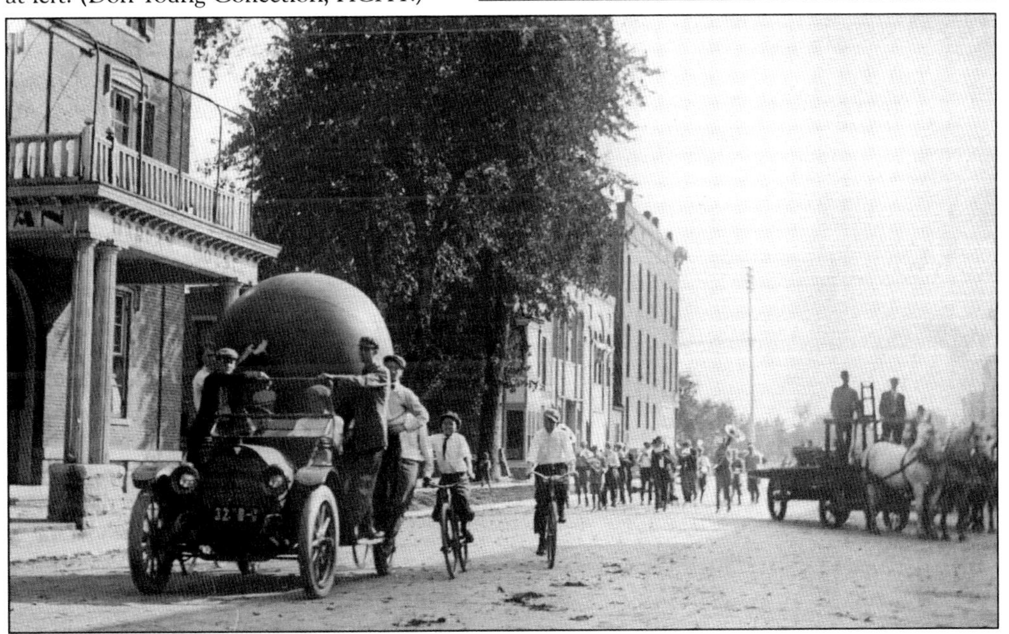

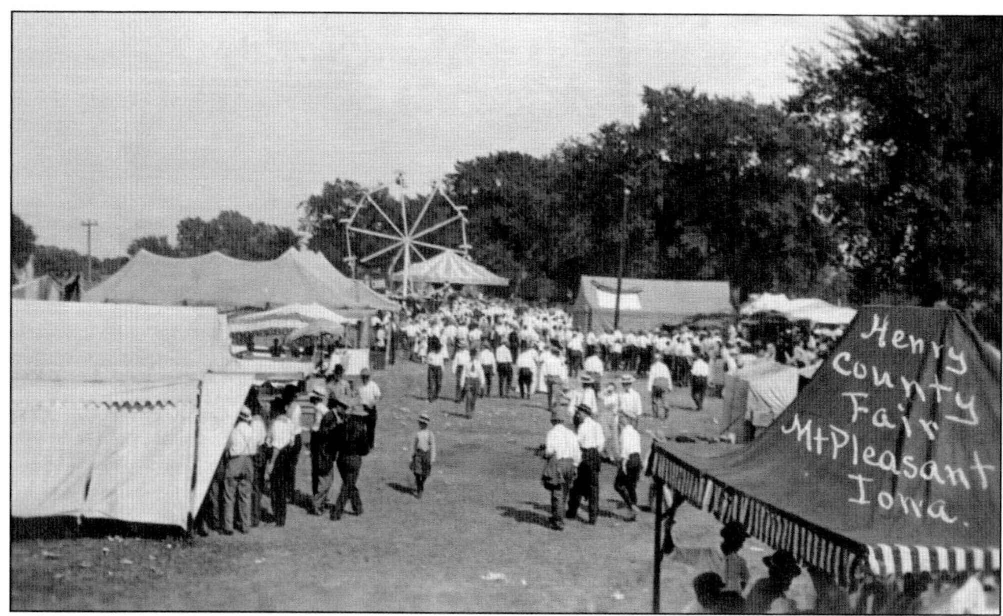

Activities abound at the 1914 Henry County Fair. Visitors move between the tents, finding shade and entertainment within the canvas shelters. In 1914, Brown's Meat Market advertised foods that are familiar to today's fairgoers, including hamburgers, pork loins, pickles, and sauerkraut. Notice the Ferris wheel in the distance. This scene is similar to today's Old Threshers Reunion. (Don Young Collection, HCHT.)

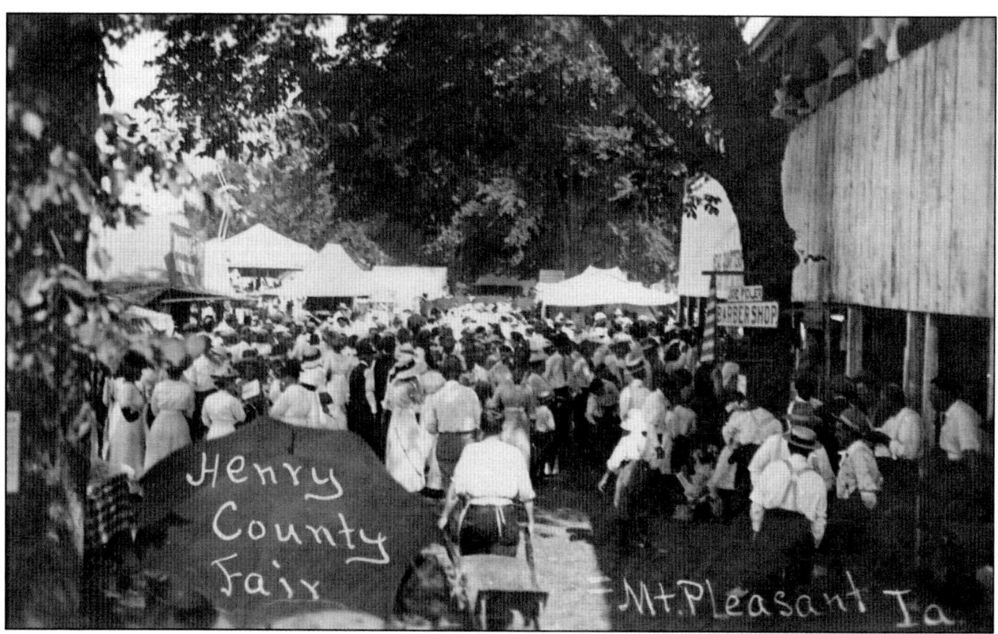

The Mount Pleasant fairgrounds have been active, on and off, since 1865. By the early 20th century, large crowds packed the fairgrounds, as seen in this photograph from about 1914. Notice the striped barber's cone near the tree at right. (Don Young Collection, HCHT.)

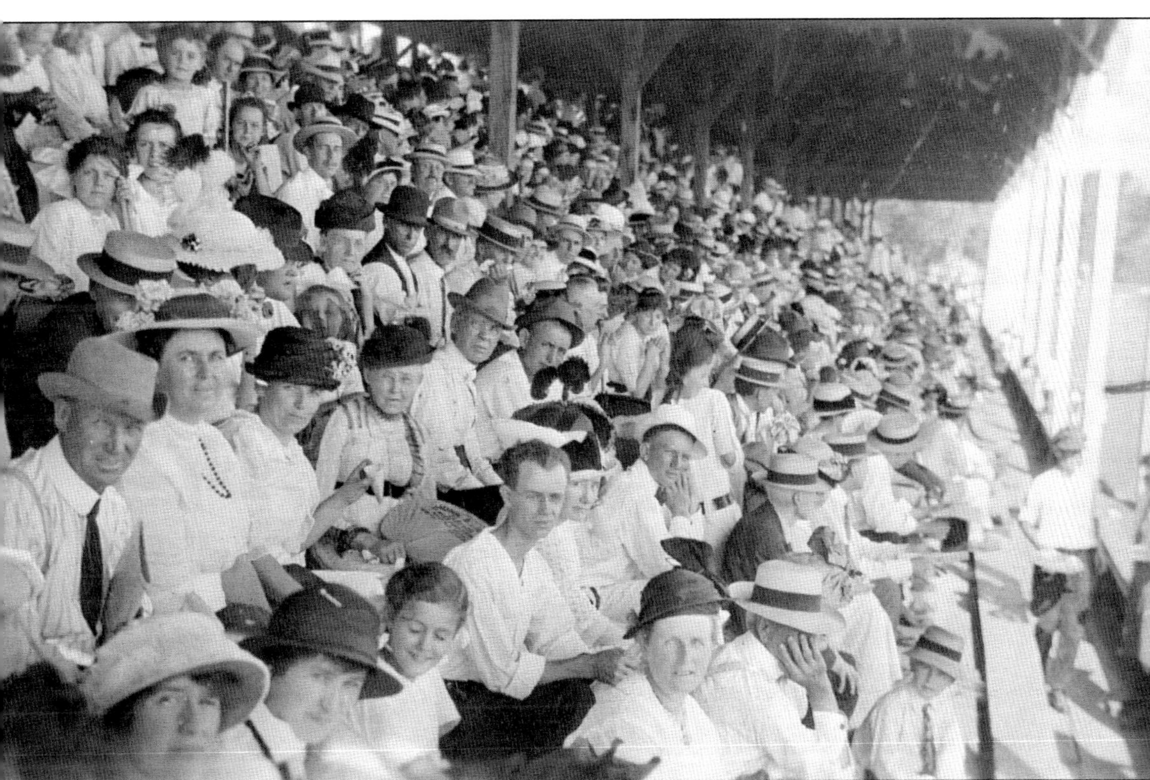

The stands are packed at the August 1914 Henry County Fair. The fair offered exhibitions of sheep, hogs, cattle, and horses. The 1914 *Mount Pleasant Daily News* noted that the fair's "horse races were good, the track being in fine condition and it took five heats to determine the result of the 2:24." Horse races carried large purses, ranging from $300 to $400. During that festival, the fair even included Fearless Greggs, a daredevil automobile act. Thousands still come each fall to experience Mount Pleasant's great fair, the Old Threshers Reunion. (Don Young Collection, HCHT.)

Consistent with our mission to preserve history on a local level, this book was printed in South Carolina on American-made paper and manufactured entirely in the United States. Products carrying the accredited Forest Stewardship Council (FSC) label are printed on 100 percent FSC-certified paper.

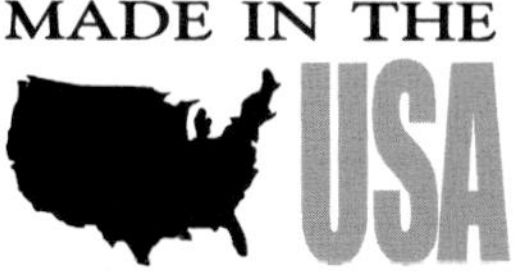